ABOUT THE AUTHOR

R oberta Morrell studied singing and clarinet at The Royal College of Music in London. In 1972 she joined the D'Oyly Carte Opera Company, spending 10 years as both chorister and principal, before pursuing a career as a freelance singer and actress. As a director, she has staged over one hundred shows for professional and amateur companies both in the UK and North America. She regularly travels to the USA to give Master Classes in vocal presentation and stage technique. Her home on the beautiful Lleyn Peninsula in North Wales provides a peaceful setting for her writing and she plans a series of crime stories, 'The Savoy Murders', with Gilbert and Sullivan as the theme, following the success of her first novel, 'Vengeance Dire'.

ROBERTA MORRELL

D'Oyly Carte

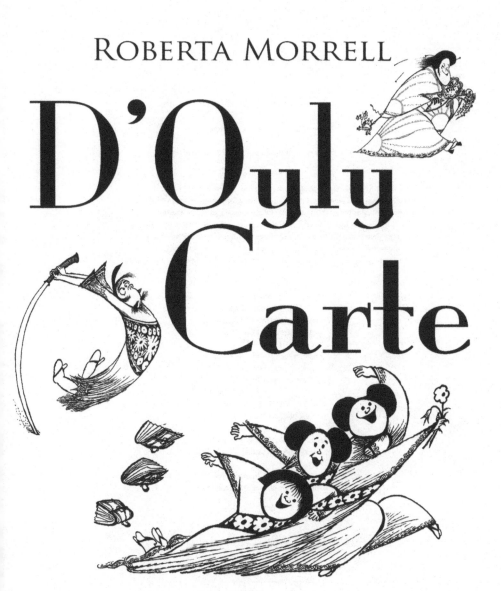

The Inside Story

Matador
9 Priory Business Park,
Wistow Road, Kibworth Beauchamp,
Leicestershire. LE8 0RX
Tel: 0116 279 2299
Email: books@troubador.co.uk
Web: www.troubador.co.uk/matador
Twitter: @matadorbooks

ISBN 978 1785893 803

British Library Cataloguing in Publication Data.
A catalogue record for this book is available from the British Library.

Printed and bound in the UK by TJ International, Padstow, Cornwall
Typeset in 11pt Palatino by Troubador Publishing Ltd, Leicester, UK

Matador is an imprint of Troubador Publishing Ltd

ACKNOWLEDGEMENTS

I wish to express my most sincere thanks to the London Gilbert and Sullivan Society for sponsoring and promoting this book. Also, to my great friends, Daniela and Richard Krupowiecki, for their sponsorship and unfailing encouragement during its two years in preparation. To Valerie Bailey, who represents the great affection in which the D'Oyly Carte Opera Company is still held by its many fans, I add my thanks for her sponsorship. Thank you to my dear friend, Gareth Jacobs, and to George Low for their eagle-eyed help with my mistakes. To my friend, the legendary American cartoonist, Arnold Roth, I add my heartfelt thanks for allowing me to use his cartoon creations for the book and to Eugene Bolt for his help in preparing the artwork. Thank you to all my former Carte colleagues who have shown such interest and belief in this project. I am truly grateful for the trust placed in me to write the family story. Lastly, I offer my gratitude to Cynthia Morey and Peter Riley for their help in my research for this book. The encyclopaedic knowledge of the company possessed by these two distinguished members of the D'Oyly Carte has been of immeasurable help to me. It is true to say that I could not have done it without them.

PREFACE

The D'Oyly Carte Opera Company was a theatrical institution for over a century, delighting audiences young and old with the Savoy Operas of Gilbert and Sullivan. Travelling year on year around Great Britain and North America, the company's visits were eagerly anticipated wherever it went. The intention of this book is to give an insight into the working life of this great touring repertory company from 1950 to its closure in 1982. Using the anecdotes and recollections of former members, I hope to create a lasting tribute to this unique company. In years to come, the many recordings of the Gilbert and Sullivan repertoire made by the D'Oyly Carte will still be available, but personal experience of how the company operated will be lost to British theatre history with the passing of its members. It was a company like no other.

The D'Oyly Carte seemed to be a permanent fixture: through Queen Victoria's long reign, two World Wars and many times of austerity, the popular melodies and hilarious satire of the Savoy Operas brought a smile to the face of the nation. It was common for company performers to meet fans in their 80s fondly reminiscing about being taken to see the D'Oyly Carte as small children. For such devotees it had been an unchanging factor in their ever-changing world, providing a predictable and consistent source of pleasure. For some, the D'Oyly Carte Opera Company became a lifelong passion, the familiar faces on the front row of the theatre in every town never failing to amaze the performers who often wondered how these addicted fans managed to fund their habit.

Throughout the 20th century, hundreds of amateur groups were founded to indulge local audiences in their love of Gilbert and Sullivan. Many still in existence today, they often provide the only access to the Savoy Operas since the demise of the D'Oyly Carte, which served as the inspiration for their performances. Unfortunately, the adherence to the traditional perception of how Gilbert and Sullivan should be performed has led to the closure of too many groups, whose ageing members are not being replaced by young people, who think of G&S as boring and old-fashioned simply because they have never been shown any other way of presenting such timeless classics. Audiences, too, need to see a fresh coat of paint on favourite old pieces if they are to continue their support of local groups. So much responsibility lies with directors, most of them amateur, to have sufficient vision, expertise and theatricality to present Gilbert and Sullivan in a style that appeals to modern-day performers and audiences alike.

Being true to the spirit of the original staging is vital, but that does not mean it can't be fun. Updating a G&S opera can sometimes work, providing Gilbert's satire is allowed to shine through the time change, but gimmicks and the liberal reworking of lyrics are not the answer. Too often audiences leave the theatre wondering why they have wasted money on a production that is clearly the product of the director's ego, full of weird ideas and stage business which makes no sense to them. If a new generation of G&S lovers is to be created, young people need to be assured that they will have a good time performing works created over a century ago. Imaginative use of a chorus whose members are valued as actors is essential, as is attention to principals' dialogue and stagecraft. Artistic integrity, more realistic concepts and a less-regimented approach to the shows are, in my opinion, essential if we are to see the continuance of the amateur G&S movement. Professional productions, too, are often at the mercy of directors whose personal ambition and lack of understanding of the genre do no service to the genius of Gilbert and Sullivan. There are many instances of opera companies presenting G&S with directors who think they can improve on the brilliantly-crafted originals, often with very dubious results. Fortunately, there are also professional companies producing Gilbert and Sullivan at the highest artistic level. Australian Opera's many productions have excellent musical standards, imagination and creativity, whilst treating the material with the greatest of respect. It is no coincidence that its G&S repertoire is hugely popular with audiences.

It was not just in Great Britain that the D'Oyly Carte made an indelible impression. From the earliest days of the collaboration of composer and librettist brought together by the impresario, Richard

D'Oyly Carte in the 1870s, North Americans readily embraced the works of Gilbert and Sullivan, flocking to theatres when the company frequently crossed the Atlantic. Such enthusiasm spawned the oldest amateur group still devoted to performing the works of Gilbert and Sullivan, the Savoy Company of Philadelphia. In 1901, it was granted permission to stage the operas in America by W.S. Gilbert himself, the original letter of authority still a prized company possession. Always endeavouring to be faithful to the original D'Oyly Carte style of performance, it still prides itself on upholding tradition and it was, for many years, the only amateur group allowed to appear at the city's venerable Academy of Music. It is interesting that G&S is popular with young people in the USA, thriving in colleges and universities, where taking part in shows is often seen as an opportunity to find a date. If that spills over to enthusiasm for Gilbert and Sullivan in later life, then long may it last. Happily, there has been an upsurge in interest in university Gilbert and Sullivan Societies in this country over the past few years, so all is not yet lost.

After the Second World War, the D'Oyly Carte enjoyed a period of sustained success. With its popularity a foregone conclusion, it continued to tour for forty-eight weeks of the year on both sides of the Atlantic, playing to enthusiastic audiences wherever it appeared. It even survived the expiration of copyright in 1961, when companies such as English National Opera took the opportunity to include Gilbert and Sullivan in their repertoires for the first time. In 1976 and 1978, even though the company was, by then, showing signs of financial instability, it successfully undertook extensive tours of the USA and Canada. A year later it embarked on a one-off tour of Australia and New Zealand, where it was warmly welcomed by the many G&S fans in those countries. It was in Perth that the D'Oyly Carte was last seen outside of its home country. By 1980, touring as many as eight shows was proving unsustainable, the cost of conveying the company and its effects from town to town proving greater than its box office takings. Although audience attendance was never a real issue, the financial gap grew to the point where it was impossible to continue and, on the 27th of February, 1982, the D'Oyly Carte Opera Company gave its final performance before an emotional audience at London's Adelphi Theatre.

It was a popular myth that the company had always been in receipt of public funding, but this was never the case. In the final years there was some small-scale sponsorship from Barclays Bank and a group called 'The Friends of D'Oyly Carte' was formed to raise money, but it was never enough to put the company on a secure financial footing. An application for funding was made to the Arts Council of Great Britain, but it came to nothing. The performers who experienced that last yo-yo year when hopes of financial lifelines were raised and dashed, remember the disbelief that such a theatrical institution could possibly be allowed to disappear, but so it proved. It can be argued that the Trustees of the company, comprised of a mix of prominent lawyers, bankers, politicians and wealthy businessmen, did their best, but it seemed to be a case of them trying to find a way to allow the company to continue as it had always existed, independent of outside influence, even as its house style became increasingly outdated.

Several years later a new D'Oyly Carte Opera Company emerged, but it was to be short-lived. When the original company closed in 1982, it was understood by the performers that the Trustees planned to reopen the company as soon as finances permitted. It was suggested to them that there would be a cross over period when the experience of some of the seasoned performers could be utilised to help introduce a new generation of principals to the tricky art of performing Gilbert and Sullivan. It seemed to be a sensible approach: a new look company with fresh ideas and a few familiar faces to please the audiences until the New D'Oyly Carte Opera Company found its artistic feet. It did not happen that way.

Members of the company were devastated by the closure of the D'Oyly Carte which, they believed, might have been avoided had the management had the foresight to reinvent the company image several years before the financial situation became desperate. For those employed by the D'Oyly Carte when it closed, it was more than losing a job; it was losing a lifestyle. The company's tough touring regime naturally encouraged a family atmosphere, when being away from home for long periods meant separation from the support of loved ones. It was a cosy club and the closure was particularly hard for those who had spent over twenty years with the D'Oyly Carte. Nonetheless, they were professional performers needing to earn a living, so most embarked on the audition circuit in the hope of securing work. There were some considerable successes, with numerous ex-Carters appearing in West End musicals and grand opera to great acclaim. Others pursued a freelance career taking what singing work they could get, frequently supplementing their income by appearing as supporting artists and small-part actors in television shows. Oddly, it was a popular soap opera that led to a new company rising from the ashes of the old D'Oyly Carte.

It was during a recording of *Crossroads* for Central Television in Birmingham, not long after the company had closed in 1982, that several D'Oyly Carte friends found themselves in the green room discussing the possibility of putting together a concert group. Their belief that there was a market for Gilbert and Sullivan following the closure of the Carte proved to be correct. A formal company was founded, G&S a la Carte Ltd., and a concert format was devised that remained popular into the next century. An application was made by its board of directors to the D'Oyly Carte Opera Trust for the use of the company name. Following a meeting with the Trust secretary, permission was formally granted for the new group, consisting almost exclusively of former company members, to appear under the title 'The Magic of D'Oyly Carte'. It was an arrangement that seemed ideal for both parties: the new group had the advantage of the famous company name in promoting its slick and fast-moving concert presentations, whilst the Trustees would see the name kept in the public eye until they were in a position to reopen the company.

For several years, audiences flocked to see their beloved D'Oyly Carte stars appear in major theatres and concert halls around the country; the family was still together and its long-standing camaraderie continued. G&S a la Carte Ltd. even presented a short season of fully-staged operas, but such large-scale productions were too costly for promoters to sustain. Nevertheless, the concerts continued to prove highly successful with the running of the company in the hands of its artistes, who could not understand why the D'Oyly Carte Trustees had not recognised for themselves the merits of this concept as an interim arrangement.

However, the day came when the Trustees withdrew the right for G&S a la Carte Ltd. to use the iconic name in promoting its appearances, because the D'Oyly Carte Opera Company was about to reopen, but the concert group continued its success under its new title, 'The Magic of Gilbert and Sullivan'. In the few years following closure, the Trustees had taken stock and decided on a very different performing company. Rightly or wrongly, just two or three of the former performers were included. Having used G&S a la Carte Ltd. to keep the D'Oyly Carte name afloat, the Trustees had no compunction in turning their backs on the wealth of experience in performing Gilbert and Sullivan so obviously at their disposal. It seems hard to believe that the D'Oyly Carte management could not see the advantage of utilising the skills of at least some of its former stars in some way. The art of performing G&S does not come overnight and the company, whose many new principals would, possibly, have had little or no experience of Gilbert and Sullivan, would have benefited enormously from the guidance of experienced artistes. If the Trustees thought the way forward was to have completely new casts for the relaunch, then it would, at least, have made theatrical sense to have artistic advisers with a proven track record working in G&S to help in making the new company as successful as possible.

The opening of The New D'Oyly Carte Opera Company needed to be absolutely right from the outset and the appointment of artistic staff would be crucial to the success of the relaunch in 1988, the Trust looking to promote, quite rightly, the very highest standards of music and staging. I think it is fair to say that they did not manage this. It is generally acknowledged that the musical standards of the new company were excellent, but the staging of the operas met with mixed reviews, ranging from good to very bad. The decision to engage a different director for each opera may have seemed a logical way to get away from the old, stilted style of production, but it did not work out that way. The various stage directors appointed, arguably, with little or no pedigree in G&S, certainly changed the image of the D'Oyly Carte, but the new company never really found a sense of identity and many of its principals, however talented, lacked the experience and charisma of their predecessors. In the new company's second year, the legendary contralto, Gillian Knight, was engaged to play the 'Queen of the Fairies' in *Iolanthe* and 'Dame Carruthers' in *The Yeomen of the Guard*, possibly suggesting that a star from the original company would prove a draw with audiences, something previously eschewed by the management.

It seemed to many fans, initially so delighted to have the D'Oyly Carte back, that some of the productions went too far in changing the old-fashioned image of the company, sometimes relying on cheap stage business which seemed to have no respect for the wonderful material created by William Schwenk Gilbert. Most D'Oyly Carte aficionados agreed that the company needed to change with the times and some of the productions were well-received, but the revolution in the look of the operettas as presented by the new company was, probably, too much too soon.

With much shorter tours than those undertaken by the original company, a programme of just two or three shows and reduced chorus and orchestra numbers, the new company pushed ahead, introducing other operettas into its repertoire, including *Die Fledermaus* and *La Vie Parisienne*. The inclusion of these popular shows attracted financial support from the Arts Council which, ironically, had been a recommendation when the old company applied for funding. It might be asked, why the about face? So, despite all the changes introduced by the D'Oyly Carte Trustees, they failed to create a stable and successful new company, its demise following in 1993. Although the D'Oyly Carte Trust is still in existence, sometimes lending its support to promote Gilbert and Sullivan performances (most recently a joint venture with Scottish Opera), there is, as yet, no sign of a return for the famous and much-loved company.

I hope that the original D'Oyly Carte Opera Company, with which this book is concerned, will live on through the wonderful stories told to me by my fellow Carters, who have been so delighted to have the opportunity to tell the story of company life as it really was.

Roberta Morrell

FOREWORD

I think I must have read nearly every book about the D'Oyly Carte Opera Company ever published, but never one like this! 'Outsiders' who have written on this subject in the past may have given their opinions of the Company, the management, the artists, and the productions, but it is only the past members of this unique organisation themselves, who, having experienced life on the inside, truly knew what it was all about. Of course, there are accounts of personal D'Oyly Carte experiences by former principals Jessie Bond, Henry Lytton, Martyn Green, Winifred Lawson and others (I include myself), but I feel that perhaps many of the less attractive truths have been glossed over, and the Company presented in a rather flattering light. Martyn Green tends to be more critical in his *Here's a how-de-do*, but there is still much left untold. Here, Roberta Morrell, herself a member of the D'Oyly Carte for ten years, gives us a true and unsentimentalised account of life in the Company and all its faults, but with sincere affection.

Our intrepid author has travelled the length and breadth of the United Kingdom seeking out and interviewing past D'Oyly Carte members, collecting memories and anecdotes that are in danger of disappearing, unless recorded for posterity. This is such an important enterprise, for as the years go by, the 'family' is inevitably decreasing. In these pages you will read stories that have never before been told, life as it really was, from the 1950s until that sad day at the Adelphi Theatre in 1982, when the Company made its farewell appearance.

There is much laughter in Roberta's book; it is also informative and highly entertaining. I chuckled frequently while reading, laughed aloud many times and was greatly intrigued by much that was new to me. There is also nostalgia, and sadness for the demise of such a unique theatrical phenomenon. Although I was not present at that very Last Night, I heard that the curtain never finally fell on the D'Oyly Carte Opera Company. I don't believe it ever will.

Cynthia Morey

CHAPTER ONE

"THANK YOU, WE'LL LET YOU KNOW."

In its history of over a century, the D'Oyly Carte Opera Company employed more than two thousand performers, as well as many others in the departments of music, wardrobe, wigs, stage management, props, carpentry and company management. How all of these people came to join the prestigious company we can't know but, during the period of its final thirty two years, it has been possible to discover some of the many and varied avenues of approach. It would be easy to suppose that an application for audition or interview made to the company office at its impressive address of 1, Savoy Hill, London WC1, was the most obvious way of getting a job with the company and this may, indeed, have been the case for many prospective employees. However, there were more routes into the D'Oyly Carte than might be imagined, some of them most unusual.

In 1955, the D'Oyly Carte Opera Company embarked on a tour of North America, opening on the 26th of November at the Shubert Theatre in New York. Elsewhere in the city, a young English baritone was appearing with New York City Opera when he noticed the advertising for the famous company's visit. Having emigrated to the USA in 1947, he was reminded of appearing with the D'Oyly Carte as a supernumerary in *The Mikado* at the King's Theatre, Southsea, just a few months before moving to the States. Since that experience of being on the stage with the great performers he had so admired as a youth, it had always been his ambition to join the D'Oyly Carte. On the spur of the moment, he went to the Shubert Theatre Stage Door and asked to see the manager of the D'Oyly Carte. Before long, an immaculately-dressed man with a military moustache appeared. He introduced himself as the Company Manager, Bruce Worsley, and asked the young man what he wanted, to which came the reply that he would like to audition for the D'Oyly Carte. With a frosty tone, Mr. Worsley stated that the company never auditioned outside of its home country and bade the disappointed hopeful a curt goodbye.

Undeterred by this rebuttal, he borrowed a tape recorder and set about making a recording of several arias from the Gilbert and Sullivan repertoire before sending it, with a polite accompanying letter, to Miss Bridget D'Oyly Carte, the owner of the company, in London. Some weeks later he was amazed to receive a letter from the lady herself telling him to present himself at the Shubert Theatre in Philadelphia, where the Company Manager and Music Director would be pleased to hear him. He duly arrived for his audition where, he noted with amusement, no mention was made of his previous encounter with Mr. Worsley. He sang for Isidore Godfrey, the company's respected Music Director, accompanied by William Cox-Ife, the Assistant Music Director. A few weeks later, much to his joy, he received a contract and letter instructing him to make his way to England to begin rehearsals. And so, on April 2nd, 1956, after sailing to Southampton on the *Queen Mary*, John Dennison became one of the few people to be engaged by the D'Oyly Carte outside of the UK.

Twenty-two years later in 1978, another expat took advantage of a D'Oyly Carte North American tour to stake a claim to a much-coveted job with the company. Jill Pert, originally from England, was living in Toronto and had recently played the 'Queen of the Fairies' in *Iolanthe* for the local Gilbert and Sullivan Society. During a party for the D'Oyly Carte hosted by the group, she was in conversation with Leonard Osborn, then the Director of Productions and Royston Nash, the Musical Director. She told them she would love to join the company and would be going to England in the autumn to do some auditions, whereupon she was told they would be delighted to hear her. Having arrived from Canada, Jill asked to audition for the company as a mezzo-soprano and sang 'Mad Margaret' from *Ruddigore* at the Savoy Theatre. Within hours she received a telephone call from the company asking her if she would do a second audition, this time as a contralto. Happy to oblige, she sang 'Alone and Yet Alive' from *The Mikado* and was duly offered a contract to sing in the chorus and understudy Patricia Leonard, the incumbent of the 'dame' roles. Jill recalls that, during a rehearsal soon after she had joined, Royston Nash told her it was not uncommon to meet people anxious to audition for the D'Oyly Carte, whom they never saw again. When she turned up at the Savoy for her first audition, he had said to Leonard, "It's that girl from Toronto. Well, I'll be damned!"

Overseas interest in joining the D'Oyly Carte Opera Company was not confined to North America. There have been many Australians who have appeared with the company, including Musical Director, James Walker; principal contralto, Christene Palmer; chorus member, Denis Olsen, who subsequently returned to his native country to enjoy a distinguished career with Australian Opera, as well as several other choristers, Suzanne Houlden and Jeanette Kearns amongst them. From New Zealand, Helen Moulder joined in 1975 for one season before returning home to pursue a successful acting career. The D'Oyly Carte, courtesy of its many recordings, was synonymous with Gilbert and Sullivan all over the English-speaking world and many a youngster learned to love the Savoy Operas without ever having seen the company.

Captain Royston Nash can definitely be said to have been in the right place at the right time and, probably, to have been head-hunted. As Director of Music for the Royal Marines School of Music in Deal, he was invited to conduct a section of his band on the stage during a Last Night performance of *HMS Pinafore* at Sadler's Wells Theatre, where the company was playing the final show of its winter season of 1970. The Last Night of a London season was, traditionally, an opportunity for a little fun, when the audience might expect anything to happen other than the usual performance. Later that year, Royston was invited to join the company as Assistant Musical Director, before being promoted to Musical Director when James Walker left the company in 1971. It was wickedly rumoured amongst company members that Bridget D'Oyly Carte had been so smitten by the sight of the dashing Captain Nash in his smart uniform and white helmet that she determined, there and then, to have him in her company. Whether or not there was any truth in this story we will never know, as the Dame can no longer speak for herself, but she must have thought his long career in military band music, which had started when he was sixteen, eminently qualified him to conduct Gilbert and Sullivan. In fairness, Royston was not completely new to G&S, having played in a pit orchestra for *The Yeomen of the Guard* as a young man, as well as conducting *The Gondoliers* whilst based in Portsmouth.

There must be something about military attire, because one of the great tenors of the D'Oyly Carte, Thomas Round, auditioned for the company wearing his RAF Flight Lieutenant's uniform. Tom, who was a Spitfire pilot, spent part of the Second World War training American Air Force pilots in Texas. During this time, he sang with church choirs, often 'borrowing' a plane for a few hours on a Sunday to fly several hundred miles to a favourite church, and also took part in an amateur production of Leoncavallo's opera, *I Pagliacci*. Whilst awaiting demob from the RAF, he and a friend went to London to see a matinee of *The Mikado* at the King's Theatre, Hammersmith. It was the first time he had seen the D'Oyly Carte Opera Company and he was entranced. At the interval, he turned to his friend and said, "I can do that!" Without further ado, he left his seat and found his way to the Stage Door where he asked to see the company manager. Repeating his assertion, "I can do that!" he asked if he could be heard. Perhaps the sight of an RAF Flight Lieutenant in full uniform so surprised the manager that he was unable to refuse, so he told Tom to come back at the end of the show. An old upright piano was pulled onto the stage and he sang 'Oh, Maiden, My Maiden' from Franz Lehar's operetta, *Frederica*. Although he does not know who heard him sing, he does recall walking back to the tube and being caught up by someone from the management who said, "They want you."

Like many others awaiting demob at the end of the war, Tom had no idea as to what he was going to do to earn a living. All he knew was that he wanted to join the D'Oyly Carte and they had offered him a job, but he had a wife and small son, so it was not just about what he wanted. Fortunately, for the many fans he delighted during his years with the company, common sense did not prevail and he was soon to prove, "I can do that!" Thomas Round took an audacious approach to joining the company, although this modest man probably did not look at it that way.

Another principal tenor who joined the company after serving time in the military was Ralph Mason. Before that, he had proved himself a talented singer at school, where his interest in Gilbert and Sullivan began when he played 'Ralph Rackstraw' in *HMS Pinafore*, his 'Josephine' being the distinguished composer-to-be, Howard Blake, whom Ralph describes as "very attractive", although not keen on the kissing at the end! Continuing to sing after leaving school, Ralph joined the Sussex Branch of The Gilbert and Sullivan Society, where he met former D'Oyly Carte stars, Leslie Rands and his wife, Marjorie Eyre, who were keen for him to audition for the company. Unfortunately, his call-up for National Service put on hold any theatrical ambition.

During his army service, he became something of a 'wide boy', always looking for ways to earn money and alleviate the boredom of being a pay clerk at his batallion HQ in Hampshire. He got to know a soldier who came in every week to be paid and learned that he was personal secretary to the great Second World War commander, Field Marshal Montgomery. When the soldier announced that he was being demobilised, Ralph managed to get himself short-listed for consideration to be the successor and was duly selected by 'Monty' himself. For the rest of his time in the army he spent a fascinating time working at the great man's home, continuing in the job after demob, before deciding to leave when Montgomery told him not to fraternise with two German girls working in the area!

Returning to his Brighton home, he worked for a time at a golf course, where he met several D'Oyly Carte golfers, including Glyn Adams, who was later to become his best friend. Attracted by the stories he heard about life on tour, he got back in touch with Leslie Rands and Marjorie Eyre, who contacted Isidore Godfrey to recommend he be heard by the company. At his London audition, Ralph chose to sing unaccompanied, but started 'Oh, My Love is Like a Red, Red, Rose' too high, almost causing himself permanent damage. Nevertheless, he soon received an offer of a chorus contract and joined the company in December 1959.

Head-hunting specific singers was not the usual way of recruiting to the D'Oyly Carte, but that is how tenor, Meston Reid, came to join the company. He was appearing as 'Schubert' in the John Hanson touring production of *Lilac Time* in 1975, when he was approached after a performance by the Carte's touring manager, who had been at the show to check him out. Asked if he would be interested in joining the company, Meston was very surprised and confessed that he knew nothing about Gilbert and Sullivan, but agreed to do an audition, for which he quickly learned 'Take a Pair of Sparkling Eyes' from *The Gondoliers*. He was immediately offered a principal contract and it was obvious to him that the company was anxious to secure his services as soon as possible, the draw of year-round work making easy his decision to accept the job. However, it was several months before he was able to join due to his contractual obligation to John Hanson. Meston had no idea as to who recommended him to the D'Oyly Carte, but he went on to become extremely popular with audiences and company members alike.

For a professional singer, auditioning is a way of life, a necessary evil for any performer wishing to find a job. Auditions are stressful by nature and sometimes unsuccessful, so the phlegmatic artiste must shrug his shoulders, learn from the experience and move on to the next one. It is not helpful, therefore, when a routine audition takes an unexpected turn for the worse. It was 1970 when Yvonne Sommeling applied to join the D'Oyly Carte. She got off the bus at the stop near the theatre where the auditions were being held and realised, to her horror, that her music had not alighted with her. Having eventually found the bus terminus and retrieved the music, she was very late arriving for her audition and was grateful that not only was she allowed to sing, but also that she was offered a chorus contract. Interestingly, Yvonne was one of five students attending The Birmingham School of Music who went on to join the D'Oyly Carte over a five-year period, the others being Michael Rayner, Anne Egglestone, John Broad and myself. But more of Yvonne's escapades in the company will follow. She certainly challenged the usual perception of 'Miss Carte's young ladies'.

In 1979, Bruce Graham, a keen fan of Gilbert and Sullivan, was living in Edinburgh when he was granted an audition for the D'Oyly Carte Opera Company. Told to go to the Grand Theatre in Leeds, where the company was appearing, he booked accommodation in the city for the previous night in order to be in good time for his appointment the following morning. Ever the conscientious professional, on arrival in Leeds he decided on a trial run to make sure he could find the theatre and park his car, so as not to be late. All went according to plan.

The next morning, Bruce threw back the curtains to be greeted by a blanket of thick fog. He set off for his audition confident of the route, but poor visibility, combined with the disorienting nature of the city's traffic system, left him hopelessly lost and late for his audition. Much to his relief, the fog suddenly lifted and the now sunny streets revealed that he was not too far from the theatre. He found a car park and ran as fast as he could up Briggate, but the heavy clothes he had donned to ward off the foggy chill of the early morning meant that he arrived at the theatre, in his own words, "sweating like a glass-blower's backside", dry-mouthed and out of breath. As he was late, he was immediately ushered up to the Dress Circle Bar and had to dive straight into 'When the Night Wind Howls' from *Ruddigore* before Royston Nash, Leonard Osborn and the Assistant Director, James 'Jimmie' Marsland. Having sung in less than ideal circumstances, he turned to leave and was surprised to be asked if he would be able to go to London the following week to be heard by Dame Bridget D'Oyly Carte and the company's General Manager, Frederic Lloyd. Fortunately, his recall was far less fraught and he was immediately offered a contract as a baritone chorister and understudy to the great Kenneth Sandford.

Kenneth's own experience of auditioning for the D'Oyly Carte Opera Company was odd to say the least. It was 1957 and he had just finished an uninspiring six-month stint in a revue called *Five Past Eight* at the Alhambra Theatre in Glasgow. One morning, at home in Chiswick, he opened a letter from Miss Bridget D'Oyly Carte in which she stated it had been brought to her attention that he would be interested in auditioning for her company. He was completely at a loss to understand how this could be, as such a thought had never crossed his mind. His only experience of Gilbert and Sullivan had been singing

'Take a Pair of Sparkling Eyes' from *The Gondoliers* with the band of RAF Cranwell when he was stationed at the Lincolnshire air base at the end of the war.

Ken had always dreamed of becoming an opera singer, but he needed to earn a living so, as he was sick to death of appearing in revue, he opted to accept the audition at the Savoy Theatre that Miss Carte had suggested. Astonished to be offered the 'Pooh-Bah' roles, which meant nothing to him, he decided to take the contract, knowing that this offered his family financial security whilst he continued to work towards a career in grand opera. He was never able to resist the lure of year-round employment, despite seasonal offers from Glyndebourne and other opera companies, so he was still with the D'Oyly Carte when it closed in 1982. However, the intervening twenty-five years shed no light on that fateful letter. He could only assume someone from the company must have seen him performing and that he had been head-hunted. He was convinced the D'Oyly Carte management wanted him to think they were doing him a favour, rather than the other way around. His long experience of the company's quaint style of management probably meant he was right.

Although the Savoy Hill office received plenty of letters from hopefuls wanting to audition for the D'Oyly Carte, there were, occasionally, times when demand outstripped supply, so adverts were placed in newspapers, colleges of music were contacted or, sometimes, company performers were able to give details of singers they knew who might be suitable. In fact, over the years, 'knowing the right people' and the 'tip off' proved very successful routes into the company for many performers. Personal recommendation often saved the management a good deal of time and effort.

In Burton-on-Trent in 1980, Christine George saw an advert stating that the D'Oyly Carte Opera Company was looking to recruit sopranos and tenors. Anyone interested was asked to write to the company office, so Christine did, soon receiving a reply saying that her application would receive attention in due course. She was a full-time teacher, but a keen amateur singer looking for the opportunity to turn professional. At the time of her application, she was rehearsing *Carousel* for the local operatic society, playing the role of 'Nettie Fowler'. It was then that fate played its part. Told by the producer that she would not be required for rehearsal until 8.30pm, she was at home at 7.30pm when the phone rang. It was Fraser Goulding, the D'Oyly Carte's Musical Director, who said he had almost given up trying to contact her (there was no voicemail in those days, of course). He told her that the company was playing at the Belgrade Theatre in Coventry, which was not too far from Burton and a convenient place for her to be heard, if she was still interested. She certainly was.

Her audition went well and she was asked if she would be prepared to go to London for a second audition at The Savoy Theatre, to which she readily agreed. Two days later she received a letter with the details of her recall and noticed, to her consternation, that the date coincided with her school's annual outing, a trip to London to see *My Fair Lady*. Initially upset by the clash, she considered the timings and soon realised that she could fulfil her commitment to the pupils and, with some crafty planning, also attend her second D'Oyly Carte audition. So, she drove a minibus full of schoolchildren down the M1, headed for a Northern Line tube station, where she got out and left a colleague to complete their journey. Despite a small panic when the tube stopped and all the lights went out, she arrived at the Savoy in good time to sing a soprano aria from *HMS Pinafore*. Having assured both Fraser Goulding and Company Manager, Gordon Mackenzie, that leaving her teaching post was not a problem, she happily accepted the chorus contract offered to her. Walking on air, she met up with her school party at the previously-appointed place in Covent Garden, took the children to the Adelphi Theatre to see the show and then drove them back to Burton-on-Trent! Christine was always a good organiser.

The D'Oyly Carte Opera Company needed many people to make sure it functioned efficiently, not just its performers and musicians. The demands of travelling all over the country with several productions required a backstage staff to ensure the safe transportation of all the company's effects from venue to venue as well as getting everything ready for each performance. Both the Savoy Hill and touring management teams were essential to ensure a smooth operation throughout the forty-eight week season. Just like the performers, these vital behind-the-scenes people also arrived in the company's employ by a variety of interesting means.

In 1964, at just seventeen, Peter Riley was working on the stage crew in weekly repertory theatre in York, when a chance remark led to an eighteen-year career with the D'Oyly Carte. He was chatting one evening with one of the part-time crew members, who mentioned that he was going to see a good friend in Leeds the following day, the D'Oyly Carte Opera Company's carpenter, Trevor Morrison. With two huge plays in production and another due to start rehearsing, it was very hard work, so Peter quipped, "Ask him if there are any jobs going." The following evening, the stage hand told Peter that there was, indeed, a job vacancy and, if he was interested, he should go to the Grand Theatre in Leeds, where the D'Oyly Carte was appearing, at 9am the next morning to be interviewed by the company manager, Mr. Bruce Worsley. Worried about the 8.30am rehearsal the next day, Peter sought the advice of his mother, who told him to go for the interview if he was serious about the job and she would telephone to square things with his boss at the rep. So, he went to Leeds and Mr. Worsley immediately offered him the job; they wanted him as soon as possible. He was delighted to be offered more than double what he was being paid at York rep, over £14 a week, and jumped at the chance of such a salary. Fortunately, his current employer thanked him for his hard work and allowed him to work a week's notice on the proviso that he took a holiday before taking up his new duties as Property and Baggage Master for the D'Oyly Carte. At that moment, he could never have dreamed he would end up as Assistant General Manager of the illustrious company. Knowing the right person certainly worked for Peter.

Many years later, in his capacity as Company Manager, Peter was responsible for hiring backstage staff. He explains that props, wardrobe and stage crew were often recruited from the theatres where the company appeared on their tours, many of which were played every year. Acquaintances were made and good workers remembered, so approaches to fill vacancies were often made in this way, particularly if interest in joining the company had been shown. In the event that a job could not be filled by knowing the right person, Peter placed an advert in *The Stage*, the weekly newspaper serving the professional theatre, thereafter holding interviews to engage the most suitable person. In 1976, Shelagh Fawcett saw such an advert for a wardrobe assistant. Even though she had trained in stage management, she applied for the job and, unusually, was interviewed at Savoy Hill by Bridget D'Oyly Carte's secretary, Mr. Albert Truelove, who offered her the job on the spot.

Peter recalls that when the company's legendary Wardrobe Mistress, Florence 'Flo' Ewbank, retired, he advertised the post in *The Manchester Evening News*. A middle-aged couple, John and Vera Carnegie, successfully applied, joining in the mid-1970s and staying with the company until it closed in 1982. These quiet, rather shy people could not have been more different from Miss Ewbank, who might best be described as a battleaxe with a heart of gold, best known for her familiar cry of, "Pick your bloody dress up!" Nevertheless, the hard-working Carnegies became very popular with company members, for whom teasing the good-natured Vera was great sport.

It could be said that the D'Oyly Carte had been recycling long before it became a familiar expression in modern-day life. Performers who had retired from the stage were often used to fill other posts within the company. In 1955, Herbert Newby dropped out of the chorus and became Assistant Stage Manager, then Assistant Director of Productions. In 1956 he was appointed Stage Director. In 1960 he then became Director of Productions, before assuming the role of company Business Manager in 1970, a post he held until his death in 1979. Similarly Gordon Mackenzie. Having served as a chorister and small-part player on and off between 1954 and 1970, he became Assistant Business Manager, then took over as Business Manager when Bert Newby died. Both were extremely popular within the company. It is true to say that long-serving stalwarts knew the D'Oyly Carte inside out, but whether or not their stage experience qualified them for senior artistic, technical, or managerial positions is another matter.

The appointment of Ken Robertson-Scott as the company's Deputy Stage Manager, or DSM as the post is usually known, in 1975, is an example of how getting to know the stage crew of a theatre could pay dividends for the D'Oyly Carte. Ken had been fascinated by the theatre since he was a small child and, by the age of twelve, he was backstage helping to run and light amateur shows. Although working in his father's undertaking firm, his real ambition was to become professionally involved in the technical side of the theatre. In his late teens, he managed this by continuing to work for his father, but also by getting a job as a part-time stage hand at the Sunderland Empire and the Theatre Royal in Newcastle-upon-Tyne.

For the next few years he got to know all of the big companies on tour in the North East, the D'Oyly Carte Opera Company being one of them. Ken remembers that Peter Riley and James 'Jimmie' Marsland were always ready to chat with him and, during one D'Oyly Carte season, he approached Peter to say he would be interested in joining the company. There were no vacancies at the time, but Peter would have taken note. A couple of years later, Ken asked again, but there were still no jobs available. However, a short time afterwards, Peter wrote to Ken to tell him that there was an opening on the stage management side and so, after an interview, the job was his. A year later, Ken's dream of becoming a professional stage manager had been realised and he was 'running the corner' on the company's 1976 tour of North America, the youngest man at that time ever to have stage-managed a show on Broadway.

Given that the music of the Gilbert and Sullivan operas has rarely been considered worthy of inclusion in their syllabuses, The Royal Colleges of Music proved to be a rich source of young talent for the D'Oyly Carte, with many members joining from The Royal College and The Royal Academy in London and The Royal Northern in Manchester. One way or another, but usually by word of mouth, students would learn that the company was holding auditions and jump at the possibility of getting a well-paid job, regardless of the fact that most of them knew little or nothing about G&S.

In 1970, Kathryn Holding was studying at The Royal Northern College of Music when fellow student, Susan Mosco (later to join the company at a second attempt), told her that she was going to audition for the D'Oyly Carte Opera Company and asked Kate if she would go with her. Kate said yes and set about choosing her audition piece. It was always a source of amusement within the D'Oyly Carte that, on arranging an audition, you were often told to bring 'a bright English song', but nobody knew why. At other times, the recommendation was to sing Gilbert and Sullivan, but there were also occasions when people were told not to bring any G&S, so they sang whatever they believed would best display their vocal talent. This confusing approach to auditioning was one of the many quirks of the D'Oyly Carte and, to this day, company members still laugh whenever the 'bright English song' is mentioned.

Kathryn, for reasons best known to herself, chose to sing a Brahms song with a fiendishly difficult piano accompaniment. Taking great care to be dressed smartly for her audition, she walked confidently into the audition room above Forsyth's music shop in Manchester and gave her music to the pianist. Looking at the small, rather nondescript little man sitting at the piano, she thought he looked as if he had been dragged in from the street and had grave doubts about his ability to cope with the demands of the piano part. As she put the music in front of him, Kate leaned forward, jabbed her elbow into his ribs and whispered, "It's a bugger to play." Her fears were unfounded, the pianist played superbly and, at the end of the song he congratulated her on her performance, stating that he would love to do more work with her. At this point, he introduced himself as the company's Musical Director, James Walker. The horror and embarrassment she felt at that moment still makes her squirm forty-six years later. The gaffe did not seem to matter, because, after a short wait, she was asked to sing again. She was then told, "Thank you, we'll let you know."

Time passed and Kate heard nothing. She had been offered a summer season in Bournemouth, but was reluctant to accept this short-term job until she knew whether or not the D'Oyly Carte wanted her. She mentioned this dilemma to her teacher who, in turn, told the Principal of her college. He immediately contacted the Savoy Hill office and was told that the company were very interested in Kate, but there was no vacancy for a mezzo-soprano at that time; only sopranos were required. He countered with, "Well, Kathryn can sing soprano." And so she did, for several months, until Brenda Atherton, who understudied Peggy Ann Jones in some of the principal mezzo-soprano roles, left to have a baby. Kate was all set to replace her as a mezzo in the chorus, but was worried when summoned to the office of Michael Heyland, the Director of Productions. Scared that she was going to be sacked, she was astonished to be told that the management wanted her to take over the understudies when Brenda left. Kate remembers some of the other chorus mezzos being very put out by this unexpected promotion. After all, they had been in the company much longer than her and certainly hadn't joined as sopranos.

In 1959, another student, Gillian Knight, was in her final year at the Royal Academy of Music with ambitions of a career in opera and oratorio. The girl with whom she shared a house knew William Cox-Ife, the D'Oyly Carte's Assistant Musical Director. He had mentioned in conversation that the company was looking for a short-term replacement for its illustrious principal contralto, Ann Drummond-Grant. Miss Grant was suffering from cancer and would not be well enough to perform for some time, so it was suggested by her house mate that Gillian might be suitable for the job. An audition was quickly arranged, which saw her immediately contracted to the D'Oyly Carte, as Gillian explains:

"Bill was such a dear and put me at my ease at once, even though he was puffing cigarette smoke at me! That was it, I had six weeks to learn six roles, the last two weeks rehearsing with Snookie Fancourt and dear John Reed for a few sessions. At the same time, I managed to complete my Royal Academy of Music exams, so all was well. John was such an inspiration and we worked so well together. I can't believe how lucky I was to join the company at that time." The job proved to be rather more than temporary because, sadly, Ann Drummond-Grant died a few weeks later. It was inevitable that illness, or difficult personal circumstances, occasionally caused people to leave the company in the middle of a tour, when it became necessary for the management to find a replacement as quickly as possible. Keeping on file the details of previous auditionees could be very useful at such times and that was how Michael Rayner came to join the D'Oyly Carte.

On completing his studies at the Birmingham School of Music in 1968, Michael joined the Welsh National Opera Company's 'Opera For All' outreach programme. Although he very much enjoyed this work, it provided only six months employment each year and, with a family of five children to support, he needed to look for a job offering year-round work. He wrote to the D'Oyly Carte on several occasions, but failed to secure an audition for a long time. Eventually, his persistent requests led to an audition in Birmingham, where he sang 'Largo al factotum' from Rossini's *The Barber of Seville*. He was rewarded with nothing more than, "Thank you, we'll let you know." A year later, he was on holiday with his family in Norfolk when it was his custom to ring his mother every day to check that everything was fine at home. One morning, she told him there was a letter for him from the D'Oyly Carte Opera Company. Michael was surprised to learn that the company wanted him to go for another audition, this time at the Savoy Theatre in London, in three days time. Having been given a specific time, he rang the company office and said that he would do his best to get there on time, praying that the train from Norwich to Liverpool Street would not be late.

That was not his only concern. He had never sung any Gilbert and Sullivan and it had been requested for the audition. With great presence of mind, he sought out the choir master of Cromer parish church and explained his predicament. As luck would have it, the choir master had all the G&S scores and suggested Mike learn 'Fair Moon' from *HMS Pinafore*. He kindly coached Mike over the weekend and even lent him the score to take to his audition. There was one final problem which suddenly occurred to him: it was summer; he was on holiday; he was wearing shorts; it was Sunday; the shops were not open for him to buy a pair of trousers!

As feared, the train to London the next day was late arriving, so when he got to the Savoy Theatre, the Stage Door keeper told him that everyone had left. Not at all happy, Mike followed his directions to the company office round the corner on Savoy Hill, where, after a lengthy wait, he was cordially received by the company's General Manager, Frederic Lloyd. He was told that, as he had travelled so far, arrangements would be made for him to be heard. There followed a bizarre few minutes, during which Mike found himself trailing behind Mr. Lloyd, Royston Nash, Miss D'Oyly Carte and her secretary, Albert Truelove, as they wound their way through a maze of passages until they arrived in one of the grand banqueting rooms of the next-door Savoy Hotel. To say that Mike felt somewhat under-dressed in his shorts is something of an understatement. Asked to go to the far end of the huge room, Mike realised that there was no piano in sight. He need not have worried. Royston Nash asked him what he was going to sing, produced a tuning fork, hummed and gave him his starting note. After his sterling efforts of the previous few days, all Mike got was, "Thank you, we'll let you know."

A few days later they did let him know and he was asked to do yet another audition, this time in trousers and with a piano. Frederic

Lloyd told him he was wanted, but they couldn't say when. It was explained to him that John Webley, the talented and popular young principal baritone, had cancer and that his prognosis was uncertain. Mike set about learning the roles, effectively on standby, without being paid a retainer. It was not long before he was told that John was too ill to continue and that he was to take over the roles forthwith. Arriving for his first day of rehearsals with the full company, he was greeted by the news that John Webley had died that morning.

Personally, I owe a great deal to Michael Rayner, whom I first met in our student days at the Birmingham School of Music. Without his recommendation, I would never have joined the D'Oyly Carte Opera Company and spent a lifetime in the thrall of Gilbert and Sullivan. It was 1972 and I was in my second, not very happy, post-graduate year at the Royal College of Music. Out of the blue, Mike contacted me asking me to meet him at Sadler's Wells Theatre, which I did after a matinee. I had known he was a principal with the D'Oyly Carte, but hadn't seen him for some time. He told me that he had arranged for me to audition for the company the following week at the Savoy Theatre. I was astonished to say the least. Although I had seen and enjoyed a couple of D'Oyly Carte performances in Birmingham when I was a teenager, I considered myself a serious classical singer intent on a career in oratorio and lieder. My response must have been somewhat lukewarm, because Mike pressed the issue, telling me I could not stay at college for much longer and that an audition would be a useful experience. Despite the arrogance of youth, what he said somehow penetrated the thick layers of my musical snobbery and I eventually agreed to have a go, but only for the experience.

Never before having been on the stage of a theatre, let alone in the West End, I was very nervous for my audition and can remember only two things about it. Firstly, that I sang 'Ruth's Song' from *The Pirates of Penzance*, which I had learned in the previous few days and, secondly, that I was taken aback to find myself singing in front of a hospital bed surrounded by screens. Being nervous was one thing, but I didn't expect to collapse on the spot! Later, of course, I realised that Brian Clark's play, *Whose Life is It Anyway?* was being performed at the theatre. Was anyone ever more naïve? Within two days, I received a letter from Frederic Lloyd asking me to return to the Savoy Theatre for a recall audition a few days later and that I should prepare a piece of dialogue from one of the operettas. Again, I remember few details, except that I was asked to go down to the auditorium and was immediately offered a chorus contract to start in four weeks. I was able to buy some time to think things through by telling Mr. Lloyd that I needed to clear it with the college before agreeing to join the company. My head was in a whirl, because this was not the way it was supposed to happen. Within a few days, thanks to Michael Rayner, my life had been turned upside down.

It was not really a difficult decision. Like most poverty-stricken students, I had little money and the lure of a well-paid job proved irresistible. The bursar of the Royal College of Music, John Stainer, told me I would be mad to turn down such an opportunity and I convinced myself that getting an Equity card was very important, that it would be most useful in the future. I decided to accept the contract, but only for a year, of course! It was some time before I realised that a mezzo-soprano had left the company mid-tour and Mike had told the management that he knew someone whom he thought would be a suitable replacement. So, I was in the right place at the right time, I knew the right person, and I will always be grateful to him.

Another reluctant recruit to the D'Oyly Carte Opera Company was Elizabeth Howarth. At twenty-three years old, she had a good job in Birmingham and enjoyed singing as a hobby, performing in concerts and shows around the Midlands. She was very content with her life. That was, until she went for a singing lesson one day, when her pushy singing teacher told her that an audition with the D'Oyly Carte had been arranged for her in Stratford-upon-Avon, where the company was appearing. With her mother equally enthusiastic, Elizabeth's protests that she was not interested fell on deaf ears. On the day of the audition, to her great delight, she and her mother somehow managed to miss the train to Stratford, leading her to believe a career with the D'Oyly Carte was not meant to be. But such a minor detail did not deter Elizabeth's mother, who immediately hailed a taxi to be sure her daughter did not miss the audition. After singing 'Softly Awakes My Heart' from Saint Saens' opera, *Samson and Delilah*, Bridget D'Oyly Carte invited her to go down to the auditorium for a chat, where she was asked if she would like to join and how soon she could start. Elizabeth saw one final opportunity to escape her fate when Frederic Lloyd told her what she could expect to be paid. She gleefully retorted that she was earning far more in her current job, but her last hope evaporated when he instantly increased the offer. Finally defeated, she heard herself agreeing to join the company as a chorister and small-part player. Perhaps it was meant to be after all because, in 1953, just a year after she joined, she married the popular D'Oyly Carte principal tenor, Neville Griffiths.

Singing teachers, anxious to see their students prosper, don't always get things right. In 1974, Thomas Scholey was studying with Arthur Reckless at the Guildhall School of Music in London. Arthur, a good friend of the D'Oyly Carte's General Manager, Frederic Lloyd, suggested that Thomas should write to Savoy Hill and ask for an audition. His request granted, he was told not to sing Gilbert and Sullivan, so Reckless suggested that 'bright English song', 'The Fishermen of England'. After his rendition at the Savoy Theatre, Mr. Lloyd asked if Thomas could sing something else, so he offered 'The Vagabond's Song' from the *Songs of Travel* by Ralph Vaughan Williams. This seemed to please Mr. Lloyd, who asked Thomas why he had chosen 'The Fishermen of England', a song which he hated. Much to the discomfort of Mr. Lloyd, Thomas told him it was the choice of his singing teacher, Arthur Reckless.

It would seem that Frederic Lloyd's dislike of the audition piece did not influence his decision, because Thomas was told by the audition panel that they wanted him to join, but they could not say when. In the meantime, Thomas successfully auditioned for 'Gilbert and Sullivan For All', the popular concert group formed by Thomas Round and Donald Adams after they had left the company. He was offered some work with them, but nothing to match the twelve-month contract the D'Oyly Carte might give him. In a quandary, he rang Frederic Lloyd and told him that 'G&S For All' wanted him, to which Lloyd immediately replied, "You start at the end of June." The opposition group full of ex-Carters, which successfully toured all over the world for many years, was considered treasonous within the hallowed portals of Savoy Hill.

Kevin West was another young man at the mercy of his singing teacher. He was twenty years old and, by his own admission, naïve and self-confident in equal measure. A would-be G&S patter man, he wrote, at the suggestion of his teacher, the former D'Oyly Carte performer, Ivor Evans, to Frederic Lloyd inviting him to see an amateur performance of *The Mikado* in Ilford, which was to star Kevin as 'Ko-Ko'. Such barefaced cheek was met with a kindly, negative reply, but the letter also contained an invitation to audition early in 1975, when his audacious approach to Mr. Lloyd was rewarded with a chorus contract and the understudy to 'The Major-General' in *The Pirates of Penzance*. He recalls that, as he left the stage after his audition, Lloyd's sonorous tones escorted him into the wings: "Give my regards to Ivor."

Abby Hadfield would surely agree that singing teachers can be a mixed blessing. In 1963, she was at college in Manchester studying singing and subsidising her meagre income by taking modelling work whenever she could. She was often in demand as a head model, allowing hairdressers to create whatever style they desired, sometimes with outlandish results. Arriving one morning at college for a singing lesson, Abby was told that she was not going to have the expected lesson, as her teacher had arranged for her to go for an audition instead. Wearing trousers, she had no make-up on and was sporting white-blonde hair plastered against her face with the sides flicked up, courtesy of a recent modelling assignment. It was no wonder Abby was worried that her appearance was hardly ideal for an audition and complained that she would have preferred to have been warned in advance. On enquiry as to where she was going, she was told that the audition was for the D'Oyly Carte Opera Company. Abby was delighted by this, because her grandfather had been a huge fan of the company and, somehow, he had always managed to get free tickets for the company's Manchester seasons. She remembers just the two of them sitting in style in a box above the side of the stage, as nobody else in the family wanted to go.

Arriving for her audition feeling less than perfectly turned out for the occasion, she sang 'Mad Margaret's Song' from *Ruddigore* and was immediately called down to the auditorium, where Miss Bridget D'Oyly Carte was eyeing her appearance with some suspicion. Having been asked a few general questions, Abby was certain that Miss Carte would soon ask the obvious one and she was right. "Your hair, Miss Hadfield, is it your own?" Having explained why she was a head model, Miss Carte turned to the other panel members in amazement. "She models her head for money to help pay for her music studies.

How interesting." Despite being rather tall for the D'Oyly Carte chorus, something about her must have appealed to Miss Carte, because she was offered a contract. Abby's delight was tinged with sadness, because her grandfather, who had died two years earlier, would never know the pride of seeing her on the stage with his beloved D'Oyly Carte Opera Company. After their first introduction, there were to be further interesting encounters ahead for Abby Hadfield and Bridget D'Oyly Carte.

The vision of voice teachers who realised the value to a young performer of joining the D'Oyly Carte was laudable. To this day, musical snobbery, so common amongst people who know nothing about Gilbert and Sullivan, means that many teachers never consider what might be learned from the technical demands of Sullivan's music. It is unlikely there was ever a principal in the company who found the music of the Savoy Operas easy to sing and the company's celebrated principal soprano, Valerie Masterson, still makes the point that G&S should never be underestimated.

Joining the D'Oyly Carte Opera Company was, for some singers, a long-cherished dream, requiring both persistence and patience. Pauline Wales had loved Gilbert and Sullivan and the D'Oyly Carte Opera Company from childhood. At the tender age of sixteen, she wrote to the company asking for an audition, but was gently told that she was much too young and that she should apply when she was older. Two years later she did audition but, to her great disappointment, was not successful. For the next three years Pauline sang in oratorio, amateur musicals and operetta, gaining valuable stage experience. When she was twenty-one, her boyfriend announced that he was going to audition for the D'Oyly Carte, so she decided to go with him and try once again to achieve her ambition. She remembers going in to that second audition with a totally different approach from her first, with a new-found confidence born of many stage appearances and the maturity she had lacked at eighteen. Ironically, this time she was accepted by the company, but her boyfriend was not. Pauline does not comment on the effect this had on their relationship!

Bryan Secombe was another youngster who very much wanted to join the D'Oyly Carte. Even as a teenager, he possessed a true bass voice, a rare gift indeed. When he was seventeen years old, he wrote to the company asking for an audition but, like Pauline Wales, was told he was too young and that he should try again in two years. This he did, but his audition was not successful because he was still considered to be too young. Not to be discouraged, at the age of twenty-one, he did a second audition at the Manchester Opera House. He sang 'There Lived a King' from *The Gondoliers*, followed by a scale up and down, before he heard the immortal words, "Thank you, we'll let you know." A week later, he went directly from work in Manchester to see a performance of *Don Giovanni* given by English National Opera. Arriving home late, he found a telegram waiting for him from the D'Oyly Carte asking him to be at the Savoy Theatre for a recall audition the next morning. Brian didn't have a car, so he arranged to stay overnight with a friend who agreed to drive him to the station early the next day to get the London train, although he was not sure he could make the appointed time. Whilst he was on the train, his friend rang the D'Oyly Carte office to explain the situation and say that Bryan was on his way. He remembers there being lots of ladies doing recall auditions, but just one other man, and that they were all asked to wait in the quick-change room, before being called to the auditorium in turn. Bryan was thrilled to be offered a contract after his four-year wait. All the girls had been successful, too. Offering his congratulations to the only other man, he was told, "I didn't get in." That man was Alan Rice, who did join the company two years later in 1979. Success or failure could depend on whether the company was looking to hire a baritone or a bass .

Unusually, all the successful candidates were immediately whisked away by taxi to Wig Creations and Gamba to be measured for their wigs and shoes, something normally done on joining. On the way back to Manchester, Bryan remembers travelling with Alison Charlton-West and Hélène Witcombe, both of whom had been accepted into the company that day. The train was packed and they had to stand all the way, but they chatted excitedly about joining the D'Oyly Carte and exchanged comments about a young woman they could see further down the carriage, who spent the whole journey without looking up from her crocheting. On joining the company a month later, Bryan noticed a woman who seemed vaguely familiar and then the penny dropped; it was the lady on the train who had been so absorbed in her crocheting. He approached her and asked if she had been on that

Manchester train and did she crochet? Elizabeth Denham, the principal contralto understudy, confirmed that she was and she did, leaving both of them amazed by the coincidence.

Someone rather less patient about joining the D'Oyly Carte was Cynthia Morey. As a teenager she played the part of 'Edith' in *The Pirates of Penzance* for the Leamington and Warwick Operatic Society, immediately falling in love with Gilbert and Sullivan. At that time, in the late 1940s, all amateur groups had to perform the Savoy Operas exactly to W.S. Gilbert's original staging, so her group went to see the D'Oyly Carte perform *Pirates* to see how it must be done. Cynthia was completely hooked by everything she saw and heard, determined that she was going to join the company one day.

Her singing teacher told her that if she wanted to become a professional singer, she must be properly trained, so she applied for, and won, a scholarship to The Royal College of Music in London. After two years of too little singing and too much music theory, she was bored by having to spend so much time studying harmony, counterpoint and everything she didn't want to know about the great composers: she wanted to be on the stage. With so little opportunity for that at the college, she joined a local G&S society and did two shows, learning more about the theatre than she had done in her time at college. Soon after, she decided to take matters into her own hands by writing to the D'Oyly Carte to ask for an audition. The letter inviting her to be heard soon followed, with the instruction to sing 'a bright English song'. She made sure to choose one that had a good top note at the end of it. Cynthia was thrilled to be accepted but, as in my own case, she had to tell the Royal College why she wanted to leave before completing her studies. Her experience was somewhat different, because the bursar told her she was mad to think about leaving and sneeringly asked how she thought she was going to get a job. She had the pleasure of informing him she already had one and that was that. Early in 1951, she fulfilled her ambition to join the D'Oyly Carte Opera Company.

In 1971, Rosalind Griffiths was nearing the end of her studies at the Royal Northern College of Music. Ready to be out in the big world of professional theatre, she applied for auditions to various companies, including Welsh National Opera. However, she knew that the D'Oyly Carte Opera Company was playing its annual season at the

Manchester Opera House and was reminded of seeing the company with her mother as a youngster, when she was inspired by the comedic talents of Peggy Ann Jones. She remembers saying to her mother, "I want to be like her." So she went to the Stage Door of the Opera House and, not having a clue to whom she was speaking, asked if it might be possible for her to have an audition. By coincidence, she was told that open auditions were soon to be held and given the date.

She arrived in good time and joined the queue of hopefuls, noticing the very short lady immediately in front of her, who had a pair of tap shoes draped around her shoulders. Somewhat startled by this, Ros found herself wondering what on earth either of them was doing there. The queue eventually ended in the wings and Ros was next to go on after the tap dancer. She remembers hearing the clickety-click of the dance steps, quickly followed by a loud shout from the auditorium: "Next!" Ros sang a Michael Head song and was asked to go to London for a recall at the Savoy Theatre, for which she was told to sing Gilbert and Sullivan. Unwisely, she chose a piece she had never done before, 'The Sun Whose Rays' from *The Mikado*. The first verse went very well, but she arrived at the beginning of the second without a word of it in her head. She could only stand in embarrassment as the accompanist, William Cowley, cigarette dangling from the corner of his mouth, sang it for her! Despite this lapse, Ros was accepted and joined the company the following year.

Advertised open auditions, often referred to as 'cattle calls', were sometimes held by the D'Oyly Carte and, as Stage Manager, Ken Robertson-Scott was responsible for the smooth running of these events. With a list of names to announce, he made sure that the next singer was always ready in the wings, took the contact details of anyone whom the audition panel might wish to hear again, or escorted people through the pass door from stage to auditorium if the panel wished to speak to someone who could be of use. Often lasting for some hours, open auditions could be very tedious and Ken remembers when, in one morning, they had to endure twenty-eight sopranos singing 'Poor Wand'ring One' from *The Pirates of Penzance*. It is at such times that one's heart goes out to the poor accompanist even more than to those having to listen. Ken recalls another occasion when a young man with no singing ability whatsoever delivered his song in excruciating fashion. From the darkened auditorium, the voice of General Manager, Frederic Lloyd, enquired, "What do you do for a living?" The young fellow replied that he was a Stage Manager at Sadler's Wells Theatre. "Ah, well, that explains it. I do think that Stage Managers should stick to stage-managing."

Time and again, it proved to be the case that people joined the D'Oyly Carte because they were in the right place at the right time, or because they knew the right people and sometimes, as in the case of John Reed, both situations applied. It was 1951 and John was out and about in Darlington when he bumped into a man called Ron Thornton, whose brother, Eric, had once appeared in a Darlington Operatic Society show with John. Ron told him that Eric had become a principal with the D'Oyly Carte Opera Company and that he knew an understudy to the 'patter man', Peter Pratt, was being.sought. Eric Thornton had told his brother he thought John would be ideal and could arrange an audition. John was very taken aback, because he was a dancer and actor, not a trained singer, so an opera company seemed way out of his league. However, he decided to have a go and Eric arranged for John to be heard at an hotel in Glasgow, where the company was playing at the Theatre Royal.

Used to quickly learning new material when he was in repertory theatre, John soon picked up 'The Nightmare Song' from *Iolanthe*, his first experience of Gilbert and Sullivan. His rendition having been met with the expected, "Thank you, we'll let you know", John chose to go to see a ballet that evening; it never occurred to him to watch the D'Oyly Carte. He was not bothered about joining the company and put the audition out of his mind. A week later, he got a letter asking him to go to Edinburgh for a recall to be attended by Bridget D'Oyly Carte and Frederic Lloyd, after which he was immediately offered a contract. He was so shocked that he accepted, on the proviso he could have two months to sort out his personal affairs and, most importantly, arrange care for his widowed mother. That evening, he bought his own ticket to see the company perform *The Gondoliers*, which only served to convince him he would not fit in. A few days later, when he had decided to turn down the contract, he took a phone call from Mr Lloyd asking him if he could possibly join in Newcastle earlier than agreed, in fact, in two weeks time. His earlier decision flying out of the window, John found himself saying, "yes". Thus, one of the truly great D'Oyly Carte performers hesitantly signed up for what proved to be an illustrious twenty-eight year career with the company.

It occasionally happened that couples joined the D'Oyly Carte together, but it took Patricia Leonard and Michael Buchan a few years to manage this. Both had been struggling to make a living as singers, so when Patricia was chatting with D'Oyly Carte principal tenor, Ralph Mason, after a concert they had done together, his suggestion was that they should write to the company for an audition. Trish and Mike followed Ralph's advice and both were auditioned on the same day, but neither was accepted. In 1971, at the same time the company re-auditioned Michael Rayner as a potential replacement for the ailing John Webley, Michael Buchan was recalled to sing for the same reason. He was to be disappointed again. However, a year later, he was again contacted by the company and asked to sing for a third time. Patricia volunteered to drive him to London from their home in Stoke-on-Trent and Mike recalls that it was a dreadful day of torrential rain, so Trish dropped him off at the Stage Door of Sadler's Wells Theatre while she went to find somewhere to park the car. After he had sung, Miss D'Oyly Carte asked if the same young lady was with him as when they had previously auditioned and if she would be willing to sing. Mike told her that Patricia was waiting for him and he was sure she would be happy to sing for them again. It was at this point he caught sight of Trish in the wings resembling a drowned rat. He dragged her onto the stage and then made a hasty exit, leaving her standing in a dripping mac, squelching shoes and with her drenched hair plastered against her head. Asked if she could sing any Gilbert and Sullivan, Trish opted for 'Alone and Yet Alive' from *The Mikado*, probably thinking that her dreadful appearance would make light work of portraying 'Katisha'!

Both were asked down to the auditorium for a chat and offered contracts, but were told that they needed to make a decision within an hour. Shocked by this totally unexpected turn of events, they retired to the pub across the road, the Shakespeare's Head, to consider their position. With drinks to hand, Mike asked Trish what she thought they should do. Her response was to burst into tears. Overjoyed to think that, after all the years of hard work, they at last had the chance to join a famous company, she knew that there would be difficulties ahead, not the least being the welfare of her young son, Andrew. But the chance for both of them to earn a good living was important, too. Another flood of tears brought the landlady over to ask what was the matter. Through sobs, Trish told her that they had just been offered jobs with the D'Oyly Carte. "Congratulations! What are you drinking?" After a couple of glasses of wine, Trish was able to think more calmly and they decided the offer was too good to refuse, so she and Mike walked back over to the theatre and accepted their contracts. It is interesting to note that, with the help of family, Andrew's education was successfully managed and he joined Patricia for the Australian tour of 1979, where he was tutored by chorister and, latterly, choreographer, Alan Spencer, a former teacher.

In 1956, the final of the inaugural Kathleen Ferrier singing competition featured a soprano aged nineteen called Jean Hindmarsh. In the audience at Westminster Hall that night was the D'Oyly Carte's General Manager, Frederic Lloyd. Despite the fact that she didn't win, he was so impressed by her singing that he got in touch with her and asked her to audition for the company. With principal soprano, Muriel Harding, leaving the D'Oyly Carte, a replacement needed to be found, so Jean auditioned twice before being offered the job. She recalls going down for a chat after singing for the second time and, much to her surprise, being asked to take off her shoes. The muttered discussion amongst the panel members produced the verdict that, with flat shoes, she was not too tall to play opposite principal tenor, Neville Griffiths. Although Jean had designs on a career in opera and oratorio, she accepted the contract, seeing it as a great opportunity to gain valuable professional experience. Sometimes, being too tall, or too short, might mean the difference between getting a job or not. It is not always solely about talent; there are sometimes practical considerations to be taken into account.

Soon after Jean joined, Mary Sansom came into the company after distinguishing herself as an amateur performer. Despite her considerable experience in Gilbert and Sullivan, Mary's audition in Bournemouth was something of a nightmare. She was so nervous that she tripped up as she came onto the stage and was barely able to sing. The Musical Director, Isidore Godfrey, taking pity on her, suggested that she go and take a walk on the promenade to calm herself before trying again. His advice must have worked, because she came back and sang well enough to be asked to join the D'Oyly Carte as a small-part player and understudy to Jean Hindmarsh.

It is difficult to explain to someone who has never been involved in the theatre how much more nerve-racking it can be to audition for a role than to play it in performance. Auditions have to be endured and it is true to say that some performers are better at auditioning than others. An audition panel may be faced with a singer who gives a reasonable account of themselves, but who, when employed, proves never to be more than ordinary, regardless of how much coaching they receive. On the other hand, someone who gives a shaky, nervous audition could prove to be a fine performer once outside of the audition situation. How is an employer to make this distinction? For experienced directors, it often comes down to gut instinct; they just seem to know the difference.

On finishing her studies in Geneva, her reward for winning the Sir Thomas Beecham Scholarship at The Royal College of Music, Jane Metcalfe returned to London and found work with the Glyndebourne Festival Chorus, the Scottish Opera Chorus and The Ambrosian Opera Chorus. It was one day in 1975 that she went to have tea with an old friend and was introduced to another guest, Judi Merri, the principal mezzo-soprano of the D'Oyly Carte Opera Company. Judi complained at length about the company and, in high dudgeon, told Jane and her friend that she was leaving. The next morning, Jane rang the D'Oyly Carte office and asked if she could be auditioned but was not expecting to be told that they would hear her two days later. A hasty visit to the library produced a copy of *The Yeomen of the Guard*. With just enough time to learn 'When Maiden Loves', she went to the Savoy Theatre, where all the senior management was present, including Bridget D'Oyly Carte.

She sang 'Che Faro' from Gluck's *Orpheus and Euridice*, followed by the song from *Yeomen* and was asked to go down for a chat. One thing she had not anticipated was immediately being offered the job of principal mezzo-soprano. She asked for time to consider the offer and remembers Michael Heyland, the Stage Director, giving her two hours to make up her mind. She knew there was a possibility of getting more work with Glyndebourne, so she rang the company office in the hope of finding out, but was told that, as it was holiday time, nobody would be available to give her an answer for a few days. Taking a deep breath, she went back in to the Savoy and signed the D'Oyly Carte contract there and then. The company must have been anxious to find a replacement for Judi Merri, because it was most unusual to be asked to sign on the dotted line at a first audition. A few days later, much to her dismay, Glyndebourne contacted her and offered her more work, including the understudy to the great Dame Janet Baker. Understandably, Jane did not wish to miss such an opportunity, so she rang Equity, the actors' union, only to be told that there was no way out of the D'Oyly Carte contract. Her fate was sealed. How typical of the theatre business; it's either feast or famine.

It was the 'tip-off' and 'in the know' techniques that led to D'Oyly Carte auditions for Christene Palmer and her future husband, Norman Wilfred Wright. Both joined the company in this way and admit that neither of them knew much about Gilbert and Sullivan. Christene's only experience of G&S was singing 'Oh Foolish Fay' from *Iolanthe* at a singing competition in her native Australia before she came to England to further her studies and look for work. Whilst in the Glyndebourne Opera Chorus, a colleague told her that Gillian Knight was leaving the D'Oyly Carte and suggested Christene might be a suitable replacement. As a lover of opera, oratorio, baroque music and madrigals, this was not at all what Christene had in mind, but year-round work being hard to find, she contacted the company and went for an audition at the Savoy Theatre, for which she learned 'I'm Called Little Buttercup' from *HMS Pinafore*. It is a source of regret to her that it proved to be the only time she sang on that stage. It must be assumed that the famous home of the Savoy Operas inspired her to make quite an impression on the company management, because one audition was considered enough for her to succeed Gillian Knight in 1965.

Norman Wright was at music college one day when the pianist for the opera class, with whom he had become friendly, told him he was due to play for D'Oyly Carte auditions in a few days time and that Norman should think of going. Having just been offered a contract for a national tour of *The Student Prince*, starring John Hanson, Norman thought it a waste of time. But his wise counsellor pointed out that, however much he might enjoy touring in John Hanson's company, he would be out of work when the tour finished, whereas a D'Oyly

Carte contract offered full-time employment. His friend, who was in the know, said that the company was looking for a chorus tenor, so it was arranged for Norman to attend at the Savoy Theatre. The first of several tenors to be heard, he was invited down for a chat and remembers Bridget D'Oyly Carte asking him if he was willing to take the job. His sympathy for the unheard tenors still waiting in the wings lasted just long enough for him to say yes.

And, finally, there was John Broad, whose repeated attempts to have a well-paid career in education were always thwarted by the good intentions of his college teachers. Studying English at university in Birmingham, he wanted to get qualified as quickly as possible in order to be earning a living. As is the wont of students, he got rather drunk with his friends one evening and ended up singing loudly in the bath in the small hours, much to the annoyance of his tutor who was in the next room. An angry knock on the door was followed by a curt instruction for John to present himself at his tutor's office at 8.30am. With a terrible hangover, he made it on time for the inevitable reprimand. Having been duly admonished, he was frogmarched to the office of the music tutor who ran the college choir. Joining a choir seemed a pleasant kind of punishment for his drunken vocal antics, but he was in for a surprise. The music tutor, in turn, frogmarched him to a crumbling old building in Dale End, at that time in the 1960s, the home of the Birmingham School of Music, later to become the Birmingham Conservatoire.

Awaiting him was the college principal, Gordon Clinton. "I've heard all about you; can you tell the difference between a major and minor chord?" John had been a boy chorister at Christchurch Priory, so was able to assure Mr. Clinton that he could. After he had sung, obviously to the satisfaction of the principal, arrangements were made for John to receive a small scholarship to cover the cost of singing lessons at the school for a year. When the year came to an end, John was happy to be getting back to the serious business of getting a job as a teacher. But no, scraping around the School of Music finances, Mr. Clinton came up with a second year of funding as John certainly could not afford to pay for his own lessons. That year duly completed, there could be no more money so John, once again, contemplated his teaching career. That was until his father announced that he had seen an article in the Christchurch Times about a local Dorset charity which helped with education costs for the children of distressed seamen. John protested that such a deception was hardly right, but his dad countered by saying that the charity would never find out. With a glowing recommendation from his singing teacher, René Soames, a successful, if fraudulent, application was made to the charity and so, the money was dishonestly found to cover a third year of singing lessons. Three years turned into four when the duped charity not only stumped up the money for more lessons, but also added a tidy sum to cover living expenses, which John promptly spent on a Triumph Spitfire sports car!

That was surely that, but René had other ideas. John, who had thoroughly enjoyed himself (as did we all) at the tumbledown Birmingham School of Music, told the college that enough was enough; it was time to get on with the serious business of becoming a teacher. However, on going for a singing lesson, he saw on top of the grand piano a copy of the Birmingham Evening Mail, open at the entertainments page. René explained: "The D'Oyly Carte are at the Alex, I have a contact there. You should audition." The contact was his former student, Anne Egglestone, who had joined the company in 1967. Resigned to the inevitable, John, yet again, did what everyone thought he should and attended the audition arranged by Anne. Surprised to be offered a contract, John quickly did his sums and realised that the salary offered by the D'Oyly Carte was more than he could earn as a teacher. He could be 'a thousand a year man', a fortune in those days. So, after all his protestations, in 1969 John became a professional singer. As things turned out, he eventually fulfilled his dream of working in education, becoming a successful Head Teacher in Somerset after six years with the D'Oyly Carte. However, he has his time with the company to thank for meeting his wife of forty-one years, soprano Rosalind Griffiths.

During the period covered by this book, of the hundreds of artistes who appeared with the D'Oyly Carte, it is likely that many more of them than it is possible to include could tell a story or two about joining the company. However, the anecdotes related in this chapter go some way towards demonstrating the company's recruitment process. For all those who were successful, it was just the beginning of their adventures with the company.

CHAPTER TWO

"BEGINNERS, PLEASE."

Sir Despard Murgatroyd (A
Wicked Baronet)

The delight felt at being accepted into the D'Oyly Carte was soon tempered by the process of being integrated into the productions and most new recruits to the company found the preparation period a real shock to the system. Nobody could have anticipated how hard would be the intensive period of work required to learn as many as eight of the Savoy Operas in a few short weeks. Generally speaking, people leaving the company finished in late summer at the end of an eleven-month tour. Those staying on had a well-earned four-week holiday, during which time the new personnel would be in London learning the music and stage business ready to be slotted into shows for the start of the new season in September. For principals and chorus alike, it was a tough introduction to company life. There were occasional exceptions to this format, mostly when performers left in the middle of a tour, requiring replacements to be found and trained as soon as possible.

Beginning any job is daunting; meeting new people and being the object of their curiosity is always difficult, even for those of a gregarious nature. Starting life with the D'Oyly Carte was no different.

It was easier to be part of a group of new people than to join alone but, for anyone of a diffident nature, it could be an awkward time. Michael Lessiter joined the company after the Australian tour of 1979, which had seen the departure of several choristers and principals. A quiet, rather shy man, he made his way in good time to the Church of the Holy Redeemer in Islington's Exmouth Market for his first rehearsal, where he saw a group of people standing outside chatting excitedly and guessed them to be his new colleagues. Too nervous to join them, Mick walked up and down the market several times before finally plucking up the courage to introduce himself. However, after two weeks of music calls in the grim church hall, he had become firm friends with the others and soon discovered the delights of that favourite D'Oyly Carte watering hole, The Angel Cafe, near Sadler's Wells Theatre.

However glamorous it might have seemed to become part of a prestigious company, the grind of learning music for many hours each day in dingy church halls, or dreary rehearsal rooms, soon brought home the reality of life in the theatre. Whether joining alone or with others, it was an exhausting experience. The work continued away from rehearsals when newcomers slogged away in their own time to memorise vast amounts of music and words. Jane Stanford, who joined the company in 1979, remembers sharing a room with fellow newcomer, Alexandra Hann, where a tape recorder was placed on the table between their beds so that they could listen to the soprano chorus lines before they went to asleep. It would be reasonable to assume that every singer joining the D'Oyly Carte was able to read music to a high standard, but this was not always the case. Those who had not enjoyed the benefits of a formal musical education could find themselves at a disadvantage if they were not as proficient at 'reading' as other new recruits.

Jeffrey Cresswell, a fine lyric tenor with a wealth of amateur stage experience, describes in his memoirs the difficulty he encountered when he first joined the company in 1968. In the early rehearsals, a repetiteur was tasked with teaching newcomers the music for the operas in the repertoire, so anyone who could not read as well as the others inevitably caused delay. In a process known as 'note bashing', the vocal line is played over and over until memorised. This way of learning is usual in amateur groups, but uncommon in a professional opera company. Jeff found it somewhat uncomfortable to keep his new colleagues waiting because he needed his notes repeated more than they did. Sight-reading tests were not a part of D'Oyly Carte auditions: it was always assumed that anyone wishing to join the company possessed the ability to read music.

Peter Lyon was lucky in that, as an amateur, he had played the baritone roles he took over from Michael Rayner in 1979. This allowed him more time to concentrate on learning the productions, although much of the stage business he already knew from appearing with amateur G&S societies which slavishly adhered to D'Oyly Carte moves. Peter, quite rightly, points out that there was just not enough time between the end of one tour and the start of the next to give every new member ideal preparation. Time was money for a company without funding, so it was essential to get new personnel into the shows as quickly as possible and trust that confident, polished performances would soon follow with the experience of eight shows every week.

Between rehearsals, arrangements were made for newcomers to have costume and wig fittings. The D'Oyly Carte wardrobe department and stores were housed just off the Walworth Road, in Camberwell, where Ruby Buckingham and her team pinned, fitted and tucked to adapt costumes for their new occupants. In latter years, Wig Creations was the favoured supplier to the company and, as with the costumes, wigs were reworked to fit new personnel or, sometimes, made to measure. These excursions brought welcome relief from the grind of hours spent sitting on hard chairs going over the music, or practising production moves.

New principals, too, had to be coached in the music for their roles and this was, usually, the responsibility of the company, but they sometimes undertook the task themselves, paying for coaching out of their own pockets if necessary. In 1956, Jean Hindmarsh was told to make her own arrangements to learn her music and paid expenses of £10 a week to cover the cost of a repetiteur during the six weeks she had to prepare before starting production rehearsals. At least she had the luxury of someone to teach her, which is more than I did. Joining mid-tour, I was given just a month to have the chorus music learned for the eight shows in the repertoire before I joined the company in April of 1972. Left to my own devices, I spent many hours in the music library of The Royal College of Music in London which, luckily, had recordings of all the Savoy Operas. Poring over the scores, headphones in place, I somehow managed to absorb the alto harmonies more accurately than I dared hope. I certainly did not receive a retainer during the month I spent swotting. The results of my labours were never checked when I arrived in Manchester to join the company and I can remember making any necessary corrections when singing with the other altos in the chorus. Over forty years later, I am amazed that I still know all that music learned in such a state of panic.

When Clive Harré joined the company in 1979, he experienced difficulties with some of his new music, struggling, in particular, with the harmony lines for 'Captain Corcoran' in *HMS Pinafore*. This was due to the fact that, before he joined the D'Oyly Carte, he had played 'Sir Joseph Porter' in the same opera. Trying to 'unlearn' one music line and replace it with another is never easy and it proved a real irritation for Clive, the Act Two 'Ring the Merry Bells' trio driving him barmy as he slipped from one character's line into the other. He also had to cope with being vocally unsuited to the 'Sergeant of Police' in *The Pirates of Penzance*. As a high baritone, the low tessitura of the great comedy role proved a real problem as he tried to adapt his technique. He recalls Fraser Goulding, the Musical Director, trying to help him but, in the finish, he decided to throw himself into the acting side of the part and try not to worry too much about the low notes.

Clive was not alone in finding the 'Sergeant of Police' too low. Kenneth Sandford inherited the 'Pooh-Bah' parts and the 'Sergeant' from Arthur Richards when he joined the company in 1957. For five seasons Ken had to play a part he came to hate. As a former tenor, the low notes were completely out of his range, so it was not unknown for him to stamp his foot on the bottom note whilst someone in the line of policemen behind obligingly sang it for him. Ken also struggled for the same reason with 'King Hildebrand' in *Princess Ida*, the rapid-fire diction required in the lowest part of his voice causing him considerable difficulty. By contrast, some of his other roles, like 'Doctor Daly' in *The Sorcerer* and 'Archibald Grosvenor' in *Patience*, afforded him the luxury of a higher tessitura which suited him much better.

Blocks of parts being handed on to new principals was D'Oyly Carte policy throughout its history. The 'patter' parts, The 'Mikado' roles and 'Pooh-Bah' roles, as well as the 'dame' character contralto parts were prime examples, with one performer, in general, playing all the parts in the set. W.S. Gilbert created a wealth of diverse characters for which Sullivan set appropriate music, so this system of allocating parts, inevitably, led to occasions of unsuitable casting, but that was the way it had always been and the principals had to accept it as part of the job. John Reed was never happy playing 'The Major-General' in *The Pirates of Penzance*, but loved all of the other comedic roles. It was several seasons before he was able to relinquish it to his understudy, on the basis that it was better for the understudy to play a role in his own right than suffer audience disappointment when a scheduled night off meant John did not appear. It is probably fair to say that the D'Oyly Carte was the only opera company to adopt a policy which systematically cast performers in sets of roles, regardless of whether or not they were suited to all of them.

It was March 1951 when Cynthia Morey joined the company along with several other choristers, in preparation for the Festival of London season which was to start in May. They were taught the music by Maude Evans, a lady in her eighties who, in her youth, had worked with W.S. Gilbert. Cynthia remembers her being a stickler for detail and woe betide anyone who missed a demi-semi quaver or dotted note. Not at that time protected by Equity rules, Cynthia describes music rehearsals as "interminable". Sat on upright chairs with few breaks, in a bleak band room in the bowels of The Savoy Hotel, the work was very hard and reminiscent of being at school. It is worth pointing out that, in later years, Equity dictated that a normal rehearsal session could be no longer than three hours and include a fifteen-minute break. Some three years later, Jennifer Toye was another young chorister who found herself being put through her musical paces by Maude Evans. Unlike Cynthia rehearsing in central London, she and her fellow newcomers had to travel by train to Maude's home near Watford, the tedium of the daily journey adding to the fatigue of intensive rehearsals, although she and her colleagues at least had a lunch break and some fresh air, watching cricket in the local park. Although their tiredness after a long day was understandable, it is, nevertheless, a great pity, as Cynthia points out, that neither she nor Jennifer had the foresight to ask for anecdotes about Gilbert from someone who actually knew him.

Amongst the D'Oyly Carte repetiteurs responsible for getting the new singers prepared, William Cox-Ife seems to have been universally popular. Before joining the company as Assistant Musical Director and Chorus Master in 1950, Bill had enjoyed a varied and successful career, including conducting many film scores, as well as orchestral concerts in Germany and Belgium. Having excellent musical credentials is one thing, but getting new recruits through the difficult period of taxing rehearsals required patience and an easy manner. Bill's charm was legendary and everyone spoke well of him. Christene Palmer spent several gruelling weeks with him learning all eight roles inherited from Gillian Knight and she still speaks highly of his work with her. His tragic death in a plane crash in 1968 was mourned by D'Oyly Carte members even though he was no longer with the company. His successors included Stuart Nash, Peter Murray, James Walker, William Cowley (who, rather quaintly, started his D'Oyly Carte career in the wardrobe department before being recycled to the music department), David Mackie, Paul Seeley and Glyn Hale. All excellent musicians no doubt, but William Cox-Ife's name always brings fond memories to those who worked with him.

Even new members of the music staff had to spend weeks learning the operas. When Royston Nash joined the company as assistant to James Walker, he was handed thirteen piano/conductor scores and was expected to learn everything about the shows from them. A full conductor's score has all vocal and instrumental lines, but the D'Oyly Carte only ever used a piano accompaniment score with important instrumental cues marked in red ink. This had been the practice of the company for many years, which seemed to make no sense, but there was little Royston could do to change things. Watching rehearsals for the new tour of 1970, he carefully made notes about the tempi used and the stage business; a music director has to know where everyone is positioned on the stage so that he knows where to look when giving them cues. For Royston, it was an intensive period of work as he got stuck into learning everything that happened on the stage, as well as what everyone did musically, both on the stage and in the orchestra pit, for all the operas in the repertoire. No mean feat.

Hard as it was for new members learning all the music for several shows before commencing production rehearsals, it must not be forgotten that principals needed to be memorising the dialogue for their roles at the same time as absorbing the music. Whereas they had help from the music staff for the latter, dialogue was always left to the performers, with no help at all coming from the production staff. Principal soprano, Susan Jackson, vividly remembers the hot summer of 1967, when she worked for hours on the roof terrace of the house she shared in Earl's Court, with her housemate playing all the other parts, sometimes having to shout to be heard above the noise of planes passing low overhead, as she crammed in the dialogue for the roles she had taken over from Ann Hood. This had to fit in between her appearances in *The Magic Flute* at the London Opera Centre and several trips to Bristol, where the company was playing, for music rehearsals. New principals were expected to know their words no matter what. No rehearsal time was allowed for dialogue, so it must be supposed that the company assumed they would be proficient in the acting department. Every performer has their own way of learning lines, but Jane Metcalfe's was most ingenious. Whilst learning the music for the soubrette parts she had inherited from Judi Merri, she came up with a novel way to get to grips with the dialogue. When studying singing in Geneva, she had become fluent in French and found that by translating Gilbert's words into French, their meaning readily stuck, making them easier to remember when she translated them back into English.

The fact that so little help in dialogue or characterisation was available to new principals and understudies was due, in no small measure, to time restrictions, but also to the fact that most of the production staff were the product of the in-house recycling of retired performers, many of them choristers or small-part players. Eleanor Evans, (aka 'Snookie' Fancourt), Robin Gibson, Herbert Newby and James Marsland, all took charge of rehearsals, but had limited personal experience of delivering dialogue whilst with the company. A former principal elevated to director status in 1978, the celebrated tenor, Leonard Osborn, made little impact. A fine performer does not necessarily make a good director, something the D'Oyly Carte management did not seem to understand. It was supposed that an experienced principal would, by default, be capable of staging a show and bringing out fine acting performances but, if anything, Leonard Osborn took the company delivery style back forty years to his own era at a time when the company desperately needed to look to the future. On the rare occasions that directors were brought in from outside, Osborn's predecessor, Michael Heyland, and Wilfred Judd amongst them, they were, invariably, inexperienced in Gilbert and Sullivan, or lacking the ability to suggest anything in the way of characterisation, either to incoming principals, or seasoned stalwarts thirsty for fresh insight into their characters.

Kenneth Sandford and John Reed were two such long-standing principals always looking to refine their performances and breathe new life into the characters played week in and week out, but no D'Oyly Carte Stage Director ever had anything to offer them. Ken and John often laughed in disbelief about the time in the 1960s when the much-favoured company designer, Peter Goffin, was brought in by Bridget D'Oyly Carte to 'freshen up' *The Yeomen of the Guard* and take charge of the production. He called John and Ken for a rehearsal, whereupon he told them to work out how they wanted to play the Act Two scene between 'Jack Point' and 'Wilfred Shadbolt', then he would look at it and tell them whether or not he liked it! Such ill-considered appointments were, sadly, typical of the company management.

Of course, there are always exceptions and it is generally acknowledged that Anthony Besch, brought in to re-stage *The Gondoliers* in 1968, created a production that was a complete departure from the usual D'Oyly Carte house style. Not only did it have a different look with its Edwardian costumes, but the characters and chorus, set free from the confines of straight lines and semi-circles, became much more vibrant under his guidance. Taken out of the traditional 'classical' design, the principals had much more freedom to express themselves and few who saw it would ever forget the quiet, sinister lechery of Kenneth Sandford's 'Don Alhambra del Bolero'. Perhaps, if the management had seen the wisdom of having more of the operas staged by a director with a proven pedigree, the closure of the company might have been averted.

Having been recycled twice within the company, Robert 'Robin' Gibson proved himself to be a capable director. He served for a year in the chorus from 1945, before being appointed Company Stage Manager, a post he held for three years. He then left to work in America, becoming the first British Stage Manager at New York City's famous Radio City Music Hall. In 1953, he returned to the D'Oyly Carte to replace Eleanor Evans as Director of Productions, his arrival in this post as mysterious as his sudden departure three years later. Known to be keen on 'method acting', Robin introduced improvisation sessions to improve acting techniques, which he dubbed 'the Chekhov class' and all chorus members were expected to attend. Cynthia Morey conjures up wonderful images of them all trying to do as instructed in one such class, having to fight their way through an imaginary forest to be confronted by a shining vision. Unexpectedly coming face to face with her great pal, John Reed, the pair collapsed into hysterical laughter. Needless to say, the classes didn't last long, although Jennifer Toye remembers Robin taking her to an improvisation class in Berkeley, California during the 1956 American tour. She, too, found it impossible to take seriously, her endeavours to be a blossoming tree coming to nothing but giggles.

In fairness to Robin Gibson, he seems to have been genuine in his desire to nurture the operas. Jean Hindmarsh remembers how he tried to help her with dialogue and characterisation when she first joined the company. Young and inexperienced, she had several soprano roles to learn and found his guidance very useful until she found her feet. She recalls that he had followed her down the street one day, later telling her she didn't have the bearing of a principal with a famous opera company and that she lacked self-confidence. His advice was that she should always think she was 'Princess Ida' when unsure of herself, advice she has followed to this day. Robin was given the task of re-staging *Princess Ida*, which brought him into close collaboration with Bridget D'Oyly Carte and the designer, James Wade. The company gossip machine suggested that Miss Carte carried a torch for Robin, but her interest was not returned. It is impossible to know the truth behind his sudden disappearance from the company in 1956, which took everyone by surprise but, for a long time afterwards, it was speculated that he fled the country to avoid Miss Carte's attentions. If true, perhaps Gilbert would have smiled at the echo of 'Katisha' pursuing 'Nanki-Poo' in *The Mikado*!

With the music under their belts, production rehearsals were the next challenge for new company members. Between 1950 and 1982, the responsibility for teaching the stage business fell into the hands of several interesting characters, all of whom had been recycled with varying degrees of success. During the early part of this period, the job of preparing choristers for the stage fell to C. William Morgan, better known as 'Billy', who was associated with the company for over thirty years. He had started in the second-string D'Oyly Carte company in 1920, transferring to the main company in 1927 as a chorister, understudy, small-part player and Assistant Stage Manager. It is not clear how he moved on from stage management to assisting on the production staff, but he seems to have been a popular character.

Joining the company at the same time as Cynthia Morey were two other sopranos, Joyce Farrer and Patricia Crossingham, alongside baritone Leslie Still. It fell to Billy Morgan to prepare them for the shows in time for the start of the Festival of Britain season in 1951. Leading them into the magnificent Lancaster Room of The Savoy Hotel, the dapper Billy started by teaching the girls the moves for the opening chorus of *Iolanthe*. With rolled-up umbrellas for fairy wands, he led by example as they balletically twirled around the room, much to the amusement of the waiters setting tables for a banquet. It was not lost on them that the flamboyant Billy was somewhat more fairy-like than the girls struggling to keep up with him!

John Dennison remembers being taught the moves and dances for the shows by Billy, whom he found to be a fascinating man, who delighted in taking his new charges to the pub after rehearsals and regaling them with hilarious tales of the old days. John still regrets that there were no handy voice-recorders in 1956 to commit such stories to posterity, because it is not now possible to have first-hand accounts of life in the D'Oyly Carte in the 1920s and 30s. Sadly, John cannot recall any specific story after all this time, only that he loved hearing them told in Billy's inimitable style.

Rather less personable was Eleanor Evans, wife of the great principal bass-baritone, Darrell Fancourt. Known to everyone as 'Snookie', for reasons that nobody has been able to remember, her grand manner was not popular with company members and she proved to be very intimidating to newcomers. Her D'Oyly Carte career had been lengthy, but unspectacular. She joined the company in 1921 as a chorister and, over the next twenty-six years, she had spells playing small principal parts, sometimes losing them to newcomers, before spending her final ten years solely as a chorister.

In 1949, she was unexpectedly selected by Bridget D'Oyly Carte to become Director of Productions, a choice which met with strong opposition from many of the established principals. Martyn Green, in particular, was unhappy about her appointment and made his opinion known to the management. Her temperamental nature and dictatorial style certainly made her unpopular amongst company members. Replaced by Robin Gibson in 1953, she was sometimes used by the company thereafter to train new principals. Very much of the 'old school', she was insistent that everything be played as it had been since the time when W.S. Gilbert himself directed the productions and she eschewed individual interpretation. Kenneth Sandford fell foul of her strict notions at his very first production rehearsal. Already taken aback by rehearsing without either fellow principals or a set of any kind, he came down the centre of a bare 'stage' for his first entrance as 'Pooh-Bah' in *The Mikado* and managed just the two words "It is" before she stopped him in his tracks.

"No, dear. Pooh-Bah is much too important to look at Pish-Tush and Nanki-Poo. He would look straight ahead and purse up his mouth to sound upper-class." Used, in his previous shows, to a natural style of acting, where characters directly addressed each other, Ken was completely bemused by this instruction, which made no theatrical sense to him. Bold enough to ask why this must be, he was told in no uncertain terms, "Because it has always been done that way". The following few weeks of training in this manner caused Ken to question his sanity in joining such a quaint organisation.

It can be argued that the policy of using long-standing company performers to prepare newcomers for the productions made good sense. Their knowledge of the words, moves and dances made them far better equipped for the job than someone brought in having to learn everything from scratch. The peril of a Stage Director coming in from the outside became frighteningly clear to Jane Metcalfe. Unusually, she was taught the moves for 'Pitti-Sing' by Michael Heyland rather than his assistant, James Marsland. Probably, he was used to seeing *The Mikado* from the auditorium, so he taught her the moves for 'Three Little Maids from School' and 'So Please You Sir' back to front. She only discovered this at her first rehearsal with the full company, when the two other 'little maids', Julia Goss and Patricia Leonard, realised, as they ran the numbers, that Jane was doing everything they did, but in mirror image. Jane was most embarrassed, but a few minutes practice on their own was all that was needed to put matters right. It must not have occurred to the Director of Productions that the business he saw from the front was reversed when on the stage.

For any new principal joining the company, learning so much stage business in a very short space of time was hard enough, but it was about more than knowing where to come on and stand, or knowing the routines. They needed guidance on the acting side, but there was never anyone on the production staff to help them dig beneath the surface of their characters, or offer advice about the timing of lines. They were left to fend for themselves and hope that, with the help of the principals whom they were joining, their dialogue and characterisation proved acceptable.

Perhaps the D'Oyly Carte performer recycled more than any other was Herbert Newby. Bert joined the company as a chorister in 1947 and ended up as Business Manager. In the intervening thirty-two years, he played small parts, understudied, played three principal tenor roles and served in various positions on the technical and production staff. In his fourteen-year tenure in charge of productions, Bert kept the shows ticking over, but the legacy of this charming man was mediocrity. He had a comfortable job, his wife, Ceinwen Jones, who was in the chorus, was at his side on tour and he enjoyed an occasional round of golf. In fact, according to the Stage Manager at the time, Peter Riley, Bert still had his clubs taken from town-to-town on the scenery lorry long after he had ceased playing. When Michael Buchan joined the company in 1972, he recalls Bert admitting he was fond of a flutter on the horses and the two of them frequently popped into the nearest bookmaker to place a small bet.

Of all those responsible for teaching the productions to new company members, James 'Jimmie' Marsland was legendary. Having been a reliable tenor chorister between 1949 and 1966, no one can remember how he came to join the production staff when he retired from the chorus, but he proved himself invaluable in getting every new performer prepared to go on. A permanently cheerful

42

and popular man who loved his work, his elephantine memory was little short of staggering. He knew every line and note of music, every move, gesture and dance for every character in every one of the operettas. With nothing but a few chairs to mark the position of the scenery on the stage, he patiently took his charges through their moves until they were drilled and confident, filling in the blanks of any missing characters with remarkable skill. Whether you joined alone or as part of a group, as a principal or chorister, Jimmie got you ready.

Pleasantly eccentric, he was totally uninhibited, equally comfortable demonstrating a swaggering march to new Dragoon Guards with two left feet in *Patience*, or dropping an elegant curtsey with a new principal lady in *Princess Ida*. Where there was principal music between chorus music lines, he sang it in without a mistake; when there was chorus music before a principal's entry, he sang the melody, giving a sense of the opera's continuity for those who had only had time to learn their own parts. Whilst rehearsing dialogue scenes, Jimmie played all the characters without reference to a libretto, his help invaluable for new principals who would not have the luxury of working opposite their colleagues until a run-through prior to their first performances. He never missed the opportunity of correcting a mistake, even out of hours.

James Conroy-Ward was once on the receiving end of Jimmie's inability to leave things in the workplace. After a three-hour understudy call for *The Gondoliers*, all concerned were walking away from the rehearsal hall when Jimmie grabbed James to tell him he had not quite mastered the dance steps for 'The Gavotte'. Oblivious to the astonished looks of those passing by, he was showing how it should be done, when he was approached by a down-and-out begging for money. Without missing a beat in the running commentary accompanying the demonstration, his dismissal of the tramp went somewhat thus: "In out, in out, down, point; in out, in out, down, point; front side, back side, front, side, piss off, down, point." Totally unconcerned by what others thought about the enthusiastic way in which he did his job, Jimmie spawned many such hilarious tales. Once a tour was under way and newcomers had settled in, he had other duties, which will be detailed later, but it is impossible to imagine how the company would have functioned without this dedicated and hard-working man whose catch-phrase was "No, no; you're doing it all wrong!" To this day, everyone who knew him has a favourite Jimmie Marsland story, a testament to the affection in which he was held.

When Jill Pert joined the company in January 1979, replacing Elizabeth Denham as understudy to principal contralto, Patricia Leonard, she was faced with a huge amount of work in a few short weeks and found it extremely hard. Not only had she to learn all the chorus music and moves but, at the same time, all the contralto roles she was to cover. Patricia played in every opera in the repertoire, but was given one performance off every week, so Jill knew that she would have to go on as soon as she was prepared. She spent interminable hours rehearsing in the ballet room of London's Sadler's Wells Theatre, either with the other new choristers, or alone with Jimmie Marsland, who taught her the principal stage business. She remembers having one session with Michael Heyland, but that was only to give her a general outline of his production of *Iolanthe*; the donkey work, as usual, was done by Jimmie. As Jill recalls, there was nothing from him in the way of character detail, just the bare bones of the production moves, but it is hard to imagine how she managed to absorb so much material in such a short time without serious melt down.

The strain on new recruits in such an intensive rehearsal period is easy to imagine, but there were two people whose reactions to the stress of preparing to go on the stage with the D'Oyly Carte were quite extraordinary. Yvonne Sommeling found the work so mentally and physically demanding that she lost twenty pounds in weight between starting rehearsals and making her first appearance some four weeks later. Unfortunately, this did not go down well with Wardrobe Mistress, Florrie Ewbank who, not with good grace, had to alter all of Yvonne's costumes which had been so precisely fitted a few weeks earlier.

The late Eileen Bruckshaw also found it hard to cope with her frenetic new life in the D'Oyly Carte. According to her great friend, Vera Ryan, the toll on Eileen's body and mind, when they joined the company together in 1959, was so great that she regularly fainted in rehearsals. Fortunately, such alarming blackouts ceased once she had become familiar with the productions and gained confidence during performances. Such symptoms were extreme, no doubt, but they clearly demonstrate the difficulties for new company members faced with such an intimidating workload.

Amongst the intake of new choristers in 1956 were Alan Barrett and John Dennison. After four exhausting weeks of rehearsals, they decided that they deserved a bit of a fling before embarking on their first tour, so they organised a slap-up night out. Alan had quickly become enamoured of one of the new girls, Mary Sansom, so he invited her, along with her friend, Anne Sessions, to join John and himself for a night at the ballet. Determined to do things properly, the boys hired a limousine for the evening at a cost of £5.10 shillings and bought dress circle seats for *Coppelia* at Covent Garden. In full evening dress, the four new Carters emerged after the performance to find the throng in the foyer parting to let them through to their limousine parked outside the main entrance! With 'royal waves' to the curious onlookers, they drove to the Savoy Grill for cocktails and supper.

Thoroughly enjoying the opulence of their surroundings, their gaiety quickly turned to horror when Bridget D'Oyly Carte and her General Manager, Frederic Lloyd, came in and sat down at the next table. Eventually, after hiding behind their menus for a whispered discussion as to what they should do, they realised that, as new chorus members still in rehearsal, they would probably not be recognised, so they were able to enjoy the meal without fear of being accused of having delusions of grandeur. Once they had dropped off the girls at their digs, Alan and John had only enough money left to pay the chauffeur, so they walked the two miles back to their lodgings, considering such extravagance worth every penny. The following day they set off to begin their D'Oyly Carte careers in Oxford. Happily, Alan's scheme to impress Mary paid handsome dividends when, a few months later, she agreed to become his wife.

Another hurdle to jump for those joining the company was being introduced to their new colleagues at the start of the rehearsal period in which they were to be assimilated into the productions. Watching the old hands chatting comfortably together was enough to make anyone feel like a fish out of water, particularly for someone joining on their own. But the D'Oyly Carte was nothing if not friendly and new recruits were soon put at ease. One exception to this was when Jean Hindmarsh was brought in to replace Muriel Harding as principal soprano in 1956.

Muriel, the wife of principal bass, Donald Adams, was very popular within the company and Jean remembers feeling the coolness of her reception when Muriel left. Conscious of the unjust resentment shown towards Jean, it was Donald himself who put matters right. Speaking to the whole company, he told them, in no uncertain terms, that Muriel's departure was not Jean's fault and that they should make her feel comfortable, for which generous intervention she was always grateful.

The use of formal manners was an essential part of D'Oyly Carte life in the 1950s, with production staff addressing performers as 'Miss' or 'Mister'. When Kenneth Sandford joined the company, he found it difficult to develop a close onstage working relationship with Joyce Wright, particularly in *Ruddigore* and *The Yeomen of the Guard*, whilst he was obliged to call her 'Miss Wright'. Such old-fashioned etiquette gradually declined over the years but, even in the late 1970s, it was not unusual to be formally addressed by the management. Respectful behaviour towards colleagues was considered essential. Chorister Jane Stanford was so in awe of two of the senior principals when she joined in 1979 that, for a long time, she could not bring herself to call them anything but 'Mr. Sandford' and 'Mr. Reed'. Quaint as it may now seem, such courtesy was the D'Oyly Carte way and not such a bad thing.

Cynthia Morey tells how nervous she felt at the thought of meeting the stars of the D'Oyly Carte she had admired for so long. As she entered The Savoy Hotel via the Embankment entrance, rather than through the staff entrance as before, the thought of rehearsing with them made her feel both excited and nervous. She followed a liveried page to the Lincoln Room, where the rehearsal for *The Mikado* was to be held, and stared in astonishment at the scene before her, which she describes as "looking more like a cocktail party than a rehearsal". Elegantly-dressed ladies dripping in jewellery, with beautifully coiffured hair, were chatting to men in smart suits, the genteel atmosphere of the room making her wonder if she was in the right place. She slipped in to join Joyce Farrer and both stood awkwardly waiting for something to happen, painfully aware that, in their dowdy clothes, they stuck out like a sore thumb. Within no time at all, Alan Styler approached them with the customary twinkle in his eye and introduced himself to the new girls. Pointing out various people he thought they should know, he immediately made them feel as if they already belonged, something Cynthia has always remembered with gratitude.

The expectation of the management in the 1950s was that company members should be smartly-dressed at all times because they were representing the famous D'Oyly Carte Opera Company. Cynthia had joined a company just returned from an American tour, so it was no surprise that the girls had come back stocked up with beautiful clothes at a time when Britain was still subject to the austerity of rationing after the Second World War. Joyce Wright remembers the strict dress code when she joined in 1947 and that 'Miss Carte's young ladies', as they were dubbed, were told they must always look immaculate, their clothes always complemented by matching accessories. So ingrained did this attitude to appearance become, that Jean Hindmarsh still laughs about how many years it took her, after she left the company, to realise she could go shopping without wearing a posh frock and full make-up!

One chorus lady who thought nothing of the D'Oyly Carte's unwritten law that its ladies must always be dressed to the nines was Yvonne Sommeling, who was to become the second wife of Peter Riley. Never a lady to abide by convention, she adopted the 1970s fashion for wearing hot pants, much to the disapproval of many company members. She also did some modelling on the side and somehow managed to appear in the Sunday Mirror wearing nothing but a bikini bottom and strategically placed feather boa! Following the outrage this caused amongst her colleagues, Yvonne fully expected to be sacked, but the reaction of General Manager, Frederic Lloyd, was not quite what she expected.

BRIDGET D'OYLY CARTE LIMITED

Cables : Savoyard, London   1, SAVOY HILL, LONDON, W.C.2   Telephone : 01-836 1533

14th February, 1972.

Dear Miss Sommeling,

       Unfortunately I don't usually read the Sunday Mirror, but I am glad to say a copy turned up in the Office today !

       It is indeed a pity we didn't know about this revealing photograph earlier as I am sure we could have incorporated you in this costume for the last night at Sadler's Wells with some considerable success !

       Yours sincerely,

General Manager.

       P.S.   I should think you are extremely glad you had the photo taken before the power cuts came on.

Miss Yvonne Sommeling,
Royal Shakespeare Theatre,
Stratford-upon-Avon,
Warwicks.

Although Snookie Fancourt was known as something of a tartar, Gillian Knight saw a kind side to the woman so often seen as difficult. Joining as principal contralto straight from her studies at The Royal Academy of Music, Gillian was informed by Snookie that she would be expected to wear smart clothes whenever she was working. She explained that she had no money, so Snookie arranged to take her to a ladies' outfitter and loaned her the money for the new clothes until she was in a position to pay it back from her wages.

This mandatory dress code persisted well into the 1960s but, with many company members by then able to buy their own cars, the traditional train calls transporting everyone from one date to another were gradually phased out and a more informal style of dress became acceptable. However, the management still expected everyone to look smart when representing the company. It is now difficult to imagine an opera company so concerned by appearances, particularly for rehearsals, when it would, surely, have been more appropriate to wear suitable comfortable clothing and character shoes as opposed to the high heels favoured by the ladies. But that was not the D'Oyly Carte way: it had an eccentric style that often defied logic. By the 1970s, common sense had prevailed and members wore casual clothing unless attending an official company event. Doubtless, there were some who regretted this fall in sartorial standards and, even today, the phrase 'Miss Carte's young ladies' is fondly used by members in memory of a time long gone.

With such distractions as getting to know new colleagues and how they should dress, the next challenge facing new D'Oyly Carte personnel after the short, but intense, preparation period, was going on for their first performances in as many as eight operas one after another. On July the 1st, 1957, Kenneth Sandford made his D'Oyly Carte debut as 'Pooh-Bah' in *The Mikado* in circumstances less than ideal. Much to his consternation, he had learned that he was to have no dress rehearsal and that he must go on without an orchestral run-through, or opportunity to become familiar with the set. Arriving early at the King's Theatre in Southsea, he plucked up the courage to ask Musical Director, Isidore Godfrey, if he might sing in his music during the band call. A harassed Mr. Godfrey replied, "If I have time, Kenneth, if I have time". Much to his relief, the time was found for him to sing his lines as the band call progressed, giving him the chance to test the theatre's acoustics. Then he 'walked' the set, frantically trying to associate the moves learned on a flat rehearsal room floor with the scenery now confronting him. With no advice offered from the production staff about make-up for his Japanese character, Ken did his best, took a deep breath and somehow managed to emerge unscathed from his debut.

Tossing and turning in bed that night, Ken wanted nothing more than to analyse his first 'Pooh-Bah', but he knew he had to turn his mind to the following night's 'Don Alhambra' in *The Gondoliers*. Desperately trying to travel to Venice, his brain obstinately remained in 'Titipu' and he slept badly. The next day, he again went to the theatre to sing his music with the orchestra and familiarise himself with the set. Aware that such preparation was completely unsatisfactory, it dawned on him that the company did not have its own orchestra and that poor Mr. Godfrey had just one rehearsal for each show in which to get the locally-hired musicians up to speed. It was no wonder he insisted that everyone watch his stick at all times. Ken's first week onstage with the D'Oyly Carte passed in something of a blur, with one debut performance following another. It was difficult, stressful and exhausting, but that was how it was for everyone joining an unfunded company which could not afford the luxury of adequate rehearsal time. But, in the early 1960s, the management made a huge leap forward when it took the decision to have its own touring orchestra, although it is not clear who, or what, prompted this move. Without the hassle of having to hire a scratch orchestra and rehearse it for every show wherever the company appeared, Isidore Godfrey had more freedom to devote to the performers and all-important dress rehearsals became possible.

My own debut with the D'Oyly Carte Opera Company was something of an ordeal. Arriving in Manchester in April of 1972, having learned all the operas on my own, no time was wasted in getting me into the productions and I was thrown on for *Trial by Jury* without a rehearsal. Never having been on a stage in my life, it was a frightening experience, but Jimmie Marsland was there for me. Having talked me through my duties as a 'box girl', he pointed out my partner for the opening chorus, told me to make my way to him, curtsey as we finished 'Hark the Hour of Ten is Sounding', before crossing to the box for 'the public' on stage left. He instructed me to hold the door open for the other ladies to enter, then go in last and shut the door behind me. All went to plan until I went to sit down.

Unfortunately, there was nothing for me to sit on. Totally flummoxed by this, all I could think to do was bend my knees and hunch down as if I was in a seated position. All very well, but I knew I would not be able to maintain this effect for another thirty minutes. Luckily, Jimmie was watching me from the nearby wings and immediately noticed my plight. After a couple of minutes with my knees already beginning to ache, I became aware of scuffling sounds behind me as Jimmie, who had managed to find a box, lay flat on his stomach to push it towards my rear end. Was I relieved when I heard him whisper, "You can sit down now". Having joined mid-tour as a replacement chorister, it is possible that the other box girls had got used to there being one less on the long bench and had spread out their voluminous crinolines to leave no space, but it was, quite literally, something of a trial for me!

The perils for a principal making their debut without a dress rehearsal became abundantly clear to Jean Hindmarsh when she went on for her first show as 'Josephine' in HMS Pinafore. Having not seen the set until just before the show, her direction to 'exit through the cabin in distress' when given a photograph of 'Sir Joseph Porter' proved a real banana skin for poor Jean. The doorway was part of the large cabin structure on stage right, which had a joining metal strip across it at floor level to help brace the two sides. Oblivious to its existence, she ran from the scene, caught her shoe on it and went flying into the wings, by which time her tears were probably genuine. Worse was to follow. She was rather scared of having to come down the steps from the deck above the cabin after singing 'Ah, Stay Your Hand, I Love You' to 'Ralph Rackstraw' in the first act finale. Her fears were realised when she missed her footing and bumped inelegantly on her backside down to stage level. She somehow managed to keep her composure, but more problems were to come. During her second act aria, 'The Hours Creep On Apace', she had been told to move away from the hatch set in the centre of the stage during the second section but, when trying to do so, found the bottom of her dress caught on something sharp. With the music punctuated by staccato yanks, she eventually managed to pull herself free, but it was a horrible moment for the debutante. At a time in the company when new principals were often given a temporary contract until they proved their worth, having so many disasters in her trial performance did not bode well for Jean, but she weathered the storm and, happily for D'Oyly Carte audiences, this popular soprano, was given a full contract.

It was not only the performers who experienced the stress of appearing on the stage for the first time. In some of the operas, supernumeraries were required and these non-speaking roles were usually filled by members of the technical or music staff. Peter Riley recalls how nervous he was about going on as one of the two marines needed in *HMS Pinafore*. Used to stage management, he found the bright lights and his first sight of a full house in a large theatre very scary. All he could think about was whether or not the audience would notice his legs shaking. The choice of which behind-the-scenes staff to use as 'supers' was usually based on which of them fitted the costumes available. Repetiteur and orchestra manager, Paul Seeley, was used as a marine and also appeared in *The Yeomen of the Guard* and *Princess Ida*. These 'extra' duties were considered to be a part of his job and were unpaid.

The D'Oyly Carte recycling system was always in evidence but, sometimes, at the expense of good production values. Adding non-performers to a professional cast, however small the part to be played, was a risky policy, which sometimes didn't work out well. Most supers did a good job, but there were occasions when someone totally unsuited to appearing on the stage had to go on, causing stifled laughter amongst the cast. It was a case of somebody having to do it and the hope that the audience would not notice the difference. The only show in which chorus members were used as non-singing supers was the *The Mikado*, with two of the men used as guards to 'Katisha', these being joined by two of the ladies to form the entourage of 'The Mikado' in the second act. Why the company chose to lose four voices is not clear, but the show surely benefitted from having professionals play these characters. It was always good to see Jimmie Marsland in his non-speaking role of 'The Solicitor' in *Patience*, his years of stage work shining through the cameo appearance.

In a touring company without financial support, economy was always of the essence and rehearsals cost money. Ralph Mason's description of his D'Oyly Carte chorus debut in December 1959, at The Royal Shakespeare Theatre in Stratford-upon-Avon, perfectly illustrates this point. "I was slung on the stage after a perfunctory rehearsal of *The Gondoliers*." During this sole run-through, Ralph placed himself for the opening scene where he had been told to go, only to be told by a veteran chorister, "You can't stand here. I've been standing here since before the war and I'm not making way for the likes of you." Such lack of generosity to a newcomer was rare in a company made up of performers who, themselves, had been under-rehearsed when they joined.

When Peggy Ann Jones made her company debut as a chorister a year earlier than Ralph, not having had enough rehearsal time was the least of her problems. Her first performance was to be in *Iolanthe* and two things bothered her more than remembering the moves. Firstly, having seldom been on a stage, she had no idea of how to correctly apply theatrical make-up and so, had to rely on the kindness of one of the chorus ladies to do it for her. Those who know Peggy will find it hard to believe that a lady who is never seen without 'full slap' once didn't know how to make up her face!

But something more embarrassing was to follow. Being an only child, she was the product of a very sheltered upbringing and had never before had to undress in front of anyone else. Finding herself in a large chorus dressing room and being expected to take off her clothes in public was the worst thing she could imagine. Staring in dismay at the green ballet dress she was to wear, Peggy put on the dress and proceeded to take off her street clothes from under it. With garments having being pulled out from arm holes and up through the bodice, she eventually took her position next to Beti Lloyd-Jones for the opening chorus. As the overture was ending, Beti looked at her and said, "What the hell have you got on under your dress?" to which Peggy replied by lifting the hem to reveal her tweed skirt! This may sound like an exaggeration, but it really happened and Peggy describes herself as having been "as green as grass". She still bemoans the lack of advice on make-up and wig-dressing given to new members, something which persisted until the company closed. What you didn't know, you had to learn fast by watching others, or asking for their help. John Dennison's company debut was in *The Mikado* and his own words make interesting reading.

"First performance with the famed D'Oyly Carte Opera Company? Terrifying! We had only been given a bare outline of the make-up required, which was in the Kabuki style, but the other chorus members kindly helped us out with the details. On the stage, the same terror. However, that wonderful man and performer, Jimmie Marsland, was there all the time whispering cues and directions to keep us in line. Between him and Jack Habbick, we got through it. Those two people looked after the newbies through most of the remainder of the tour."

Such stage fright was probably felt by everyone going on for the first time. If it was nerve-jangling for a chorister, how much more so for new principals so lacking in adequate rehearsal time? Jennifer Toye was so paralysed by fear as she stood in the wings waiting for her first ever entrance as 'Mabel' in *The Pirates of Penzance*, that she was convinced she was going to be sick. Just as the chorus ladies responded to the pleas of 'Frederic' with 'No, no, not one', she started to head back to her dressing room, but one of the chorus men, who was kindly waiting with her, stopped her flight. Turning her round, he shoved her onto the stage just in time to sing 'Yes, one', after which initial panic, she sailed through the vocally-taxing 'Poor Wand'ring One'.

The courage needed by principal performers should not be underestimated. A fine voice and good technique are, of course, essential, but having the temperament to be able to control nerves so that they do not get in the way of singing difficult music is quite another matter: it is a great gift and one much-coveted by those not so blessed. The Victorian theatrical convention of having principals make a 'big entrance' was adopted by Gilbert and Sullivan when they wrote the Savoy Operas, which are liberally sprinkled with such cruel and terrifying moments. They should have tried it for themselves. In fact, for some, the fear of coming on cold to face an audience before a big number never left them. Jennifer's words sum up such trauma.

"John Reed and I dreaded *Pirates*, he for 'The Major-General's Song' and me for that terrifying first entrance and aria without any warm-up. We used to meet in his dressing room beforehand and clutch each other, declaring how fabulous we were going to be."

If the performers were under pressure for their first performances, spare a thought for a new Assistant Music Director conducting his first shows and carrying the responsibility for every note of the score.

Royston Nash watched every rehearsal and performance in the early part of the 1970 tour before making his debut in the pit in November of that year. Thereafter, he was blooded at the rate of one or two shows each week, until he had conducted all the operas in the repertoire. Looking back, he remembered his biggest challenge was setting the right tempi needed for dances such as the 'Cachuca' in *The Gondoliers*, which required great concentration, so that the performers were able to dance the choreography at the right speed. It was a year later, as newly-appointed Music Director, that he conducted *Princess Ida*, but there had, at least, been plenty of time for him to learn the score and production. However, it was not a nerve-free occasion with Valerie Masterson returning to the company to play the title role. He loved every moment of it and the show was always his favourite.

Michael Buchan certainly needed to keep his nerves under control when he made his company debut at the start of the new tour in 1972. Due to go on in the chorus for the first time in *The Mikado* at the De Montfort Hall in Leicester, he found himself playing 'The Mikado' instead. Unusually, John Ayldon was not well enough to appear. Asked by the management if he could do it, Mike said yes, as he had played the role as an amateur. However scared Mike may have been, it must be remembered that the other principals were faced with working with someone who had not had a rehearsal. Mike clearly remembers Ken Sandford telling him that once 'The Criminal Cried' was over, he was not to move an inch during the following dialogue scene and to let the other principals work round him.

Having safely negotiated his big song, 'A More Humane Mikado', Mike got stuck in the dialogue section that had concerned Ken and had to be rescued by John Reed when he could not think what came after 'All this is very interesting', which he repeated several times. Having to go on again for John Ayldon in the following performance of *Mikado*, he dried up in exactly the same place and John Reed dug him out for a second time. Whilst Mike's self-assurance in accepting such a challenge was commendable, the pressure on the other performers was just as great because they had no way of anticipating what might happen. Had the company had plenty of time and money at its disposal, it would have been able to prepare its understudies to go on right from the start of the tour, rather than hoping the principals would not be ill before their covers could be rehearsed as the tour went along. Such were the practical difficulties of a shoestring operation.

Time after time, it was the artistes who stepped in when the production staff was invisible, generously giving of their time and experience to help new members. Clive Harré's concerns about his debut as 'The Sergeant of Police' in *The Pirates of Penzance* proved well-founded. It was a matinee day, so he had two chances to prove to himself that he could make a good job of the part, but so worried was he about the low notes he couldn't reach, that he stood in the wings, ready to lead on the line of policemen, shaking from head to foot. By the time he had completed a circuit of the stage and arrived down centre, he could not think of a single word except 'Tarantara'. His humiliation completed by the embarrassed chuckles coming from the policemen behind him, Clive couldn't wait to get back to his dressing room to lick his wounds. As soon as he was off the stage as 'The Pirate King', John Ayldon poked his head round Clive's door to see how he was coping after such a dreadful start. He went on to catalogue his own disasters and assured Clive that all would be well.

Cheered by the words of consolation, Clive felt a little better about having to get back on the horse for the evening performance. Second time around, he remembered all the words and suddenly became aware of audience laughter, the reactions to his cowardly antics all he could wish. Thereafter, he never worried about playing the part to which he felt so unsuited and much of this newly-found confidence was down to the thoughtfulness of John Ayldon. The question must be asked, why did none of the production staff see the need to bolster Clive's deflated ego? Were any of them watching out front? But it was ever thus: the performers, with very few exceptions, looked after each other during the long tours. D'Oyly Carte folk still consider themselves to be part of a closely-knit family and that will not change until every past member has gone.

CHAPTER THREE

ON THE ROAD

With the stressful rehearsal period behind them and first performances out of the way, new D'Oyly Carte members were faced with starting life on the road. Tour dates were arranged several months ahead, so everyone knew where they were going to be playing. Small cards with venues and dates printed on them were given out in good time, so there was plenty of advance notice when it came to booking accommodation. From its earliest days, the company travelled from town to town by train, the practice of the 'train call' only gradually declining through the 1960s when, for many, buying a car became affordable. This considerably simplified getting around the country and often made it possible to get home at weekends. Up until then, the Sunday train call was so much a part of company life that, despite the disadvantages of performers and staff spending a rare day off cooped up for hours in a railway carriage, stories abound of the fun and camaraderie engendered by this D'Oyly Carte travel ritual.

It was essential that everyone be dressed to the nines on gathering at the station; after all, they were in public and representing the famous D'Oyly Carte Opera Company. The ladies were expected to wear elegant coats and hats, with matching accessories, whilst the men sported smart suits and overcoats. Surrounded by their luggage, company members arrived at the station by bus or taxi to begin the journey. For those experiencing their first train call at the beginning of the tour, it must have been an exciting and colourful moment. Vera Ryan's first journey in 1959 had an extraordinary start. Walking across the concourse at Waterloo to meet up with her new colleagues for the train to Southampton, she almost bumped into a tall young soldier in the uniform of the Horse Guards. It was her brother, Terry, on the way back to his barracks in Windsor and she considered this delightful coincidence a very good omen.

More than sixty years later, the strict protocol for who sat where on the train calls of the early 1950s is difficult to imagine. The carriages segregated the company into sections, with management, principals, ladies of the chorus, gentlemen of the chorus, wardrobe, technical and music staff members seated in separate compartments. This quaint arrangement continued for as long as the train was in the station but, as the journey progressed, everyone changed places and sat with their friends, although principals were discouraged from fraternising with the chorus. Gillian Knight's description of her first journey with the company, in 1959, delightfully sets the scene.

"I remember my first train call so well. The ladies were in one carriage and the men in another, with Bruce Worsley puffing up the platform making a performance of organising things. The girls were such a jolly lot. At one point, Anne Sessions went along to see if there was any 'new talent' in the men's carriage. She came back enthusing about the handsome young props master. He turned out to be Trevor Morrison and we were married six months later!" By the start of the 1960s, seating restrictions had been relaxed a little, due in no small measure to the feisty Jean Hindmarsh rebelling against being told she couldn't sit with her friend, Anne Sessions, who was in the chorus.

Until 1966, when the company turned to road transport, all the sets, costumes, props and music travelled on the same train as the cast. The bonus of this arrangement for the D'Oyly Carte management was that having paid the train company to transport its substantial effects, the performers travelled free of charge. On arrival at the destination station, a crew of ten men was engaged to unload everything from the train onto lorries hired from a local haulage company. The substantial cargo was then taken to the theatre, where another team of ten, this time from the theatre, was required to offload it. This worked well as long as the train arrived on time, otherwise transferring everything into the theatre scenery dock carried on late into the evening. Sometimes, if backstage storage space was limited, items from some of the shows were left in carriages which had been shunted into sidings, for collection as needed. Peter Riley remembers one occasion when spears used in *The Mikado* were accidentally left behind, needing somebody to dash back to the railway sidings to search freight carriages for them.

Much as happens today, travelling by train on a Sunday in the 1950s and 1960s was often fraught with delays, hardly ideal when everyone needed to get to their digs and settle in before their 'day off' was over. Usually, there was no buffet car, so most people carried bags containing sandwiches and thermos flasks to keep them going, particularly on a very long journey. Alan Barrett tells of how he and his wife, Mary Sansom, enjoyed friendly competition with some of the others as to who could produce the best picnic. A typical menu started them off with a flask of hot soup, followed by a large salad and then dessert, with a second flask containing coffee to finish. He and Mary seldom came second in the travelling grub stakes. As might be expected, the need for diversion on travel days spawned lots of ways of passing the time, some of them not quite as obvious as one might expect. Of course, books, needlework, correspondence and card schools were much in evidence, but one or two people engaged in rather more unusual pastimes. According to Cynthia Morey, two of her lifelong friends, John Reed and John Fryatt, both had hobbies rather ill-suited to train travel.

"John Reed once decided to take up basket work and turned up on the Sunday train call with the products of his new occupation. There he was, in his usual elegant outfit, baskets of every shape and size over his arm and trailing sheaves of willow in every direction. How he disposed of all these, I can't remember, but he must have found (perhaps reluctant) recipients in order to pursue his next equally cumbersome hobby. John Fryatt settled for the gentle art of marquetry, at which he became very accomplished. He most often pursued this activity in his digs, but was known on occasion to bring out his current piece of work on the train, balancing it skilfully on his knees. He was busy on a large design of *The Mikado* and endeavouring to insert tiny pieces of veneer into the picture as the train rocked and swayed on its way. Apart from occasional mishaps with the glue and some sudden stop-starts which sent fragments showering all over the compartment, he seemed to cope extraordinarily well. The finished work of art was certainly a success."

The most popular compartment on a long journey was the one labelled 'wardrobe', where Wardrobe Mistress, Cis Blain and her assistant, Flo Ewbank, along with Stage Carpenter, Harry Haste, ran a well-stocked bar. It seems that invitations to this event were highly prized and often required at least several years of service to the D'Oyly Carte before admission was granted to this pleasantly boozy inner-sanctum. Such stories of ways to pass the time on a tedious train journey were courtesy of the number of great characters who made up the D'Oyly Carte Opera Company. One such was Alice Hynd, a Scottish lady who was the understudy to principal contralto, Ann Drummond-Grant. Notorious for the large number of tartan suitcases she took with her on tour, she could sometimes be a thorn in the side of station porters. It was usual for company luggage to be piled onto trolleys which the porters then took to the train. The usual tip everyone paid for this service in the 1950s was two shillings. On one occasion, according to Alan Barrett, Alice was standing in the corridor outside her compartment when a porter spotted her. Holding out his hand containing one shilling and sixpence, he shouted to her through the small open section at the top of the carriage window. "Is this right, Miss?" Eyeing the coins, her response was not what he was expecting: "No, I gave you sixpence too much." Thrusting an expectant hand through the window, the poor porter had little option but to reach up and return the overpayment.

It was not always a direct train to the next town or city where the D'Oyly Carte was to appear so, in that event, the company, quite literally, changed trains. If this was necessary, the company's reserved carriages were uncoupled and shunted into a siding until the train for its destination arrived to hook them up and continue the journey. It was one such occasion that led to an amusing incident involving the company's touring manager, Bruce Worsley. It has not been possible to find out why Mr. Worsley was alone in the management carriage when the train arrived to pick up the company, but it didn't take him long to realise that all the other carriages had been attached to the train receding into the distance, whilst his was still stationary! He was eventually rescued, but his predicament proved a source of much hilarity amongst the company.

Not all train journeys were from one venue to another. Sometimes, getting to the theatre from home or digs was best managed by rail. On one such occasion, Donald Adams was travelling by train to the theatre in Wimbledon when it came to a shuddering halt. The following lengthy delay was an irritation for all the passengers, but a lady with her small son, seated near Donald, seemed particularly agitated as the time passed. Repeatedly checking her watch and tut-tutting, she eventually turned to Donald and bemoaned the hold-up because she was taking her little boy to see *The Mikado* and it was looking increasingly likely that they would be late for the performance. In his inimitable lugubrious style, Donald replied, "I don't know what you're worrying about, madam, I am The Mikado." A favourite anecdote amongst D'Oyly Carters, Thomas Round confirms this to be exactly what Donald told him when he eventually made it to the theatre.

Donald's wife, Muriel Harding, might have wished she had taken a train on the evening of her day off, when she took a bus to the theatre to meet him after a show. Their digs being in an area frequented by ladies of dubious repute, Muriel was carrying the sort of patent handbag often favoured by such working girls, because they reflected car headlights and announced their presence. Much to her surprise, a car stopped next to her while she was waiting at the bus stop, the window was wound down and a man stuck out his head. Looking her up and down, he offered her 'thirty bob' (around £1.50 for those too young to remember pre-decimal currency), to which an insulted Muriel replied, "I beg your pardon?" Pondering for a moment, the man reconsidered: "Alright, then, two quid."

Although the traditional train call continued into the 1960s, there were early signs that such an outdated mode of transporting the company did not suit everyone. Change was in the air. As early as 1955, two company members had bought cars, for which they received a petrol allowance in lieu of train tickets. Principal comedian, Peter Pratt, acquired a maroon MG Magnette, although he could not drive it, that duty being performed by his wife, the principal soubrette, Joyce Wright. By coincidence, his understudy, John Reed, also bought a car. Having been a driver for some years, John splashed out on a brand new Ford Popular in a brilliant shade of blue. It didn't take him long to persuade his great pal, Cynthia Morey, to abandon the tedious train call ritual in favour of joining him for rather more leisurely trips. Sadly, John's pride and joy did not have a heater, so cold winter days proved a little uncomfortable, requiring hot water bottles to keep their circulation going. As the years passed, more and more D'Oyly Carters joined the road show until the balance had changed and those travelling by train were in the minority. However, driving the length and breadth of the country did not always fulfil the dream of freedom and convenience.

When Madeleine 'Caroline' Hudson joined the company in 1976, her faithful old red mini was her pride and joy and it saw her through many a long journey on tour. Travelling home to London from Newcastle late one Saturday night after a long week of performances, the rain on the motorway was torrential. Suddenly, to her consternation, the wipers began to stutter and work intermittently, so she could see hardly anything through the rain-streaked glass. Thinking quickly, she put on a glove and opened the window, somehow managing to hunch forward over the steering wheel to reach outside and push the wiper with her hand. Within minutes the wipers completely stopped working, so Caroline could only slow down, move onto the hard shoulder and clear the water away with her hand every few seconds, much to the detriment of her steering. Fortunately, there was a service area nearby, so she was able to crawl into the garage area, where a kindly attendant managed to get the wipers working again. Such a frightening experience was not a common occurrence, but few in the D'Oyly Carte could afford the luxury of a new, reliable car and so ran the risk of breaking down, sometimes in dangerous situations.

The two-seater sports car, acquired courtesy of the charity his father had duped in John Broad's student days, did him very nicely until one night in Glasgow. Driving back to his digs after a show, the engine blew up in the middle of the Gorbals. This notorious area still boasted a tough reputation in the early 1970s and John was not a little alarmed by being marooned in what he thought to be a no-go area.

With the option of staying in his cramped car until morning or walking the two miles to his digs, he decided to take his chances and set off on foot, praying that he would not be set upon by the thugs he imagined lurking in every shadow. Fortunately, he got home unscathed but, the following morning, he did not relish having to go back and wait for a local garage to come and tow the car away. More to the point, he was not sure it would still be there. Summoning his courage, he made his way back through the Gorbals and was pleasantly surprised to find that not only was his car where he had left it, but it still had its wheels. Needless to say, that was the end of his beloved sports car, which he replaced with a second-hand VW Beetle, but at least he had gained respect for the folk of that deprived area.

The disadvantages for any D'Oyly Carter running round the country in an old car must have been obvious, but lack of money meant that most of them did just that and tenor chorister, Edwin Rolles, paid a heavy price for having an old banger. After a Saturday night performance in Bristol in the mid-1970s, Eddie got into his trusty Hillman Avenger and set off for his home in Bournemouth. Crossing Salisbury Plain in the small hours, he had a dreadful shock when flames suddenly shot out of the dashboard. Slamming on the brakes, he jumped out and watched in horror as fire engulfed the car containing all his belongings in what seemed like seconds.

Alone in the pitch-black countryside with no means of alerting help, Eddie had no idea what to do. Very soon, a car appeared and, much to his relief, two young men stopped to help, although that had not been their original intention. They had been looking for UFOs and thought they had found one when they saw the bright light in the sky! Their disappointment on discovering Eddie's conflagration was quickly forgotten as they drove him to a nearby village, where he was able to phone the emergency services. With the fire brigade and police having come and gone, the two lads got Eddie, along with the sole item he had salvaged from the burned-out wreckage of the Avenger, into their car and drove him home to Bournemouth, which was not too far out of their way, as they lived in Ringwood. The selfless actions of these young men has always stayed with him.

When the news of this disaster got back to company members the following Monday in Brighton, their response left Eddie overwhelmed by the generosity and care of his colleagues. Singers and orchestra had a 'whip-round' and gave him more than enough money to buy clothes and other essentials. He has never forgotten the kindness shown to him and considers it typical of the D'Oyly Carte family. And the single item that survived the flames? The last few pages of his copy of *The Messiah*, the 'Amen Chorus'.

On a principal's salary, Kenneth Sandford had managed to afford to run a small car from the start of his D'Oyly Carte career in 1957. Happy to avoid the stifling formality of train calls, which were not at all his scene, he loved being able to drive home for a short weekend break when within striking distance of London. However, he was not immune from the inconvenience of a temperamental car. During one Manchester season, he was staying with his favourite landlady, Mrs. Leech, whose husband ran the funeral parlour at the front of their house. After the usual fine dinner, Ken went to his car but found it wouldn't start. He was thinking about ringing for a taxi to get him to the theatre when Mr. Leech came to the rescue with his hearse. Somewhat startled when invited to get in, Ken did as he was told and was whisked away to the Stage Door of the Opera House in dubious style, much to the astonishment of the few company fans waiting to see their favourite performers arrive. Although he was grateful for such kindness, Ken could not help feeling embarrassed by this eccentric mode of transport, but it could have been worse; at least there wasn't a coffin on board!

It was not always the car that proved to be the problem, sometimes it was the driver. Principal contralto, Lyndsie Holland, had something of a reputation as a girl racer. In the 1970s, she toured in a Saab, which had plenty of punch to suit her taste for speed. According to company members who, for a very short time, accepted lifts from her, she was not unknown to drive in the wrong direction up a one-way street, or go anticlockwise at a traffic island. In fact, it was always considered a miracle when she arrived at the theatre in one piece, because she had been known to have accidents. What a pity she is no longer with us to be able to deny, or confirm, these unkind allegations.

Taking a passenger along for the ride was an option adopted by many D'Oyly Carte car owners, who were glad of company on the long journeys during the course of an eleven-month tour. Comfortable conversation helped the time pass quickly and it was nice to be able to help out those without transport of their own. Sometimes, company members living near each other would travel together and share the petrol costs. When Clive Harré was approached by a fellow principal asking to join him on his drive to Manchester, with the promise to keep him company and have a good natter, he was happy to oblige. Both lived in Essex, so he picked her up at her home and they set off on the long drive north.

Within a couple of minutes, Clive noticed a strange noise in the car and asked his companion if she could hear an odd rumbling sound. Receiving no answer, he glanced to his left to see her fast asleep and obviously responsible for the droning noise that was bothering him. Several hours later, the reverberation inside the car finally stopped when he pulled up at a set of traffic lights in the centre of Manchester, when she opened her eyes and said, "Oh! Are we here then?" The next time she asked for a lift, he knew he was in for another noisy trip because, this time, she brought along a pillow to make herself more comfortable. Ever the gentleman, Clive wishes to spare the lady's blushes by not naming her, but it has not been difficult, given that this happened in 1980, to work out that the only other female principal living in Essex travelled with her husband, so the snorer must have been the popular principal mezzo-soprano, Lorraine Daniels. Sorry, Clive!

In the 1960s, the many D'Oyly Carte car owners spawned a remarkable new group within the company, 'The Tinkers' Club'. Its members now find it difficult to remember who first came up with the idea, but Pauline Wales says it was she and her husband, Thomas Lawlor. The year-round chore of finding somewhere to stay was an issue for everyone, particularly with the rapid decline of traditional theatrical digs, so it was suggested that having a small caravan would provide a solution to this problem. Not only that, it opened up the possibility of having pets, something previously unthinkable for most itinerant thespians. And so, the caravan club was formed, its numbers gradually swelling over several years. Touring in a caravan was not an easy option, but it at least offered the stability of a home, privacy and freedom from the accommodation lottery.

Finding somewhere to park the caravans was not usually an issue, as there were camp sites on the outskirts of every town and city in which the company appeared, even in London, where Tinkers not based in the capital circled their wagons on the municipal site at Crystal Palace for the annual winter season at Sadler's Wells. Sometimes, outside of towns and cities, the nearby countryside provided an idyllic setting for the caravans in a farm field. The camaraderie engendered by such a lifestyle was phenomenal and the adventures of this hardy breed of D'Oyly Carters are fascinating.

The practical difficulties of towing a caravan became a weekly, or fortnightly, routine for the Tinkers; securing all their belongings, loading heavy gas cylinders inside their roaming homes, raising the jacks and linking up, all of which had to be reversed on arrival at the next destination after a long journey. Peggy Ann Jones had several scrapes with the caravan over the years, including running her much-prized Daimler into the back of a lorry, but her worst experience came when the Tinkers were en route from Glasgow to Edinburgh in a winter gale, something she has never forgotten.

"As I was the least experienced, my co-caravanners had put me in the middle of the seven-vehicle fleet, but I was terrified. I could see the vans in front swaying from side-to-side, and soon I was snaking along with hardly any control on the steering doing about 15mph. We could only pray nothing would come towards us at the wrong moment." Despite such occasional hairy moments, Peggy loved the gypsy lifestyle and the social life that went with it. Cooking meals for others, having breakfast in the next-door caravan, or getting together for a drink and nibbles after a show all made for a happy life on tour, but having her Jack Russell, Judy, with her was best of all.

Another near-disaster occurred when Jeffrey Cresswell was leading the caravan convoy during a rare journey undertaken at night. None of the Tinkers can now remember why they decided to move camp in the dark, or where they were heading, but John Broad relates seeing Jeff 's car and caravan go over a bridge on a narrow country road. A sharp bend came immediately after the bridge, which Jeff misjudged, resulting in both car and caravan ending up in a ditch. After much debate, the Tinkers devised a plan to get Jeff out of the mire. With only headlights and torches to illuminate the scene, tow ropes were attached to the caravan and one of their cars. After careful reversing, much pulling and shoving, they somehow managed to drag the caravan and car back onto the road. Much to Jeff's relief, the Tinkers were able to continue on their not-so-merry way.

Pets were certainly an incentive for some of the Tinkers to put up with the trials and tribulations of caravanning. John Reed's main reason for joining the club was being able to have his beloved dog, Sheba, on tour with him. A quiet-natured brindle boxer, she and John were inseparable. It would have been impossible to always find places to stay where a large dog would be made welcome, so a caravan was the ideal solution. She was certainly no problem when in the theatre, happily snoozing in John's dressing room throughout the performance. Perhaps orchestra leader, Geoff Short, should have joined the Tinkers' Club. He toured with his German shepherd dog and sometimes chose to sleep in his car rather than be in digs without his canine companion. Pauline Wales was never happier than when surrounded by her pets during long tours. Not only was there her Dalmatian, Jane, but also two Siamese cats, Suki and Leila, who never seemed fazed by the close attendance of a boisterous spotted dog. Any D'Oyly Carte driver passing the caravan convoy might well have seen the cats ambling across the top of the dashboard, or rear-window shelf of Pauline's car!

Unfortunately, Pauline's husband, Thomas Lawlor, dubbed 'the bull of Kerriemuir' by Alan Styler, because he was always raging about something, was not always pet-friendly and his fiery temperament sometimes spooked the youngest cat, Leila. On one occasion, the Tinkers were camped in a farmer's field outside Stratford-upon-Avon and, with Pauline at a morning rehearsal, Tom was left in charge of their menagerie. As he opened the caravan door, Leila shot past him and headed straight up the nearest tree. No amount of gentle coaxing would persuade her to come down, so Tom, muttering rude words and threats, trudged off to borrow a ladder from the farmer. Precariously balanced, he edged towards the gloating cat, who climbed ever higher up the tree as soon as he got near her. Making a despairing lunge in her direction, the ladder wobbled and Tom plummeted to the ground, just in time to see Leila leap down from the tree and stroll nonchalantly back into the caravan! Needless to say, he was raging.

When John Broad joined the Tinkers' Club, he bought a tiny caravan, just ten feet long, which his VW Beetle just about managed to pull. Free from the chore of finding accommodation all over the country, he was happy, enjoying the friendship and mutual support the club offered. Despite the small size of his new home, he was amazed by how much space he had for his belongings and he loved the flickering cosiness of the gas lights when he came in at night. It was the perfect bachelor lifestyle. Then, Rosalind Griffiths came onto the scene and space was suddenly a factor. A bigger caravan and car to tow it was a small price to pay for the lady in his life, although he does remember how grumpy she was on moving days, when a lie-in would have been preferable to packing up and securing everything ready for moving on. Ros, of course, denies she was anything less than angelic, but does recall getting fed up with the chore of airing bedding on a daily basis, particularly in winter, when condensation was a problem. On the bright side, they had a battery-operated television and, fortunately for John, her cooking improved considerably after an indifferent start.

There were many adventures for the Tinkers, both funny and hair-raising but, perhaps, the most amusing involved Peggy Ann Jones encountering a 'flasher'. With the company appearing in Cardiff, the Tinkers were parked on a caravan site in Llandaff, close to fields and woodland. One day, Peggy was walking her dog, Judy, in the woods when she saw a man ahead of her fiddling with the front of his coat. Ever naïve, she carried on until he was right in front of her, whereupon he opened his coat and exposed himself. Petrified, she turned tail and ran back to the caravans, hysterically alerting the others to this unpleasant experience. With the girls anxious to commiserate, Peggy soon began to calm down, until Michael Tuckey and John Broad came along to see what was going on. When Peggy tearfully explained what had happened, prankster Mike went to unzip his trousers and said, "It's not your lucky day, is it?" Once the giggling men were shown the door, the girls advised Peggy to report the incident to the police, who duly came along to interview her. She still remembers their guffaws of laughter when they asked what the flasher looked like. "I don't know; I didn't see his face."

Not everyone took to life on tour in a small caravan. Musical Director, Royston Nash, found it hard going, even though his wife often travelled with him, so it was not long before he sold his van and went back to staying in pubs or small hotels. But he did remember enjoying being camped with the Tinkers at a farm in the Cheshire countryside, where he was able to walk to the farm every morning to get fresh milk for breakfast. Despite the disadvantages of taking their homes with them, most of the Tinkers have many happy memories of wonderful times together, although the owner of the black rubber groundsheet often seen hanging from the communal washing line has remained a source of speculation to this day!

The joys, or otherwise, of D'Oyly Carte travel were not confined to Great Britain. From its earliest days, North American tours were a regular feature of company life, when sailing across the Atlantic was the only option for getting to New York and from there, to all points in the States. As late as 1955, getting the company to America was effected by sea. The excitement felt by those members about to go on their first company overseas tour was enhanced by news that they were to sail on the *Queen Mary*. Large cabin trunks were purchased, roomy enough to cope with clothes for all seasons, from the heat of California to the biting cold of the Canadian winter, not forgetting the obligatory evening dress for official functions. Make-up and everything required for the dressing room was carried in the hold with the sets, costumes, props and orchestral parts. As the trip drew nearer, the intense anticipation of going to America was only tempered by the realisation of a long separation from family and friends, but that had to be accepted as the nature of touring with a famous theatre company.

After a drinks party at The Savoy Hotel, the D'Oyly Carters set off for Southampton, boarding the great cruise liner to find flowers, champagne and telegrams in their cabins. After an evening of great excitement and conviviality, sleep did not come easily, but everyone was anxious to be up early to enjoy setting out to sea. On waking next morning, there was a noticeable absence of activity on board and it was not long before they were told the horrible truth: the ship's staff had gone on strike and the *Queen Mary* was going nowhere. With rumours flying round about the future of the tour, the disconsolate group was taken back to The Savoy, where the company's General Manager, Frederic Lloyd, informed them that they would be flying to New York in two days' time. However, there was a problem: they were only to be allowed forty-four pounds of baggage.

The practicality of downsizing from a huge cabin trunk to a suitcase proved a real headache for everyone. Trying to decide what to take and what to leave behind from their large wardrobes was mind-boggling, but it had to be done. At least those living in London could easily offload what they could not take to America but, for anyone far from home, what were they supposed to do with the surplus clothes and personal items so carefully packed for a seven-month tour? Maureen Melvin, Jennifer Toye and Cynthia Morey took a room in a small hotel off The Strand to make the impossible happen, trading in trunks for cases and arranging storage for their leftovers.

At least the frantic reorganisation of luggage took everyone's mind off the terrible disappointment of not sailing on the *Queen Mary* and soon the excitement of flying to New York kicked in. For many, it was to be their first flight, so exhilaration was mixed with trepidation as they climbed aboard the huge Boeing Stratocruiser, a luxurious plane which even boasted beds and a downstairs lounge, doubtless for management only! The flight took an exhausting eighteen hours, with stops at Shannon and Gander, so everyone was shattered by the time they arrived in New York for an overnight stay. Despite the long transatlantic journey and five-hour time change, the company assembled at Penn Station the next morning to board a train bound for Denver, from where they were taken by bus to Central City, high up in the Rocky Mountains, for a month-long season at its bijou Opera House.

Within a few years, air travel had become much more commonplace, so it made far more sense for the D'Oyly Carte management to dispatch the company to America by plane. It was quicker and less expensive than sending them by sea, although far less glamorous for its employees. Kenneth Sandford had to wait five years to go on an American tour and once he had organised family matters for the duration of his five-month absence, he began to look forward to the trip. Many years later, he found a dog-eared diary in his attic, which vividly describes his first journey to the States on August 9th, 1962.

"At 7pm I said goodbye to my darlings and proceeded to The Savoy Hotel by way of taxi and tube, arriving there in good time. There were the usual crowds of fans and friends, including Sir Malcolm Sargent, to wish us 'bon voyage'. We boarded two coaches and proceeded to the airport, arriving there about 9.30pm. There was very little formality and we all had a very good meal. We embarked on our plane, a piston-engined DC7 of the Royal Dutch Airlines, KLM. So began a very uncomfortable and unnecessarily long journey to New York, relieved only by the kind attendance of the stewards and excellent food and wine. The aircraft was obviously not of the newest design, seats were uncomfortable and the engine noise was such that real sleep was impossible. Consequently, few of the company slept, I for only two or three hours, and that broken.

"At 9 o'clock GMT we had breakfast, then at 11 o'clock champagne and caviar, nicely presented, but much too near our previous meal and, as it turned out, much too near the commencement of the aircraft's descent. I had quite a few odd moments during the bumpy passage through the cloud. We landed at Idlewild airport at 8am local time, having already had breakfast and lunch! The Customs proved a little difficult insofar that most members of the company had to present each piece of baggage unfastened. By the time all had gone through, tempers were a little frayed. They were even more tested when we learned that we had to wait until 1.45pm before taking off to Los Angeles. The long flight to the West Coast was to be by Astro jet (the very latest in jet travel) and we were delighted by the prospect of a short journey. It was a truly lovely aircraft stewarded, naturally, by a bevy of American beauties. The journey was quite a dream. In no time we were at 35,000 feet, travelling at more than 400mph. There was not a trace of vibration. What a contrast to the fourteen-hour ordeal of a few hours before! On the coach journey from the air terminal to Pasadena I have never seen traffic like it. The roads are quite fantastic, almost Jules Verne in their conception. Flyovers fly over one another from every conceivable angle and the poor driver has to contend with four lanes! I had considered hiring a car but, until I learn a little of California's peculiar Highway Code, I think I'll remain a walking visitor!"

Such wonderment at being in the USA was shared by everyone on their first visit. Susan Maisey, who joined the D'Oyly Carte in 1964 just in time for an American tour, describes herself as a naïve country girl from the New Forest who had grown up in the depressing post-war years, to whom being in America seemed like a dream. Travelling by train to glamorous cities she knew only as names on a map, or from movies she had seen, seemed quite surreal. She has fond memories of a three-day rail trip from Seattle to the East Coast, during which she witnessed spectacular scenery, often from the comfort of her bed. On another occasion, she was astounded to find herself travelling through a salt lake. It was a fantastic experience and, as all cross-continent journeys on the 1964 tour were by train, Susan and her colleagues certainly got to see the country. It must not be forgotten that getting from venue to venue in such a huge country meant travelling on days when the company was not performing, but the excitement of being in America made up for missing the chance of a lazy day with nothing to do. The many long journeys also provided the opportunity to cement friendships and reinforce company spirit; a good thing, given that everyone was constantly thrown together for months on end.

Although luggage was handled by porters on train journeys and whisked way on check in at airports, company members were responsible for getting suitcases to and from their hotel rooms. Most people carried their own bags and this led to Kenneth Sandford finding himself in an awkward situation on the 1968 tour. Stepping into the elevator on the way down to the lobby to check out of his hotel, he found himself standing face to face with the world heavyweight boxing champion, Muhammad Ali. Feeling overawed by his proximity to the famous man, Ken was taken by surprise when Ali spoke to him. In an uncharacteristically quiet tone, he said to Ken, "Excuse me, sir, do you think you could take your suitcase off my foot, please?" Not a little embarrassed, Ken mumbled his apologies and did as he was asked, counting himself lucky not to be on the receiving end of a left hook! How Ken loved to relate that story.

The nature of air travel has always meant cramped, uncomfortable conditions when travelling long haul and, for those company members of a nervous disposition, it could be rather scary. The D'Oyly Carte Opera Company needed to get to and from many cities on a lengthy North American tour but by the late 60s, flying across the huge continent was the norm. Most of these journeys were accomplished without too many alarms, but several Carters recall one flight which stayed long in their minds and Abby Hadfield, in particular, has good reason to remember it. She was in the small toilet compartment when the aircraft hit an air pocket which sent it plummeting for several seconds. The descent was so sudden that her legs headed towards the ceiling and she was later able to boast that she was the only mezzo-soprano ever to pee uphill! Once she had sorted herself out, she emerged to a scene of chaos, with everyone mopping up, their drinks having shot up in the air and showered the cabin on the way back down. She is adamant she saw that great D'Oyly Carte servant, Jon Ellison, with ice cubes on his head! She also remembers overhearing the unperturbed Wardrobe Mistress, Cis Blain, who had been enjoying a quiet tipple or two with her assistant, Flo Ewbank. "Bit bumpy today, isn't it?"

By the American tours of 1976 and 1978, air travel had become commonplace and journey times across the Atlantic were half that of the 1962 tour, making the trips in modern Boeing 747 'jumbo jets' a much pleasanter experience. For those undertaking their first tour to the States, the excitement was intense as they soaked up the atmosphere of the traditional departure from The Savoy Hotel. The upmarket meeting point, with its historic connections to Gilbert and Sullivan, made the gathering seem very special, but it was about more than drinking the odd glass of fizz and a send-off from the management. Having the company together for the distribution of travel documents was managed more easily there than in the chaos of Heathrow's departure terminal. Passports, which had been taken well in advance to the American Embassy, were returned to their owners containing the necessary work permits and everyone was given a cash allowance in dollars to start them off.

As ever, the buses taking the company to Heathrow Airport were waved off by friends, family members and D'Oyly Carte fans, the latter doubtless bemoaning the upcoming drought of G&S whilst the company was away. Luggage check in for the large group was handled by the company manager, so there was little to do but enjoy duty-free shopping and wait for boarding. The company always travelled cabin class, but the large jets were relatively comfortable and everyone enjoyed the free bar. In the late 1970s, smoking on board was still allowed and the company's many smokers occupied the back rows of the aircraft and happily puffed their way across the Atlantic. On arrival in America, buses conveyed everyone to their hotels. Usually, there was a choice of accommodation ranging from budget to more expensive, members having made their selections several weeks in advance of the company's departure. All hotel bookings were made by the American management responsible for the tour, such as the

James M. Nederlander organisation on the 1978 tour, and were, mostly, of a good standard, so everyone enjoyed the bonus of not having to find digs for five months. With rare exceptions, travel from one city to another was by air, the flights and hotel transfers handled by the Americans.

For me, the most memorable flight of the 1978 tour was from San Francisco to Los Angeles. Many of the company had family or friends visiting for the California leg of the tour and my parents were among this group, for whom arrangements were made to travel with the company between venues. Taking off in perfect conditions, with no fog to obscure the view of the iconic bay, the plane soared high over the Golden Gate Bridge. As one D'Oyly Carte voice started to sing 'I Left My Heart in San Francisco', the rest of the company picked up the melody to give a thrilling rendition of the famous song, much to the astonishment of the other passengers, who cheered and clapped as we hit the big finish. The only person not applauding was my mother, who was in floods of tears. It had always been her ambition to visit the city she had seen in movies, but she never seriously thought about it actually happening. Thanks to the D'Oyly Carte, I was able to help fulfil that long-cherished dream, something for which I shall always be grateful.

Until 1970, D'Oyly Carte overseas tours had been confined to North America, but a chance conversation between two Danish men led to an interesting week away from the company's usual routine. Ingvar Blicher-Hansen was told by a friend how much he loved the operettas of Gilbert and Sullivan. Intrigued, Ingvar made trips to England in 1968 and 1969 to see several of the shows, which he found enchanting, so he contacted Savoy Hill to see if it might be possible for the company to visit Denmark. With his contacts, Mr. Blicher-Hansen aided the company management in organising four performances in Copenhagen and two in Aarhus, with *The Mikado* and *HMS Pinafore* the chosen operas. Flights were booked to get everything needed to Denmark and, in October of 1970, the D'Oyly Carte set out for what was to be a wonderfully different week. Unfortunately, details are a little sketchy due, in no small part, to the amount of liquid hospitality shown to the company, with the Carlsberg brewery and the NATO fleet the main culprits. Peggy Ann Jones, however, remembers everything very clearly. Her mother accompanied her on the trip, so she spent a quiet, rather sober week as everyone else had a ball.

Four years later, another European jolly was arranged, when the Accademia Filarmonica Romana hosted the D'Oyly Carte for a memorable week in Rome. The Accademia's director, Lanza Tomasi, had always been interested in English operettas, particularly those by Gilbert and Sullivan. Wishing to promote something other than the works of popular Italian composers, he approached the company with the idea of a week at the Teatro Olympico, seeing this as an ideal opportunity to share his own love of G&S with his fellow Italians. *The Mikado* and *Iolanthe* were the shows selected to be performed between November 11th and 15th, 1974.

Arrangements for getting the company personnel, orchestra, sets and costumes to Rome fell to Peter Riley, who went for an overnight stay in May of 1974 to look for suitable hotels and check out the theatre facilities. On his return, he consulted Equity, the actors' union, for their approval of his choice of hotel and travel plans. Protecting its members' interests gave Peter a few headaches as he tried to implement all union requirements. He was told that performers should not be expected to make their own way to and from the theatre, but the Accademia Filarmonica Romana refused to pay for the necessary bus transfers, so he approached the British Council and British Ambassador to Rome. Between them, they agreed to cover the cost of the transport, their generosity ensuring the D'Oyly Carte visit to Rome could go ahead, but it was a close call. That was not Peter's only problem with Equity. When told that the flight he wished to book was over an hour long, the union insisted that company members must be served a full meal, not just a snack. Alitalia did not have such a service on the Rome route, so he was forced to book a charter flight to Ciampino airport, with meals specially provided by Forte Inflight Catering. Eventually, Peter completed the complicated arrangements and the engagement went ahead.

After a wonderful week in Rome, the company returned to Gatwick airport on the Sunday, quite literally coming down to earth with a bump as the plane clattered onto the runway in wet weather and finally skidded to a stop. It seems hard to believe, but the D'Oyly Carte was scheduled to open the following day in the somewhat less eternal city of Bradford and everyone had to travel almost half the length of the country on the Monday morning to be there in time for the show. The rain in the south of England turned to snow as the exhausted company members drove northwards, the contrast between the balmy autumn sunshine of Rome and the wintry conditions of Yorkshire proving to be from the sublime to the ridiculous. It is a tribute to the professionalism of the company that everyone made it in time for the show, but it was particularly hard for the principals; unlike the chorus, with nowhere to hide, they probably got through the performance on adrenalin and caffeine.

With the D'Oyly Carte away on tour in North America in 1978, final negotiations were taking place between the Savoy Hill management and the Michael Edgley Organisation's London representative, Derek Glynne, with a view to taking the company to Australia and New Zealand the following year. If an American tour was exciting, how much more so the prospect of touring on the other side of the world? By the time the company returned from the States, the Australian tour was confirmed and, for the management, the daunting task of getting the company to Australia began in earnest, with Technical Director, Peter Riley, in the thick of things.

According to Peter, planning travel arrangements for the performers, management and staff was the easy bit. The first tour date was to be Canberra, so a flight to Sydney, via Bombay and Brunei for refuelling stops, was booked, followed, after a brief wait, by a short flight to Canberra. There was to be no stopover, because the Australian organisers deemed the expense too great. Organising the transport of everything needed for the shows to be taken, *The Mikado*, *HMS Pinafore* and *Iolanthe*, was not so straightforward, the logistics of shipping large amounts of scenery, costume baskets, wigs, props and everything else needed for the three operas proving to be extremely complicated.

With it taking nearly five weeks to get everything to Sydney by sea, it would be necessary to take the shows out of the repertoire for later UK tour dates. *Iolanthe* and *Pinafore* were to be dropped after the first week of the Manchester season in March of 1979. However, as the company had two *Mikado* sets, it was possible to keep performing the perennial money-spinner using the alternative set. Three sets of scenery would have to go to the company paint shop to be refurbished, before being shipped to Sydney, along with costumes and props for *Iolanthe* and *Pinafore* on March 18th. Costumes and props for *The Mikado* were to be packed after the last performance in Leeds on April 16th, before being sent by air freight at the end of the month. However, the 'Three Little Maids' costumes would be kept back, to be taken on the company flight and used for a photo opportunity. On arrival in Sydney, everything for *Iolanthe* and *Mikado* was to be taken by road to Canberra, with the *Pinafore* effects being stored at the Regent Theatre ready for the company's season there, which followed Canberra.

The Australian side of things organised, plans had to be made to get the sets to New Zealand and back, which proved to be a real headache for Peter Riley and the tour organisers. Shipping would take too long, so air freight was the only option. Air New Zealand offered a DC10, but the hold was too small to accommodate everything required for two operas, so a Qantas 747 cargo plane was chartered to get *Pinafore* to Auckland and a similar British Airways plane to take *Mikado*. Getting everything back for the Melbourne season was going to be even more complicated, with road, ferry and air transport needed to bring the company from Christchurch. From Peter's point of view, it was a good thing *Iolanthe* was not going to New Zealand to complicate matters further.

Whilst the D'Oyly Carte management and Edgley Organisation were dealing with such transport nightmares, company members were busy getting ready for the trip of a lifetime. Sets and costumes being sent to Australia by container ship meant that it was possible for everyone to send an advance suitcase, even if choosing what to take was something of a problem. The tobacco company, Benson and Hedges, one of the tour sponsors, had advised that there were to be numerous formal receptions during the tour, so evening dress would be essential. Temperatures in Brisbane would be warm, but winter in New Zealand called for warm clothes, so packing for a five-month tour was not easy. On top of that, it was necessary to make sure that all financial and family matters were in hand for the duration of the long trip. Bills would need paying, cars stored and gardens tended in the summer months, so there was much to organise.

Early in May, with everything finally in place and farewells said, everyone convened at The Savoy Hotel for the traditional departure before setting off for Heathrow Airport. The long flight was broken by four hours in the terminal of Bombay airport, when there was a welcome chance to stretch legs. The second refuelling stop was in Brunei, but nobody was allowed to leave the plane. By this time, everyone was very tired, but still in good spirits. After a flight of over twenty hours, the sight of the Australian coast as the plane descended brought home the reality of being on the other side of the world and excitement mounted as The D'Oyly Carte Opera Company landed for its one and only tour of Australia and New Zealand.

First to come down the steps from the aircraft, in full costume and make-up, were the 'Three Little Maids', a pre-arranged publicity stunt for the benefit of the waiting Sydney media, which had been made aware of the importance of the tour. All very effective it may have been, but the practicality of this was not the concern of the waiting reporters, who probably gave no thought as to how Barbara Lilley, Lorraine Daniels and myself had managed to change on the aircraft. We were tired and grubby after such a long flight, so putting on our *Mikado* costumes was not much fun, but we knew it was a nice gimmick for the start of the tour. Spare a thought, too, for Wardrobe Mistress, Vera Carnegie and Wig Mistress, Heather Perkins, who had to bring our costumes and wig boxes on board with their hand luggage. Using the toilet on an aircraft is difficult enough at the best of times, but such small compartments were certainly not designed to apply Japanese eyes and don kimonos. In turn, the three of us got changed with Vera's help, before Heather put on our wigs. Putting on the large 'fried-egg' hats in the loo was a non-starter, so they had to wait until just before we exited the plane. Meanwhile, our own clothes were gathered up by Vera so that we could change back into 'civvies' in the terminal toilets, much to the amusement of other passengers using the facilities for normal purposes.

Such publicity was necessary at the start of an important tour and, however exhausted we felt after the long journey, it was part of our job as professional performers, so we just got on with it. Nevertheless, it was an enjoyable experience. Meanwhile, by the time we had waited a few hours for the connecting flight to Canberra, everyone was getting a little tetchy, the tiredness really kicking in. The tour organisers had sensibly planned for the company to open a week after arrival, so we had time to adjust to the twelve-hour time difference and catch up on some sleep. It was a gentle start to a tour which took the D'Oyly Carte to some wonderful cities: Canberra, Sydney, Brisbane, Adelaide, Melbourne and Perth in Australia; Christchurch, Auckland and Wellington in New Zealand. The flight between the latter two places was spectacular. We saw mountains, forests and smoking volcanoes as the plane flew south at low level down the west coast of New Zealand's North Island. The last date was Perth and it was from there that the company returned to the UK after a memorable tour. The D'Oyly Carte Opera Company never again appeared outside of its home country.

CHAPTER FOUR

IT'S A FULL HOUSE

The most difficult part of life with the D'Oyly Carte was, undoubtedly, having to find accommodation when away from home for forty-eight weeks of the year. For anyone who was with the company for many years, it was possible to build up a network of good digs, so the problem was not so great, merely requiring contact to be made with familiar landladies or landlords. Even then, there were times when a new touring date for the company meant starting from scratch. Sometimes, landladies had retired, or lodgings were fully-booked. For those new to life on the road, knowing where to begin the search for somewhere to stay was daunting. The only respite from this constant hassle was the welcome chance to stay at home, or with friends and family, when the tour brought them close enough to such luxury. As has been previously mentioned, in the late 1960s, many took matters into their own hands by buying small caravans, which eliminated the constant search for accommodation.

It was usual for every theatre to have its own list of recommended digs, but the D'Oyly Carte management took responsibility for helping its employees find suitable places within easy reach of theatres. Several weeks prior to the company's visit to a town or city, adverts requesting offers of rooms with meals provided, or self-catering flats and bedsits, were placed in local newspapers, the resulting letters being made available to members on a first come, first served, basis. During the period covered by this book, one thing that changed very little was the ritual of queueing for digs letters. In the 1950s, they were pinned onto the theatre notice board, or placed on a table during a rehearsal. By the 1970s, these letters were available from the Company Manager's office, usually for perusal between a matinee and evening performance, the tannoy announcement of their availability causing a stampede from the dressing rooms. Those at the front of the queue got the pick of the letters and were allowed to keep two before passing back the rest, so anyone at the end of the line was left with the least attractive-sounding lodgings. It would be unkind to suggest that the Company Manager always had excellent accommodation, but we did wonder.

Sometimes, a little subterfuge was used to gain advantage in the digs stakes, when someone heard a hint that the letters were about to be made available and used it to their advantage. Cynthia Morey, who often shared with Alice Hynd, remembers being on her hands and knees in the chorus, with head bowed, during 'The Mikado's Entrance' when Alice, in the alto line directly behind her edged as close as she dared before whispering, "The digs letters are up!" Once they had backed obsequiously off the stage at the end of the scene, the two of them picked up their kimonos and ran like the wind to get to the notice board first. It was not always necessary to gain an unfair advantage, the process of getting digs letters was normally a patient and good-natured business. One incident which sparked much hilarity in the queue involved Lorraine Daniels. With the company due to go to Scotland, the digs letters for Edinburgh were being passed around and Lorraine, who was sharing with Barry Clark at the time, found herself looking at a postcard of Edinburgh Castle. Without thinking to turn it over, she caused gales of laughter when she nudged him and said, "'Ere, Barry, this place looks nice."

The types of people who wrote to the company offering accommodation were many and varied, from traditional theatre landladies, to people who thought it might be interesting to have show business people staying with them, and even D'Oyly Carte fans, although the latter invariably meant being unable to get away from work. Lodgings in the 1950s were mainly with professional landladies used to the needs of theatre folk, who liked a late breakfast, midday meal and a supper after the show. Some would even offer to do laundry, a perennial problem for anyone on tour before the days of washing machines and laundrettes. The girls often washed clothes in the theatre, going in early before a show to do their 'smalls'. With the rigging up of temporary washing lines around the room, there were frequent jovial complaints about nether garments dripping on the heads of those directly below. Many of the men parcelled up their laundry and sent it home for their lucky wives to wash and iron. That done, it was posted to the company's next port of call.

For a longer season such as in London or Manchester, small flats were in great demand, because they had fewer house rules and gave more of a feeling of home. It was not unusual for company members to hire houseboats on the river in Oxford, or caravans and holiday chalets when playing a seaside resort. The trick to surviving eleven months on tour was to think of digs as being home. Most people managed this successfully, but there were some who never settled to the prospect of being away from home for long periods, so their D'Oyly Carte careers were brief. Kenneth Sandford always preferred digs where he could cook for himself and feeling at home meant baking his famous apple pie, or a pineapple upside down cake large enough to last a week. He became an excellent cook and quite innovative when faced with a lack of cooking utensils in kitchens which were often very basic. Rolling out pastry with a Coca Cola bottle was quite usual for Ken but, on one occasion, finding something in which he could cook his pineapple cake needed a little more thought. Finding a colander under the kitchen sink in his digs, he lined it with aluminium foil and added the sponge mixture before successfully baking his second-favourite pudding.

Theatrical landladies usually lived near town or city centres, within walking distance or, at worst, a short bus ride from the theatre and the best were prized for their ability to provide clean, warm, rooms and home-cooked food. In the 1950s, it was common for the toilet facilities to be outside in the back yard of the house, which was not much fun in the middle of winter. In the 1960s, the residential areas surrounding traditional town centre High Streets were gradually demolished as urban regeneration kicked in and retail premises began to dominate the inner cities. By the end of the decade, few traditional theatre landladies remained and the emphasis shifted away from their 'mother hen' style of hospitality to self-catering, or rooms in private houses. Staying in hotels or pubs was generally too expensive to be considered, unless a deal could be struck for a weekly rate, but this rarely happened. There were a few remaining establishments which specialised in providing accommodation for performers, but they were geared more to club entertainers than theatre people. I once stayed in one such place, where the guests included veteran Australian yodeller, Frank Ifield, and Freddie Garrity, lead singer of the famous 1960s pop group, 'Freddie and the Dreamers', which was, by then, well past its heyday. One morning, as I was tucking into my cooked breakfast, Freddie came over to my table to tell me he had recently had his appendix removed and was worried that the wound had become infected. Without further ado, he dropped his trousers and said, "Have a look at it for me, will you?" Very embarrassed, I took a quick peek and assured him that, as far as I could tell, it appeared to be fine. Fortunately, I had already eaten my chipolata sausage, but I did push the tomatoes to the side of my plate.

Given the difficulties of always having to look for somewhere to stay, it is hardly surprising that one of the perks of an American tour was having someone else book accommodation and not having to think about it for several months. Even whilst Britain was still in the grip of post-war hardship and rationing, the D'Oyly Carte went to America, where everyone enjoyed the warmth and comfort of large hotel rooms. After being used to sharing toilet facilities, a private bathroom with a shower was luxury indeed. The fact that breakfast was not provided in American hotels only added to the sense of good living. Company members sampled the numerous coffee shops and diners adjacent to their hotels, where huge breakfasts could be consumed for a small amount of money. Excellent lunches and dinners in cheap, pleasant restaurants were easy to find and nothing like the greasy spoon cafe meals which were all most people could afford when eating out back at home. It was a very different world and everyone enjoyed the change. Jennifer Toye was on the 1955 tour and still remembers her amazement at American food.

"We couldn't believe the variety of meals we got in restaurants and diners. On one occasion, we were having breakfast in San Francisco when a man leaned over and asked if we had eggs in England! We must have looked like refugees!"

The most unusual date on American tours in the 1950s and 60s was Central City in Colorado. Looking like a typical town in any cowboy movie, it nestles high up in the Rocky Mountains and, surprisingly, boasts a beautiful little opera house which, for many years, hosted an annual festival of opera, ballet and operetta. On two occasions, the company's appearance was part of the festival's extensive programme. As might be imagined, accommodating the company performers, management and staff in such a small place was not easy. Hotel rooms were limited, so many people stayed in private homes and enjoyed the great western hospitality of their hosts. Noted for always being dressed in smart clothes, the D'Oyly Carters soon got into the swing of things, with cowboy boots, fringed jackets and stetsons replacing their usual apparel. Everyone loved socialising in the Teller House with its saloon-style bar, which had a painting of a woman's head on the floor that was reputed to have mysteriously appeared overnight. In fact, some company wag managed to make a large copy of 'The face on the bar room floor' which, equally mysteriously, appeared overnight at the bottom of the hatch on the set of *HMS Pinafore*! Purely for the benefit of the performers, of course, it caused much merriment on the stage. The pre-show festival entertainments and socialising in the town after performances made the Central City seasons a firm favourite with all those lucky enough to be in the company at the time. It is interesting that oxygen was always available in the wings of the theatre. At a height of 8,000 feet above sea level, it took everyone time to acclimatise to the altitude, so singing a rapid patter song, or having to dance energetically during a performance, could lead to breathlessness.

By the company tours of North America in 1976 and '78, hotel living had changed very little, with the exception of everyone having a television in their room, always a plus for D'Oyly Carters. It was rare to have self-catering accommodation in the States, although, in 1978, many people stayed at the El Cortez Hotel on Geary Street in San Francisco, which boasted kitchen facilities, making rooms more like small flats. This was hugely popular with those who had family or friends visiting for the Californian leg of the tour, affording the opportunity to indulge in favourite home-cooked dishes. The hotel also boasted a large function room, which was the scene of a memorable party. When away from home for months on end, birthdays were an important part of company life and always celebrated. Alto choristers, Susan Cochrane and Elizabeth Denham, had birthdays on consecutive days in early June, so arrangements were made for a joint party after a show with two cakes being ordered from a local bakery. With the company gathered for the festivities, soprano Suzanne O'Keeffe took responsibility for bringing in one of the cakes. As the operatic singing of 'Happy Birthday To You' rang round the room, Suzanne teetered in on high stiletto heels, tripped and dropped it! With cream splattered all over the floor and Suz in great distress, the company's initial dismay quickly turned to sympathy for the mortified cake-bearer. The remains were scraped up, distributed and devoured as if nothing had happened. How typical of the spirit of the D'Oyly Carte.

On the same tour, some of the hotels could definitely be described as 'budget'. In New York, the Empire Hotel was within a couple of minutes walk of the prestigious Lincoln Center, where the company was to appear, so most people opted to stay there. Small and stuffy, its rooms were blessed with complimentary cockroaches, truly knocking on the head any idea that show business is glamorous. In Boston, the Avery Hotel was another low-cost establishment chosen by some in the company, although it had other residents, whose nocturnal activities proved it to be little short of a brothel. There was something of an adventure in this cheap and cheerful place, when the building next door caught fire and D'Oyly Carters were woken from their slumbers in the small hours by hotel staff knocking on doors to tell them to quickly make their way to the reception area. This was a precautionary measure and everyone soon gravitated to the hotel bar, where those who had money with them paid for the many drinks consumed until the all-clear was given several hours later. Beti Lloyd-Jones, who was in high spirits, later denied trying to buy a drink for any fireman venturing into the lobby. This incident was, quite naturally, the subject of chatter in the ladies' dressing room the following evening, as those not staying at the Avery were filled in on the details. Somewhat puzzled, Lorraine Daniels, who was staying in the hotel, said, "Fire? What bleedin' fire?"

Her extraordinary capacity for deep sleep meant that she had snoozed her way through the whole drama.

Following the successful New York season, the company moved on to Saratoga Springs in Upstate New York. However, for the day off between venues, members were given the choice of staying in New York for an extra day to enjoy themselves in the Big Apple, or moving on to Saratoga for a rest. The numbers were evenly split and those who decided to remain in town missed one of the most famous events ever to disgrace the company, the D'Oyly Carte Olympics. The small hotel in Saratoga was in a quiet, almost rural setting and it had a large grassy area surrounding its swimming pool. The idea for a sports day is generally reckoned to lie at the door of Wig Mistress, Heather Perkins, but the wacky notion soon caught on and everyone agreed it would be a great way to have some fun on their day off. With Heather organising such traditional events as an egg and spoon race, tug of war, three-legged and wheelbarrow races, plus a five-a-side football match, the scene was set for a pleasantly different afternoon's entertainment. Somehow managing to source the props for these games, Heather did a great job, with a little help from her friends.

However, it being the D'Oyly Carte, things did not turn out quite as expected due, in no small part, to the alcohol acquired at the same time as the bits and bobs for the games. With all participants in their swimsuits or shorts, the races began sedately enough. The pairings tied together for the three-legged race included Meston Reid and Heather Perkins; Beti Lloyd-Jones and James Conroy-Ward; Ken Robertson-Scott and Ceinwen Newby, the former company mezzo-soprano and wife of the Company Manager, Herbert Newby; and Patricia Leonard, bound to husband, Michael Buchan, in more ways than one. It was a hot, sunny afternoon, so liquid refreshment was essential as the races continued and by the time the five-a-side football started, things were getting a little boisterous, with cheating and foul play in no short supply. Even Bert Newby, by no means a young, fit man, was seen to trip faster players, but the worst offender was Ken Sandford. Confined by a troublesome Achilles tendon to keeping goal, he was sent off for moving the posts of his goal closer together when he thought nobody was looking. The other players were Ken Robertson-Scott, Beti Lloyd-Jones, Jon Ellison, Gordon Mackenzie, Peter Riley and his wife, Yvonne

Sommeling, Billy Strachan and Julia Goss. I vaguely remember being the referee.

The final event was a men's tug of war across the swimming pool and that was where the real trouble started, a ducking being the least of their problems for two of the participants. All the pulling and shoving led to crashing falls, leaving Assistant Musical Director, David Mackie with a cracked rib and Stage Manager, Ken Robertson-Scott with a broken wrist! Despite these injuries, the D'Oyly Carte 'Olympics' concluded with a prize-giving, during which Bert Newby made an incoherent speech, and a closing ceremony, when the contestants, by now rather inebriated, paraded round the precincts of the hotel singing the company's anthem, 'Hail Poetry', from *Pirates*, whilst waving the fly swats from their rooms. It was all so ridiculously serious, the hotel staff looking on in utter disbelief. After mopping up some of the alcohol with a meal in the restaurant, the evening concluded with a party in one of the rooms, where everyone collapsed onto beds, chairs or the floor to finish off the day in style.

The following morning, the many aching limbs, bumps, bruises and fractures were complemented by sore heads and there was some concern as to how the broken bones were going to be explained to the rest of the company due to arrive from New York later that day. The decision was taken to play down the whole thing and everyone pretended they had enjoyed a peaceful day of rest lazing by the pool, but the truth came out when it became clear that David Mackie would be unable to conduct for some time and Ken Robertson-Scott's broken wrist meant there would be no scenery shifting for him for a while. Needless to say, the management could not take disciplinary measures, because most of them were involved! Never mind the cracked bones and other injuries, it was a wonderful, silly, crazy day; the sort of impromptu shindig that characterised D'Oyly Carte tours, made possible because the hotel allocated to the company had the facilities for such a crackpot escapade. Nobody who took part would have missed it for the world.

Such rumbustious fun was not unusual. Given that everyone enjoyed relaxing in the hot weather experienced during a summer tour of North America, hotel swimming pools were always a popular meeting point during periods of free time. The 1978 tour included a date at The Greek Theatre, a delightful open air venue in the hills above

Los Angeles, best-remembered for the helicopters 'buzzing' the shows, the raccoon sitting at the feet of 'Private Willis' in *Iolanthe*, and the large spider ambling round the rim of arachnophobe Beti Lloyd-Jones' straw hat during a performance of *HMS Pinafore*. Most of the company were housed in a motel in Hollywood and afternoon gatherings round the pool were a must. One day, Michael Buchan decided that things needed livening up a little, so he pushed Suzanne O'Keeffe into the deep end of the pool. Unfortunately, he didn't know that Suz could not swim. As he waited for her to splutter to the surface and give him hell, he realised she was struggling under the water. She was quickly rescued by everyone diving in to get her to safety, but Mike was mortified that his prank had caused her such a fright. It is typical of Suz's generous nature that she forgave him so readily, although she never let him forget it!

Back in the UK in the late 1970s, nearly all company members opted for digs where they could look after themselves. There were a few exceptions, Thomas Scholey being one of them. With no family commitments or mortgage payments to hamper him, he preferred to find small hotels or pleasant pubs which meant he did not have to worry about looking for somewhere to eat. Herbert Newby and Royston Nash also preferred this option. With the demise of landladies who provided meals, it was far too expensive to eat out every day, even assuming there were any good cafes or restaurants nearby, so cooking facilities in a flat meant being able to eat whatever you wanted whenever you wanted it. This was the preferred choice of accommodation right until the company closed, although it was sometimes necessary to take rooms in private homes, an option not always free from incident. Not long after taking over from John Reed as principal comedian, James Conroy-Ward chose to stay in a house close to the Theatre Royal in Norwich. As a non-driver, being able to walk to work was a rare bonus. On arrival at the beautiful property in a Georgian crescent, he was greeted by the lady of the house, who showed him to his room. It was comfortably furnished, but the wall opposite his bed was adorned with a large crocodile. Knowing that there were two rooms available, he asked to see the other, but that, too, was decorated with reptilian wall art.

As she showed him round the rest of the house, the landlady

proudly explained that her son loved hunting game in Africa. Leading him into a private sitting room, James was astonished to see a coffin lying against a wall. Unable to disguise his surprise, she hurriedly explained that her husband, a solicitor dealing with estates and wills on a daily basis, had ordered it in advance to remind himself of his own mortality. She went on to assure him that it was a source of much amusement for the family and that her children used it as a toy chest. When the other guest arrived, James was able to warn her of the strange things they would have to live with for the next week. Ever the joker, James proceeded to have fun at her expense during their stay in the odd house. On retiring one night, she turned down the covers to be confronted by a crocodile, which James had taken from his bedroom and stuffed into her bed to give her a fright. It worked. Later in the week, she returned from the theatre after a performance of *Pirates* to find the lounge empty and assumed that James had retired early on his night off. She had just settled down with a drink to watch the television, when she heard a creaking noise coming from behind her. With the hairs on her neck standing up, she turned to see the lid of the coffin slowly lifting. Petrified, she watched in fascinated horror as it was raised just enough for her to see James lying in state, with a cup of tea resting on his chest! He had waited until he heard her arrive home before adopting his macabre pose and she did see the funny side of it several months later. And, of course, the poor soul on the receiving end of this practical joking was me.

Unlike America, where everyone stayed in hotels, the 1979 tour of Australia and New Zealand gave the opportunity to stay mainly in self-catering apartment hotels, which were very popular at that time. This suited the D'Oyly Carters very well, because they had kitchen facilities and, more importantly, space for the get-togethers and parties that were so essential for keeping company morale high whilst 12,000 miles from home. In Sydney, the city-centre building in which most of the company stayed boasted excellent modern apartments, from studios to palatial flats with several bedrooms. It was an ideal place for the three-week season. Exactly a year after the cake-dropping incident in San Francisco, Sue Cochrane and Liz Denham held another joint birthday party, which proved to be one of the most celebrated in modern D'Oyly Carte history.

The girls decided on a fancy dress do and everyone picked up the spirit of the occasion with great gusto because, being so far from home, it was good to have something to occupy their off-duty hours. With plenty of notice, there was lots of time to consider what costumes to wear and many were ingenious. Downtown Sydney had a large Woolworths store, which was stripped of anything suitable to make costumes from a Naughty Nun (Beti Lloyd-Jones), to an inhabited champagne bottle (Alan Spencer). The latter took days to create a frame from wire coat hangers, which he covered in green cellophane, before making a cork from cardboard covered in foil, with yellow and white balloons for bubbles, which was worn as a hat. The finishing touch was a label marked '100% poof'. Unfortunately, when it came to party time, his wonderful creation proved too wide to get through the door of his room, so he had to climb out of it, wearing just his underpants, and squash it through the doorway into the corridor, before getting back in to waddle to the elevator. Luckily for Alan, nobody was around to witness this bizarre behaviour.

How he happened on the idea for his costume is not known, but Ken Sandford decided to go to the party as Dame Edna Everage, the famed Australian housewife character created by Barry Humphries. He cheated a little in that he borrowed a long kaftan-style dress from one of the girls and also a wig, but shoes to fit him were a problem, until he thought about the white ones worn by the peers in *Iolanthe*. With long silver gloves on loan from one of the *Iolanthe* fairies, all he had to do was make some outrageous spectacle frames. Making him up was another matter, so it fell to James Conroy-Ward to apply the eye-shadow, mascara and lipstick. Not in the least perturbed by the astonished looks on the faces of several butch Aussie men he encountered in the elevator on his way to the party, he merely raised his voice an octave or two and bade them a camp, "Good night, boys", as he got out. So impressive was his impersonation, that he won the prize for best-dressed female.

Not everyone made their own outfit; some of the men, John Ayldon and Guy Matthews amongst them, somehow managed to get hold of costumes from Australian Opera. Another was Thomas Scholey, who arrived as an eastern potentate complete with gold face make-up, which was still visible, despite much scrubbing, during the following evening's performance of *HMS Pinafore*, much to the hilarity of everyone on the stage. The birthday girls turned out as Minnie Mouse and Count Dracula. Amongst many other memorable characters was the koala bear created by bass chorister, Patrick Wilkes, who was led round on a leash by his future wife, Patricia Anne Bennett, dressed as a zoo keeper. Everyone provided food for the party and an echo of the previous year's disaster with the birthday cake occurred when Philip Potter, who had rejoined the company for the tour to play 'Nanki-Poo' in *The Mikado*, made a large lasagne and managed to drop the dish, depositing its gooey contents all over the floor of the elevator en route to the party! He was not popular that night.

It is important to understand that such socialising was vital for surviving a long overseas tour and keeping the company bond strong. Having a 'home', where large or small gatherings after shows were possible, was particularly important during the four weeks spent in New Zealand, because every bar or cafe was closed by the time the show had come down and television finished for the night at 10pm. The row of small houses in Christchurch, dubbed 'Coronation Street', went down really well with the company, providing plenty of room for the D'Oyly Carte poker club nights, which saw its members take turns in providing drinks and snacks before the serious business of playing for pennies began in earnest. The players were Peter Lyon and his wife, Barbara Lilley, Susan Cochrane, Beti Lloyd-Jones, Jane Stanford, Gordon 'Mike' Mackenzie and myself. In another house, Suz O'Keeffe excelled herself in the food department. Once known to try making a meringue with hard-boiled eggs (according to her best friend, principal soprano, Vivian Tierney), Suz cooked a stew and put it on a low light when she left the little home-from-home to go to the theatre for a matinee. Having invited three friends to join her for dinner, they arrived with good appetite to find smoke coming out of the windows and the last vestiges of the stew indelibly burned onto the bottom of the saucepan! Fortunately, they were just in time to avoid the need to call the fire brigade.

The weather in Christchurch was cold and frosty, which seemed very strange given that it was July, so some bright spark suggested that, as the weather was what might be expected in December in Britain, a Christmas dinner would be a good idea. Peter Lyon volunteered to cook turkey with all the trimmings for his wife, Barbara, Bryan Secombe, Sue Cochrane and Suzanne O'Keeffe who, happily for the others, was relieved of cooking duties. When word of the seasonal feast spread amongst the company, Ken Sandford and I came up with an idea to surprise the revellers. He took his make-up box back to his little house and painted an intricate blue design on my face in the distinctive style of the indigenous New Zealand population. Wearing a borrowed hooded red coat and with a stuffed pillow case over my shoulder, I burst in on the festive five as they tucked into their meal and shouted, "Maori Christmas!" before disappearing as quickly as I had arrived. By the time the astonished diners had stopped laughing, their festive meal had nearly gone cold. Happy days indeed.

The penultimate venue on the Australian tour was Adelaide where, once again, the company was in comfortable self-catering accommodation. The 'aparthotel' had a separate function room outside of the main building, which could only be accessed by a ladder up through an aperture not much bigger than a trap door. Undeterred by this strange entrance arrangement, Beti Lloyd-Jones decided to celebrate her birthday, on August 25th, with a swish party. The many formal functions, requiring evening dress, promised by the tour sponsors had not materialised, so posh frocks and dinner jackets had lain creased in suitcases. Having sent out formal 'black tie' invitations, Beti made sure that everyone got to dress up at least once on the tour, although many of the girls went rather over the top, sporting tiaras and outrageous costume jewellery. It must be said that the other hotel residents could only watch in total bewilderment as the strange group of British people ascended the ladder to the party venue wearing full evening dress, the ladies with their long skirts hoisted around their waists as they made the precarious ascent. Only in the D'Oyly Carte.

The final date of the 1979 Antipodean tour was Perth, where another self-catering hotel was selected for the company's stay. Its name, Mountside Serviced Apartments, sticks in the memory after more than thirty years because it was so inapt; the dreary, sparsely-furnished rooms earning it the prefix of 'Un'. After the excellent accommodation selected in every other city, the Mountside was a great disappointment, giving everyone the feeling that it had been a very long tour and it was time to go home. James Conroy-Ward recalls the fright he got whenever he passed the gas water heater on the wall of his room, because it had a nasty habit of shooting flames out of the aperture on its front. He told his colleagues he had a most unusual cigarette lighter in his room, as well as flying carpets, as the tatty rugs regularly sent him skidding across the wooden floor. Despite this let-down, the D'Oyly Carters had few complaints about the accommodation provided during their five-month sojourn in Australia and New Zealand, which had given them the opportunity to live comfortably and enjoy socialising whilst so far from home. The D'Oyly Carte never performed outside of the United Kingdom again. For the company's final three tours, it was back to the grind of having to find somewhere to stay.

Of all the stories told by company folk about life in the D'Oyly Carte, those about their digs have always been the most popular. There are far too many to include in these pages, but it would not be a fair reflection of company life not to tell some of the more memorable individual accommodation anecdotes, many of which are extremely funny, although some not so; but all give a fascinating insight into touring life. They also show how much everyday life advanced during the period covered by this book, from the cold, bleak rooms rented in Britain of the 1950s to the centrally-heated apartments and comfortable houses available in the early 1980s.

Jennifer Toye joined the company in 1954, but still has a clear memory of the trials and tribulations of the accommodation lottery and her words paint a wonderful picture of a time gone by.

"Arriving at digs was sometimes a nightmare. Not knowing the town, we took a taxi to the lodgings and our hearts sank as we passed the nice houses and turned into a dark street. Entering the house, we were greeted by the smell of cabbage, which had been on the boil since early morning! Mostly, however, we stayed at some wonderful places, although the cabbage was still there. We had a 'combined room'. This consisted of, usually, a front room containing beds, a table, sofa and chairs and a roaring fire. The landlady would trail upstairs with breakfast, lunch and a cold collation to have after the show. There was an amusing time when one of the meals was a mystery to us and didn't taste quite right, so we consigned it to the fire and it produced a large green flame! Another time, we found that the bathroom was occupied by builders when we weren't there, all sleeping on the floor!"

In the early 1950s, the D'Oyly Carte played seasons over Christmas at the Shakespeare Memorial Theatre in Stratford-upon-Avon, where many of the company stayed at the Old Red Lion Hotel. A fascinating old building, with low, beamed ceilings and a multitude of period features, it was a certainty for early booking. It was the perfect place to spend Christmas for those who were unable to get home for the Festive Season. With a performance on Christmas Eve and a matinee on Boxing Day, it was impossible for most people to join their families, so the D'Oyly Carte surrogate family was there to fill the void. The warm hospitality of the landlord and his wife helped create a party atmosphere, with management, staff, principals and chorus happily making decorations together in the lounge, or creating hats for competitions. Cynthia Morey remembers the year when principal tenor, Neville Griffiths, made rice wine in his bedroom, but nobody was invited to sample the fruits of his labour! As always, when it was impossible to get home, those separated from the people they loved came together to support each other and make the best of a difficult time, something that was a constant feature of D'Oyly Carte life right to the end.

A three-week season in Belfast saw several people, including John Reed, Alice Hynd and Cynthia Morey, book into lodgings which proved highly entertaining. The landlady, Mrs. Mack, was a kindly soul, whose eccentricities were matched by those of her helpful, but rather flatulent daughter, Gertie. The large house had rooms which were cheaper at the top than the bottom, but John was pipped to the attic room by Alice and Cynthia, who almost knocked him flying in the charge for the stairs. With John consigned to a small room on the first floor at an extra five shillings a week, the girls' room boasted twin beds and an odd, narrow wardrobe, which turned out to be a grandfather clock from which the workings had been removed and replaced by a rail. A noisy water tank completed the furnishings, but at least they had a skylight, out of which they somehow managed to rig up a washing line. Mealtimes were a hoot, in more ways than one, when their food was served by Gertie, who broke wind with alarming regularity, causing stifled hysteria amongst the diners. With her charges fed and watered, Mrs. Mack, who 'liked a few jars', would go to the pub directly across the road from her house and get a taxi home. Her guests always looked out to see if they could catch her staggering into a cab on one side of the street and tumbling out of it on the opposite side! It was an experience they would not have missed.

The living conditions of lodgings the 1950s were often harsh; sometimes rooms were unheated and the bedding damp, but D'Oyly Carters were a hardy breed and managed to survive without too many colds and coughs which, as professional singers, they were always anxious to avoid. In some digs, baths were only available once a week and that at the cost of an extra shilling on the rent. On the rare occasion of there being a bathroom in the theatre, it was a popular place. It is hard to believe in the twenty-first century, but that was the reality of life on the road in those days and it was not always the cheapest digs that were so primitive. On a salary which had to cover both theatre and living expenses, money was tight for company members, so cheap digs were always tempting. Sometimes, the least expensive accommodation turned out to be a real bargain. Alice Hynd and Cynthia Morey had booked a place in Aberdeen during a bitterly cold fortnight in winter and were surprised when their taxi deposited them outside a 'prefab' house, the sort quickly built at the end of the Second World War to help ease the housing shortage. The tiny house was warm and comfortable, so they were cosy, whilst many of their colleagues suffered freezing conditions in their digs. An added bonus was the wonderful fresh fish brought home every day by their fisherman landlord and all they paid was thirty-five shillings a week each, less than £2 in today's currency.

Many theatre landladies were absolute treasures, looking after their guests' every need to make them feel at home and they were popular year on year. Some were a little less obliging and Joyce Wright remembers arriving at her digs, fresh from an American tour, with her wardrobe trunk in tow. The lady of the house stood on the doorstep and eyed the large piece of luggage with some suspicion, "You're not bringing that bloody thing in here." So that was that, Joyce had to find somewhere else to stay. Some, like Mrs. Mack in Belfast, were great characters and Alan Barrett recalls one who claimed to be psychic. It was early in 1959 when he and his wife, Mary Sansom, booked into the digs in Wolverhampton with John Reed. One morning at breakfast, the landlady came in looking very pleased with herself. Pointing at Mary and John she mysteriously said, "You're going to get some good news today. I see two brown envelopes." Dismissing her weird prophecy, they went to the theatre later that day, to find two brown envelopes, the contents of which informed Mary and John that both of them had been made principals. Only after their initial excitement had subsided did they think about the uncanny prediction made by their landlady. Strange, but true, according to Alan.

In Norwich in the mid-1960s, Peter Riley and his wife, Abby Hadfield, encountered a fearsome landlady, one Miss Evans. Joining them at the address Peter had taken from the Theatre Royal digs list were Abby's sister, who was working in the company's wardrobe department, and their golden labrador, Cindy. Having contacted the landlady to confirm their booking, they turned up after the show for their first night, to find the door locked. Not best pleased, Peter pushed open the letterbox and shouted through it to let the lady of the house know they had arrived. There followed a bizarre navel-level exchange as Miss Evans responded from the other side of the gap, "Those are my house rules: ten o'clock or you don't come in." Peter pointed out that it was not yet 11pm, but to no avail; the lady was not for turning.

A hurried discussion brought the conclusion that it was too late at night to find somewhere else to stay, so the three of them huddled together under a thin blanket in the back of Peter's car, Cindy providing a little extra warmth as she snuggled in. After a cold, uncomfortable night, the intrepid quartet eventually dozed off, to be woken by banging on the windscreen early the next day. "Good morning, Mister Riley, I've brought you some tea. Breakfast will be ready when you come in." By this time very annoyed, Peter got out and told her in no uncertain terms that he would make sure her name was removed from the theatre digs list, pointing out that if she was going to take in theatricals, she must learn to deal with the hours they keep. With that, he drove his charges away to find alternative accommodation and, after such a terrible start to the Norwich season, everything turned out well when he managed to hire a mobile home on the Norfolk Broads. Abby remembers an idyllic time on the waterside and Cindy had no complaints either, jumping into the water for a doggy-paddle whenever she felt like it.

Before he married principal contralto, Christene Palmer, Norman Wilfred Wright remembers once sharing digs with fellow chorus tenors, Jeff Cresswell and David Rayson. Boys being boys, their smutty, schoolboy humour was not confined to its usual place in the dressing room when their delightfully innocent landlady, Mrs. Bates, introduced her much-loved dog, 'Master'. Every time they heard him being called, they collapsed into uncontrollable mirth and even recounting the story some forty years later made him laugh. Norman and Christene were married in 1970, despite him being told by Musical Director, James Walker, that she was too old for him and being warned by Beti Lloyd-Jones, "You make sure you look after her." Little did they know that it was Christene who set her cap at Norman! Whilst playing a rare season in Shrewsbury, they were staying at a pub in the centre of the town and Norman, never much of a drinker, decided to have a whisky before they went to bed. He woke up around dawn convinced he could hear sheep and nudged Christene to ask if she could hear them. She told him not to be stupid and went back to sleep. Having convinced himself the whisky had made him delusional, he heard the sound of bleating again. This time, certain he was not imagining it, he went to the window and was relieved to see a flock being taken to market. He vowed to avoid the demon scotch in the future. Despite predictions to the contrary, Norman and Christene are still as happy as ever.

When the D'Oyly Carte set off for Denmark in October of 1970, if the gentlemen of the chorus thought they were in for a week of partying, they were in for a terrible disappointment. When they arrived in Aarhus, they found themselves accommodated in a temperance hotel! The lack of a bar was a blow but, not to be deterred, they found a shop selling alcohol and stocked up with after-show drinks, hiding the incriminating bottles in wardrobes and drawers. John Broad remembers the childish delight the men showed when they left the booze-free hotel. Having saved up all their empties, they piled them into the waste bins in their rooms and hoped the staff would be suitably appalled when the damning evidence was discovered. In Copenhagen, they felt left out when the company ladies were lavishly entertained by the officers of the NATO fleet who, for some reason, did not seem so keen on showing hospitality to the men. At least the reception given by the Carlsberg brewery gave them a chance to indulge in what was, probably, the best lager in the world.

One of those ladies who remembers having a whale of a time in

Denmark was Kathryn Holding. However, she usually preferred to stay away from the bustle of towns and cities, choosing to find quiet accommodation in the countryside whenever possible. For one of the company's visits to The De Montfort Hall in Leicester, she had not booked any digs, so she drove around some of the pretty villages within striking distance of the city in the hope of finding a B&B or pub. Unfortunately, she was out of luck and beginning to get a little concerned. Driving through one small place, she saw a rather strange middle-aged woman wearing brown overalls and a blue hairnet, leading a sheep along the road. Kate stopped and asked the lady if she knew of anywhere she might be able to stay, explaining that she was appearing in Leicester with the D'Oyly Carte Opera Company. The lady told her there was nowhere locally, but suggested she could stay with her. By now desperate, Kate thought it was worth a try and followed the lady to her bungalow, which was surrounded by farmland. It was the start of a unlikely friendship which lasted for many years.

Betty Bishop, as she introduced herself, worked the farm on her own, looking after her herd of Charolais cattle and milking them by hand. Something of an eccentric, she nevertheless made Kate welcome in her home, which was basic, but clean. Not someone to worry about the lack of a plug in the bathroom sink, or other simple amenities, she and Kate made an instant connection and the unexpected stay was great fun for both. Of the many odd things to happen in Betty's home, Kate talks fondly of her host's inability to grasp the idea that theatre folk work until late and don't get up early. Nevertheless, she politely drank the cup of tea brought to her at 5am every morning. Swimming with fat from the fresh milk, which often boasted udder hairs, it was not exactly what Kate would have chosen, but it was delivered with generosity. Breakfast was a newly-laid egg boiled in a kettle on the stove, the water from which was always later used to make tea for the postman! Arriving home late one night after a show, Kate saw a large pan bubbling away and asked Betty what she was cooking. "I ain't cooking, I'm boiling me knickers. Yours are in there as well." Meaning only to be helpful, she did not realise that going into Kate's room to look for underwear to wash was an intrusion, but Kate let it pass, bemoaning the grey fate of her pristine white underwear in silence. The two became firm friends, keeping in touch for many years and

Betty even attended Kate's wedding. She was not the usual landlady type, but Kate would not have wished her any other way.

A favourite place for D'Oyly Carters to stay in Edinburgh was Gray's Apartments in Portobello, so early booking was a must. Mr. and Mrs. Gray provided comfortable flats within their large house and often tempted their guests with a little post-show liquid refreshment in their own apartment. In 1977, Michael Rayner was booked into a flat right at the top of the Gray's house, accessed by an awkward spiral staircase. Having retired to bed after a performance, he awoke in the small hours with a searing pain in his chest. He immediately alerted his room-mate, who sympathetically told him he probably had indigestion and to go back to sleep. Unconvinced, and with the pain getting worse, Mike made his way with difficulty down the spiral stairs and knocked on the Gray's door. Alarmed by his appearance, they told him to go back to bed whilst they telephoned for an ambulance, which meant him crawling back up the spiral staircase. Within a short time, the ambulance arrived and his worst fears were confirmed: he was having a heart attack.

Unfortunately, the ambulancemen told him there was not enough room for them to manoeuvre a stretcher down from his attic room, so he had to make his way, yet again, down the spiral stairs whilst they waited for him on the landing below. Finally settled into the ambulance and anxious to get treatment, his ordeal was far from over. On the way to the hospital, the driver got a message to say that a man had fallen into Leith docks and they were diverting to pick him up. Mike acknowledges that the man was in a bad way, but the detour was no fun for him. Finally getting to the hospital, the ambulance driver decided that the badly injured man took priority and he was immediately taken into the emergency department. Expecting them to come straight back for him, Mike waited for what seemed like an eternity, in increasing pain, before deciding that if he had managed to walk to the ambulance, he could get himself into the hospital. Wrapped in a blanket, he struggled inside to be greeted by a nurse who realised that he needed treatment right away. He never saw the ambulance crew again. Not sure how he had managed to survive, he went on to make a full recovery and resume his D'Oyly Carte career. One should not laugh at such a frightening experience, but the way

Mike related the story, in a passable Scottish accent, to Pauline Wales, who had joined us for the day, and myself, had us in stitches. Just a few months later, Mike died suddenly, aged eighty-two. I am so very glad I had the chance to reminisce with him for a few hours and I mourn the passing of the man who set me on my way to a career in the theatre.

Another interesting digs story comes from Edinburgh in the 1970s, where principal soprano, Pamela Field, and her husband, baritone David Porter, had rented a room in a large apartment. It was warm and comfortable, so they were looking forward to a pleasant stay. During their first night, both woke up suddenly and remarked how cold they felt; the air seemed to be freezing. They were discussing this when David noticed two bright, oval lights above the wash basin in the corner of the room, which remained there as they tried to convince themselves that they must be caused by light coming through the curtains, although this seemed unlikely as the heavy drapes showed no chink of light. By now rather unnerved, David was getting out of bed to investigate, when they heard a low note sound three times on the piano in the hall of the apartment. "David, somebody just played three E flats!" Pam having perfect pitch seemed irrelevant when he went to the door to find nobody in sight. Still shivering, they put on the electric fire and tried to make sense of what had just happened. They peered through the curtains, but the dark night sky showed nothing that could have made the lights on the wall. Thoroughly perplexed, they returned to bed, but slept little, the two lights having disappeared when they finally put out the bedside lamp. The next morning, with their room warm again, they decided to leave rather than face another scary night, although explaining their sudden departure to their landlady was not easy. It is hard to imagine two more sensible, down-to-earth people than Pam and David; they could never be described as fanciful. They have no explanation for what occurred that night, but one thing is certain, two people would not have imagined the same thing.

Edinburgh, such an elegant city, seems to have provided a wealth of D'Oyly Carte digs stories and one might reasonably suppose that accommodation there would always have been of a high standard. Susan Jackson and Louisa Kerry found to the contrary. They joined the company a few months apart in 1967 and often shared a room, but found themselves in horrible accommodation in the Scottish capital. Cold and dirty, it was truly depressing. In the theatre that night, they mentioned this in conversation with Assistant Musical Director, William Cowley, who told them he was in a very nice place and that there was plenty of room. The girls decided they could not bear to spend more than one night in their squalid room, so they got up in the small hours and did a 'moonlight flit', leaving the house without paying. On arrival at the digs recommended by Will, they found it to be even worse than the place they had just left. Not wishing to offend him by moving out of a place he had assured them was fine, they spent a miserable two weeks in freezing, damp conditions. Susie recalls meeting Valerie Masterson and her husband, Andrew March, who was the principal flautist in the D'Oyly Carte orchestra, in a cafe near the King's Theatre, where they spent a lot of time keeping warm. Such a glamorous life!

Another landlady to find herself out of pocket was encountered in 1974 by Maggie Bourgein, Caroline Baker and Gareth Jones. Maggie perfectly captures the scene.

"Gareth, Caroline and I shared digs in Liverpool. Caroline and I were in one room and Gareth in another. The landlady had written to the Carte, saying that her place was very clean and homely. When we got there, there were a lot of tracts on the wall about 'Cleanliness is next to Godliness' etc. but, in fact, it was anything but clean and rather squelchy around the loo and sheets. Because she kept telling us how clean it was, we felt we just couldn't tell her otherwise. In the morning, we decided we couldn't stick the place for another night, let alone the three weeks we were supposed to be there, so we left money for a night and slipped out quietly to Gareth's car, but it wouldn't start. Eventually, he got it going and we drove off with the woman standing on the doorstep shaking her fist at us. We headed straight for the nearest pub. Several days later, Freddie Lloyd wanted an explanation as he had heard from the landlady but, when we explained, her name was removed from the digs list." Maggie also briefly mentioned Mrs. Tibbs, in Nottingham. "The saying was that you always knew what was for supper by the stains on her jumper!"

On the salary paid by the D'Oyly Carte, nobody expected to have luxurious places to stay. Economy was of the essence in the days before a touring allowance was introduced in the mid-1970s, so sharing digs often made things cheaper for everyone, as well as giving companionship. As long as accommodation was clean and warm, people were willing to put up with shabby surroundings, often in the worst part of a town or city. 1A, Ashfield Terrace East in Newcastle-upon-Tyne was one such place. Offered in response to a management advert placed in the local newspaper in 1973, it was a dilapidated terraced house behind a second-hand furniture shop. Sleeping six people, it was booked by John Ayldon, Guy Matthews, James Conroy-Ward, Malcolm Coy, Judith Rees and myself. On arriving, we were shocked by the condition of the neglected exterior, which had a window boarded up, and fearful of what we might find inside. First impressions were not good. It was very basic; the wallpaper in the tiny sitting room, where it was still attached, had stains suggesting damp and a rickety wooden drying rack was strung from the ceiling. The kitchen's main feature was an ancient cast-iron cooker which would have been state of the art in the 1930s. With the bedrooms and bathroom equally unimpressive, we were not sure about staying there, but it had been cleaned and was not cold, so that was the main thing. We decided to see how we got on and it turned out to be a memorable two weeks.

On the first night, the legs at the bottom end of my single bed broke off as soon as I got into it, much to the amusement of Judy Rees in the other bed. A little ingenuity soon sorted out the problem and I spent the whole of the stay with my bed propped up on a stack of books and a large saucepan! It was such fun in that dilapidated house, which we soon dubbed 'grotty 1A'. Every time one of the men went out, they were accosted by the local prostitutes, who sat on our garden wall waiting for clients, to whom they 'attended' behind the bushes on the waste ground opposite the house. John Ayldon found a solution to this dilemma when he went out one day to the nearby shop. With the rest of us crowded onto the stairs to look out of the cracked window above the door, John, raised his deep bass voice a couple of octaves, swung his hips and told the ever-hopeful tarts, "Don't think you've got anything in my line, girls."

We cooked up great meals; we held parties; we laughed for a fortnight and voted the shabby digs a great success. So much so, for the company's next season in Newcastle in 1975, we booked again. The only change to the merry lodgers was Anne Egglestone, who shared with me, Judy Rees, by then, having left the company. The second visit was equally uproarious and one party was so noisy that John Reed, who was late arriving, knocked on the door for ages, but we never heard him. At the theatre the following evening, he was rather cross about it, but accepted our sincere apologies. It must be supposed that 'grotty 1A' has long since been demolished, but there are still photographs to remind us. Touring was what you made of it. In the words of Vera Ryan, "Digs were varied in comfort and quality, but what did we care? I was set free from strict Catholic parents and the noise of family life with seven other siblings. We worked hard, but had a ball."

In the late 1970s, in response to a letter sent to the company, ten D'Oyly Carters arrived at a large Victorian house in Bradford. They were Peter Lyon, Barbara Lilley, Meston Reid, Elizabeth Denham, Alan Spencer, John Ayldon, Guy Matthews, Patricia Leonard, Mike Buchan and Suzanne O'Keeffe. Mike describes the house as being a complete dump, with springs sticking out of the sofas, but Barbara says it must have been regularly frequented by theatre folk judging by the many photographs of celebrities lining the walls in the hall. Despite the shabbiness of the old house, they decided to make the best of it and Suz O'Keeffe tells of an embarrassing incident which still makes her blush to this day. As there was only one bathroom in the house, ablutions were something of a marathon so, with most of the group being out at a rehearsal, she took the opportunity to have a leisurely soak in the large, antiquated bath. Somehow, she managed to make the classic mistake of getting her big toe stuck inside one of the taps and, try as she might, she could not release the trapped digit. Luckily, Meston, the only other person in the house, was within screaming distance and he soon arrived outside the bathroom door for her to explain her predicament. Without further ado, he got a towel from his room and draped it over his head, reassuring a panic-stricken Suz that her modesty would not be compromised. Blindly groping his way over to the bath, he kept his back to her and was eventually able to release her toe, before retreating under cover of the towel. Grateful not to have been trapped there all day, Suz remembers him saying in his soft, Aberdeen accent, "It's no often I get asked to rescue a maiden in distress."

Not long after, Trish and Mike arrived outside their digs in Cardiff with a sinking feeling. The house did not look very appealing so, remembering their experience in Bradford, they decided to check it out before taking in their luggage. In the event of having to do a quick flit, Mike decided to turn the car round and keep the engine running whilst Trish took a look inside. By the time he had completed his three-point turn, she was back. Quickly jumping in, she slammed the door and said just one word, "Drive."

Another multi-occupancy house of horrors was in Birmingham and Suzanne O'Keeffe was once more in the thick of the action. She remembers there being nine girls who booked the digs from a letter sent to the company office. Barbara Lilley and Jane Metcalfe were amongst them, along with Glynis Prendergast and five other members of the ladies chorus. They all arrived after the show and, once inside, were surprised to meet four rough Irish navvies who were also staying in the house. But that was not all: instead of there being several rooms for them to share, all nine were to be accommodated in a large room full of bunk beds, which resembled a Victorian school dormitory. There were no wardrobes or cupboards, just hooks on the wall. They were aghast, so Barbara, taking the lead, went to confront the landlady but, before she could do so, she met one of the Irishmen, who told her that the house cat had just given birth to kittens under the kitchen table. This proving the final straw, she went back to the girls to announce, "We're not staying here." Leading them out into the Birmingham night, they got to the city centre and eventually found an hotel which could take all of them. At a cost of £9 a night, a fortune almost forty years ago, it was more than they could afford, but anything was better than staying in such a 'doss house'.

It is probably fair to say that everyone in the company remembered the bad digs rather than the good ones, because there was often an amusing story attached to them. However, there are many instances of happy times, whether staying in self-catering accommodation, or in private homes. Music Assistant and Orchestra Manager, Paul Seeley, tells that his favourite digs were in London in the late 1970s and early 1980s, which were memorable for many good reasons. As a non-driver, he always tried to stay within easy reach of the theatre and was delighted to be offered accommodation in Islington, close to Sadler's Wells Theatre, where he had an upstairs room in the home of artist and fashion expert, Elizabeth Suter, whom he describes as "lovely".

"Living there, I became part of a bohemian Islington set. I would get back from the Wells, or latterly the Adelphi, and sometimes find she had guests in for drinks, all fellow artists, and happily join them. Sometimes Elizabeth's partner was there. This was Colonel Dick Stuckey, OBE, a veteran of three Para who, really, in bearing and manner could not have been imagined as anything other than a military man. Dick and Elizabeth became extraordinarily good friends. They moved to Oxfordshire where Fiona and I visited them, and they came to our wedding, too. From Elizabeth and her friends I learned a lot about the appreciation of art. On my few hours of free time in London I could be back at her place and there she would be, with her sketch pad, drawing designs for Hardy Amies which she was in a rush to get delivered. When there was a big event, like a royal wedding, e.g. Princess Diana, and the newspapers were wanting to print drawings of the dress, it was usually to Elizabeth they turned. I was shocked to read in a Times Obituary of April 2012 that Elizabeth had died, aged eighty-five. But what a lady!"

Clive Harré has happy memories of his digs in Aberdeen, where he stayed with a delightful elderly couple in their quaint, terraced cottage close to Her Majesty's Theatre. They had hosted many D'Oyly Carte performers over the years, their home being popular with artistes appearing in the Granite City. At breakfast on his first morning, Clive was surprised when the milkman came in carrying more than milk and eggs: he also brought a bottle of whisky, courtesy of his brother, who had an illegal distillery in his garage. After the performance that evening, Clive was offered a 'wee dram' and, naturally, was too polite to refuse. The first taste of the smooth, smoky spirit was followed, after a few minutes, by a burning sensation which left his mouth on fire and his head ready to explode. Mentioning this to some of his colleagues in the theatre the following evening, there was much interest in sampling the fiery liquid, so the milkman did a roaring trade for the rest of the company's stay, as Clive ferried bottles to and from the dressing rooms. As he says, "It was naughty, but oh, so nice!"

Many company members had a list of comfortable, familiar places to stay, whilst others were lucky enough to have friends or relatives around the country who made them welcome. Christine George fell into this category and she really enjoyed being on tour when she was able to reconnect with old pals. On the few occasions she had to find digs, she usually shared with fellow soprano, Margaret Lynn-Williams, with whom she had joined the company in 1979. They sometimes encountered interesting digs, which included a holiday cabin in a forest near Inverness. There were several cabins occupied by D'Oyly Carters and everyone thought it a great place to stay, until they all got back after the first performance at the Eden Court Theatre. The car park was a short walk from their forest homes, but there was no lighting to guide them and they were in absolute darkness. Needless to say, nobody had a torch. Chris relates that it took some time for them to grope their way through the total blackness to the cabins, but then they could not remember which was which. They eventually sorted themselves out by a process of elimination, but she recalls it being an unnerving experience.

Another memory Chris provides was from the time when the Yorkshire Ripper, the infamous serial murderer, was at large. The company was playing at the Grand Theatre in Leeds, not far from the scene of many of the gruesome killings. Most unusually, Company Manager, Peter Riley, made an announcement over the tannoy regarding personal safety. He discouraged the ladies from walking alone in the city on the way to and from their digs and warned them to be vigilant. Even the men were advised not to be out on their own after dark, because they might be stopped by the police. This actually happened to tenor, Tom Marandola, who was questioned by officers wanting to know his reasons for being alone in the city late at night. For theatre people used to being out and about after a performance, it was sobering to think that mortal danger could be around any corner at that dreadful time.

In happier times in Leeds, many members of the company stayed at Novello House, one of the last examples of true theatre digs. Set in imposing gardens, the large house was owned by Basil Hartley who, as might be guessed, was a devotee of the composer, Ivor Novello, his home little short of a shrine to the great man. Warm, comfortable and totally geared to the needs of theatricals, it was a great place to stay, the many signed photographs of celebrities adorning the walls a testament to its popularity. Basil understood theatre folk and enjoyed chatting to them after a show without ever seeming like a 'fan'. John

Reed, who was often besieged by adoring fans, loved staying there, enjoying a drink and good conversation with his host to help him wind down after a tiring performance, when he could be himself and not 'Ko-Ko' or 'Sir Joseph Porter'. As a rule of thumb, staying with fans of the company was usually avoided because, however well-intentioned and solicitous as hosts, keen supporters of the D'Oyly Carte loved nothing more than to sit up half of the night chatting about Gilbert and Sullivan and their favourite company performers. This made getting away from work very difficult and, with the same problem often arising at breakfast, it was not easy to relax, so it was better not to accept such offers of hospitality. Having said that, principal tenor, Geoffrey Shovelton, sometimes stayed with fans and never seemed to mind talking shop for a week or two.

All in all, there were far more good digs than bad. Finding accommodation was nothing more than a routine part of touring life. Down the years, every D'Oyly Carter took the rough with the smooth and has tales to tell about their experiences on the road. However, there are some anecdotes which have lived long in company folklore because they are so funny. Everyone knows these stories and has, probably, put their own spin on the facts, so it is almost impossible to ascertain the exact details of what occurred, or to whom they happened, so long ago. Although individual versions may slightly differ, the gist of the following two famous digs stories will always remain the same.

Sometime in the 1950s, two D'Oyly Carte men were staying in digs in Glasgow with a landlady who made them very comfortable and was an excellent cook. There was just one problem, their bottle of sherry. A favourite after-show tipple for them at that time, each day they noticed the level in the bottle seemed to have gone down a little. Thereafter drawing a line in pencil on the bottle after each drink, they always found it had gone down by the next evening, so it became obvious they were not imagining it. The boys were rather annoyed. That the landlady should help herself to their drink did not seem right, so they decided to teach her a lesson. Downing the remainder of the sherry after a show, one of them then went to the toilet and used his own amber liquid to fill the bottle back up to the mark they had made. Giggling like naughty schoolboys, they went to bed and looked forward to seeing what happened the next day. Sure enough, the level in the sherry bottle had gone down again, so they continued to 'refill' it each night, finding the whole thing hugely funny. On the final day of their stay, the landlady brought in dinner and made a confession: "I kept meaning to tell you, but forgetting, and I hope you don't mind, but I noticed your bottle of sherry and I've been putting a wee drop in your soup every night." Now that's what I call getting your own back!

Some years later, two more D'Oyly Carte men ran foul of a landlady with a bottle. Arriving at their digs on a Sunday afternoon, they repeatedly knocked but got no reply. Noticing the door was slightly ajar, they went in, calling to the landlady to announce their arrival. Silence. Finding the kitchen, they were astonished to see the lady of the house slumped in a chair, obviously the worse for drink. Unable to rouse her, the boys took their luggage upstairs, found what they assumed to be their rooms and hoped she would sober up in time to cook their Sunday roast. After a while, with no tantalising aroma wafting through the house, they went down to see what was happening. Nothing. They gently nudged her awake and asked what time their meal would be ready, to which came the mumbled reply, "I've lost the joint. Know it's here somewhere, but can't find it." With that, she passed out again, leaving the hungry pair to search for their supper. Eventually, one of them opened the cupboard underneath the sink, which was right next to the oven, to find the missing joint of beef, all ready in its pan, nestled amongst the cleaning products and dusters! There was nothing for it but to cook their own dinner and retire upstairs to consider the position. Deciding to wait and see what happened the next morning, their decision as to whether to stay or go was made easy when they went down to an empty kitchen; there was no sign of landlady or breakfast. Having packed their cases and, rather decently, left money to cover their night's lodgings, they left the house. The man next door was clipping his hedge. As they bade him good morning he said, "You're off then. They always leave on Monday."

CHAPTER FIVE

IT'S OFF TO WORK WE GO

With all that was involved for its employees in travelling between venues and finding accommodation, it is hard to believe the company actually managed to go about its business of presenting the Savoy Operas of Gilbert and Sullivan throughout the year. Like any commercial organisation, The D'Oyly Carte Opera Company had a set routine and this pattern varied very little over the years covered by this book. It was a Monday to Sunday business and every department within the touring company was involved on a day-to-day basis; the theatre was a hive of activity from early morning to late at night.

For the singers, the working week started with a Monday evening performance. If it was the start of a new date, most people got in early to set out their places in the dressing room, unpacking make-up boxes, towels, mascots and the all-important tea mugs. The latest time chorus members were allowed to arrive was 'the quarter', in other words, a quarter of an hour prior to the start of the show. This was traditionally called over the tannoy by the Stage Manager twenty minutes before curtain up or, in earlier times, by the 'call boy', who ran around the theatre knocking on dressing room doors to give the warning calls.

Most people liked to be in by 'the half', called at thirty-five minutes prior to curtain. The familiar announcement, "Good evening ladies and gentlemen, this is your half hour call. Half an hour, please." would bring a flurry of activity for those who had been busy chatting. Arrival time depended on whether it was the ladies or gentlemen of the chorus who were on first in the show. For example, with the men opening *The Mikado* and *HMS Pinafore*, they were required to be in by the half, whereas the ladies were allowed to come in on the quarter. Conversely, in *Patience* or *Iolanthe*, it was the ladies who were on first, so the men did not need to arrive until later. Other shows, like *The Yeomen of the Guard*, *Princess Ida* and *The Gondoliers*, opened with both choruses, so everyone had to be in by the half. The management took a dim view of anyone coming in late without good reason and miscreants could expect to be reprimanded if caught out. It was expected that everyone acquire the Stage Door telephone number of the theatre being played, in case of late arrival or sickness.

Principals were usually in early, giving themselves plenty of time to warm up their voices and go through dialogue, whilst those who played 'Act Two roles' drifted in during the first act. However many times they had performed their roles, principals avoided the temptation to assume that a performance would take care of itself. There was no formal group 'warm up', a common practice in other companies, so vocal preparation was left to the individual and some of the noises emanating from the principal dressing rooms were quite bizarre. As well as the predictable scales and arpeggios, it was usual to hear snippets of arias from the show to be performed, the most difficult moments being practised several times over. Kenneth Sandford liked to warm up by singing his favourite operatic arias, whilst Geoffrey Shovelton might be heard singing, "Ninety-nine naughty nuns kneeling down knowing nothing" over and over to focus his voice and get his diction sharp. John Reed, however, would shout, "Hip bath, hip bath!" followed by, "That'll do." He never did consider himself a trained singer in the same way as the others! If it was a *Pirates* night, 'Mabels' down the years would practice the difficult runs and cadenza from 'Poor Wand'ring One'. Anyone unfortunate enough to pop into James Conroy-Ward's dressing room prior to a performance was likely to find him standing on his head against a wall making strange noises.

Nobody ever liked to ask why. For chorus members playing small parts, warming up in the dressing room was not the done thing unless they got in before their colleagues. They had no alternative but to do their vocal exercises in their digs, or in the car when driving to work. Failing that, the toilet was the only place to loosen up their voices.

Everyone did their own make-up; if you didn't know much about it when you joined the company, it was a case of relying on the kindness of the more experienced performers to tell you what you needed, where to buy it and, most importantly, how to apply it. It was common for newcomers to be made up by one of the old hands until they got the hang of it, particularly for a more specific design such as was required for *The Mikado*. New men were shown how to use soap on their eyebrows which, when dry, could easily be blocked out with the same base colour used on the face, allowing the familiar up-slanting eyebrows to be drawn on in black. It might be reasonably supposed by an outsider that there would be someone on the production staff responsible for this job, but it was rather like dialogue, everyone was left to fend for themselves, or rely on the unfailing generosity of their colleagues to show them what to do.

In time, most people became proficient in the art of making up, but some, such as John Broad, Ken Sandford, John Reed, Alan Barrett and Jon Ellison became experts, capable of completely transforming their faces to suit the characters they were portraying in a matter of minutes. Abby Hadfield and Peggy Ann Jones can remember making false eyelashes by cutting thin slashes into black tissue paper, before winding it around a pencil to get the curved effect. They can't recall who came up with the idea, but it certainly saved them money. Such resourcefulness was not unusual given the low wages paid by the D'Oyly Carte. The ladies appearing in the 1977 Queen's Silver Jubilee production of *Iolanthe*, designed by Bruno Santini, were given simple sketches of the 'fairy' make-up requirements, but no demonstration was given, so it was a case of trying it out and comparing with colleagues to achieve a consistent effect.

After applying make-up, came the tricky business of putting on wigs. In the early 1950s, wigs were 'dressed' at the start of a tour, then left in the care of their wearers, another skill needing to be acquired on joining the company, although it is hard to imagine the state of them after forty-eight weeks on tour! By the end of the decade, a full-time Wig Mistress had been appointed, making life a little easier for the performers. From 1970 onwards, Heather Perkins occupied this position and she was an indispensable part of touring life. Not only did she look after all the wigs, but she also had a nice sideline as hairdresser to anyone needing a trim, set or perm. She dressed chorus wigs at the beginning of each week, but the ladies were expected to put them on for themselves and keep them in good order. Each wig had its own cardboard box and, at the end of every performance, they were carefully put back and packed with tissue paper to help keep their shape. Ringlets were a perennial nightmare, because they quickly became untidy. Everyone learned the trick of winding them round a finger to achieve the tubular effect, before using a hair grip to secure the shape. When there were six or seven shows in the repertoire, wig boxes were piled up under the girls' places in the dressing room, or on shelves above them, if there were any. In the men's chorus dressing rooms, the wig boxes were fewer in number as *Mikado* and *Yeomen* were the only shows in which they all needed a wig, other operas calling only for a few individual 'character' wigs. Smaller boxes containing beards, sideburns and moustaches were found only in the male chorus rooms!

Principal wigs were dressed for every performance and most of the ladies chose to have Heather fit them. Many of the men fitted their own wigs, which required much less teasing than those worn by the women, and became extremely adept at it, although the Wig Mistress was always on hand if needed. However, when an understudy had to go on, having their wig put on meant one less thing for them to worry about. They were always happy to sit comfortably in the dressing room of the principal they were replacing and let the expert deal with it. There were a few instances where principal parts were played by chorus members. Those playing 'Old Adam' in *Ruddigore*, for example, remained in their own dressing room, but had the Wig Mistress come in to put on their wig. When I had to go on for Patricia Leonard, as 'Cousin Hebe' in *HMS Pinafore*, I was expected to use her dressing room, where Heather came to me but, when I took over the part, I stayed in the chorus room for Heather to fit my wig, where I had dealt with my wig the night before. The first part of the process saw Heather place the wig on my head, whilst I held it down by the net along the front of the hairline. Next, the feathered 'tricorn' hat went on at a jaunty angle, before she dressed the hair around it. Small details, perhaps, but they help demonstrate the company's need for professional specialists to make its performers look good when they went in front of the audience.

With make-up and wigs sorted out, the last job before going on was getting into costume. The D'Oyly Carte always used the professional dressers provided by the theatres, the best of which understood the importance of the job they did. It was not just a matter of doing up the hooks and eyes on the back of a dress or doublet; it was about knowing how the costume worked, or that they must start fastening at the waist and work up if the garment was to hang correctly and the performer feel comfortable. The principals, in particular, liked to develop a good relationship with their dressers, who needed to be efficient and friendly, but know when not to chatter on. Always waiting in the corridor outside dressing rooms, they had to be ready to spring into action as soon as called. It was normal practice for dressers to be given a tip after the final performance at a theatre, the chorus taking a collection in their dressing rooms, whilst principals paid individual gratuities.

Dressers were sometimes required to help a principal in the wings, perhaps with a quick change, such as needed when 'Ralph Rackstraw' had a only a couple of minutes to get out of his sailor costume and don the full uniform of a Captain towards the end of the second act of *HMS Pinafore*. Such a change would be almost impossible without the help of a calm, well-organised dresser, but one of my duties as 'Cousin Hebe' was to double-check that all the buttons on his uniform were correctly fastened when he came back on. On one occasion, Meston Reid crossed to me and I noticed a long strand of red cotton protruding from the flies of his trousers. I tried to discreetly remove it, but it got longer and longer, proving to be a thread of elastic from his underpants! As I let go, it disappeared whence it came, giving both of us the giggles.

'Archibald Grosvenors' over the years needed the aid of a reliable dresser for their lightning-quick change before their entrance in the second act finale. Perish the thought of what might have happened if the dresser forgot to be there with the costume over his arm.

Sometimes, waiting in the wings with a glass of water for a performer was a useful service. Very occasionally, an inexperienced dresser caused embarrassment and there is a story about one who took her duties a little too seriously. When carrying the heavy train of the 'Katisha' first act costume in *The Mikado*, she was supposed to hold it whilst 'Katisha' went up the steps onto the rostrum at the back of the set, ready for the entrance which required her to dramatically rush onto the stage. The idea was to let go of the train once the principal was clear of the wings but, on this occasion, the dopey dresser not only didn't let go, but also followed 'Katisha' onto the stage! Sadly, it has not been possible to discover which principal contralto shared this double act. Another incident in the same show saw a male dresser cross the stage carrying a tray of drinks, unaware that the curtain was open.

One dresser story which can be verified also happened during a performance of *The Mikado* and involved the irrepressible Lorraine Daniels. The D'Oyly Carte was playing the first night of a season at The Cliffs Pavillion in Southend-on-Sea in the late 1970s, where Lorraine was sharing a dressing room with Patricia Leonard. The dresser, who was German, came in before the start of the show and introduced herself as 'Audi'. When Lorraine, who was playing 'Pitti-Sing', was ready to get into her kimono, she popped her head out of the dressing room and said, "Can you come in please, Honda?" Trish, who was convulsed with laughter, reminded Lorraine her name was Audi, to which came the reply, "Well, I was close, wasn't I? I knew it was a bloody car!"

With preparations completed, all that was left to do was go on the stage at 7.30pm, although in some places, performances started at 7.45pm, or even 8pm in seaside towns, to accommodate dinner time for audience members staying in hotels. Notes taken by production staff at the previous performance of the show were given and, if the show was *Pirates*, it was usual for Jimmie Marsland to announce the formation for the ladies' chorus, for example: "Four threes and a two at the back, please." It was then up to the ladies to organise themselves accordingly. Considering that Monday performances took place after many company members had travelled long distances and had to check into digs, it is a tribute to their stamina that they were able to perform at a high professional level. This was just as well, because opening at a new venue usually meant the show being reviewed by the local press. Good or bad, reviews could have an impact on audience attendance. Even if the critique was cobbled together by a football reporter who hadn't bothered to attend, anyone not having booked a ticket would think twice about going if they read a bad review. At the end of the show, all that was left to do was take off costumes, it being a requirement, in later years, that chorus members carefully hang up their own, whilst the principals' dressers did this for them. Then, of course, make-up had to be washed off. Being seen outside of the Stage Door in theatrical make-up was a cardinal sin and the management took a dim view of anyone flouting this rule. The week had begun.

For the performers, a D'Oyly Carte Tuesday usually meant an understudy rehearsal, giving the principals and most of the chorus a welcome morning off. The opera to be rehearsed was determined the previous week and a 'call sheet' posted on the notice board, so the covers required had plenty of time to take a look at the music and dialogue of the parts they were understudying. Through the 1950s, Snookie Fancourt, Robin Gibson and Bert Newby took charge of cover calls but, after 1966, these rehearsals were, almost invariably, supervised by Assistant Producer, James Marsland, whose astonishing capacity for memorising all the words, music and moves of every part made him the ideal man for the job. The emphasis was on practising the music and moves rather than the interpretation of a role. Either the Assistant Musical Director, or a repetiteur would be playing the piano. Rehearsals started at 10.30am and ran for three hours, the maximum allowed under Equity rules, with the exception of a dress rehearsal, which could last for no more than four hours. Sometimes, they were held in the theatre, often in a front of house bar or, in the case of Sadler's Wells Theatre in London, in the opera and ballet rooms at the top of the building, an ideal situation which was all too rare, as most theatres did not have such facilities. Mostly, calls were held in dingy church halls, which had to be organised in advance or, as in Birmingham and Manchester, in rooms above music shops. Few people, outside of the company, would have any idea of the planning required by the D'Oyly Carte management to make sure that rehearsal rooms were located, booked and prepaid in every town and city on the tour.

On rare occasions, the full company was called in to rehearse a show if the Director of Productions deemed that stage business had become untidy. The lengthy periods of sitting around whilst others were working called for disciplined, professional behaviour; a room full of people chatting would hardly be fair to those going over a scene, so any conversation was limited to a whispered exchange. Most people read newspapers and books to pass the time, or wrote letters home. John Reed was well-known for his addiction to trying to complete the *Daily Telegraph* crossword. By the time those called for a Tuesday rehearsal got back to their digs, there was little time for resting and getting something to eat before having to go to the theatre for the evening performance. Such days were long, but that was the nature of the job. There was always the nearest pub in which to have a relaxing drink after the show, The Harlequin, next to the Stage Door of Sadler's Wells Theatre in London and The Grapes, in Manchester, being particular favourites.

Wednesday was the usual mid-week matinee day, although there were rare exceptions, when two performances were given on a Thursday, so there were never any morning rehearsals. In the 1950s, Equity membership was optional and contract details were by agreement between the artistes and Bridget D'Oyly Carte, but rehearsals were usually sensibly arranged. By the 1960s, D'Oyly Carte contracts abided by the standard Esher Opera Contract rules, which did not allow three sessions in a day. In the event of an understudy having to go on for a matinee day, it was usual for principals to get to the theatre early in order to run through their scenes with the person 'going on', particularly if it was for their first appearance in a role. Such time was unpaid, but in everyone's interest. On a day with two performances, some of the cast liked to go out between shows to get something to eat, or enjoy some fresh air, but this involved the chore of having to remove make-up and re-apply it an hour or so later. For that reason, many chose to stay in, bringing a picnic meal and enjoying a couple of hours with their feet up. For these folk, electric kettles were an essential item in their theatre case or skip, superseding the earlier days of the Thermos flask. Matinee days were particularly tough on the principals, who needed to pace themselves in order to have enough vocal stamina to get them through two shows. Unless there was a particularly vociferous audience in for the afternoon show, it was usual to cut encores, which was always appreciated by the performers. However, if the conductor did decide to do an unscheduled encore, he ran the risk of starting the music with the cast on their way back to the dressing rooms! Wednesday was another long day, but all part of the weekly routine.

It might be supposed that, after two demanding performances on the previous day, Thursday mornings would be free, but there was, usually, another understudy call. With up to eight of the operas out on tour, it was essential that limited rehearsal time was used to give the covers the opportunity to run through their music and moves. Although they watched the principals they were covering from the wings and made notes of the moves, it was no substitute for getting on the floor to work with other actors. In an ideal world, the understudies would have been able to rehearse with the principals with whom they were to appear, but this would have meant several rehearsals for every opera, which was not practical. D'Oyly Carte performers were contracted to work a maximum of ten sessions in a week, but with eight of those being performances and two understudy calls, even one extra rehearsal would have put the company into overtime, money it could not afford.

The Thursday evening show was often the fourth different opera of the week, which certainly kept the company on its toes. The change of opera on a daily basis was easier on the chorus than the principals, simply because the weight of individual responsibility was so much less. For lead performers, playing a different role every night was both mentally and vocally challenging. The company employed two principal sopranos and two principal tenors, so the division of their labour meant they would, usually, expect to do no more than five shows in a week, the exception to this being in a London season, when the company often played the operas for a week-long run. Incumbents of 'The Mikado' roles, Darrell Fancourt, Donald Adams and John Ayldon, had a night off when *The Gondoliers* was being played. Of the 'patter men', Peter Pratt played in all the full operas, but John Reed and James Conroy-Ward, later in their careers, did not appear as 'The Major General' in *The Pirates of Penzance*, so they had the opportunity to take a rest, particularly if it was played on a Saturday or Monday, giving them a long weekend break. However, the principal contraltos, from the 1950s through to the late 1960s, appeared in every opera. Ann Drummond-Grant, Gillian Knight and Christene Palmer were contracted to do every show, although Christene, later in her Carte career, was the first to get a scheduled night off. After this, Lyndsie Holland and Patricia Leonard were given a night off each week. With the exception of Ann and Patricia, their understudy in the 'Dame' roles was Beti Lloyd-Jones, who took this extremely important job from 1961 until 1977, although she had a year out whilst recovering from a serious car accident. The length of her tenure pays tribute to her reliability. Joyce Wright was cast in most of the operas when she became principal mezzo-soprano in 1951 but, when she left the company in 1962, her roles were shared out, with Peggy Ann Jones and Joanne Moore the main beneficiaries.

Friday was the one day of the week when all of the performers could expect to have a free morning, giving time for the chores of daily life, or to indulge in their favourite pastimes. For some, a round of golf was popular; others enjoyed visiting local places of interest; many of the girls loved shopping, particularly in the large cities which the company often played. It was a brief chance to get away from the confines of the theatre or rehearsal room for a few hours. By the time Saturday came, the D'Oyly Carte's working week was coming to a close with two performances. If it was the last day of the date, everything that had been unpacked for the first performance had to be repacked ready to move on to the next town. Those within striking distance of home made a swift exit from the theatre, whilst the rest went back to their digs to pack for the Sunday move, or a welcome day off. Such was the life of a touring repertory company.

While the singers had their routine within the D'Oyly Carte business, every other department had its part to play in keeping the organisation running smoothly on a weekly basis, starting at the top. The responsibility for deciding which operas would be performed in any week fell to the Savoy Hill management, the choice and order of the shows depending on several factors. Most importantly, the Box Office receipts for the previous season at a venue were studied to determine which of the shows had proved most popular, these being prominently featured for the return visit. The company invariably started a run with one of the 'strong three', *Mikado*, *Pinafore* and *Pirates*. The choice of shows for the matinees always took into account the appeal of a show to school children, coach parties and retired people, so that, again, meant choosing one of the better-known operas, *The Gondoliers* often falling into this category. It would certainly have been a surprise to the performers if *Ruddigore*, for example, was chosen for a matinee, although they would have enjoyed the change. This, along with *The Sorcerer* and *Patience* never did good Box Office, although, oddly, the rarely-performed *Princess Ida* often sold out. *The Yeomen of the Guard* and *Iolanthe* were the middle of the road shows which were, usually, performed on Tuesdays, Thursdays or Fridays. Another important factor to be taken into account is explained by Peter Riley.

"We also had to consider the logistics of moving. For example, if we finished in town A with *Mikado*, we couldn't open with it in town B. It was a logistical nightmare trying to arrange all this, but no one in the playing company ever realised." Once the tour dates and order of the performances had been finalised, small cards featuring all the details were printed by Echo Press in Loughborough, Leicestershire, for distribution to company members and venues. The tours were planned around the annual big dates of London, Manchester, Birmingham, Liverpool and Leeds, with other theatres being slotted in once these had been confirmed. This often led to some awkward journeys for the company, again described by Peter Riley.

"Before I moved up into the office, I used to think it was all done with the aid of a large map of the British Isles, a pin and a blindfold as, with regard to travel and transport, it never seemed to make sense. In fact, it was, generally, carefully worked out. I remember one of the worst moves was from Wimbledon to Sunderland, i.e. close in Wimbledon Saturday night and 'get-in' at Sunderland 9am Sunday morning. Not easy from a road transport point of view, in fact, damned nigh impossible, but we did it!" Tours of Scotland were arranged every other year, with Newcastle or Sunderland added, either on the way up, or coming back south so, as Peter suggests, logic did play a part in the arrangement of dates, wherever possible.

Whilst the working week for most D'Oyly Carte employees began on a Monday, the technical crew was not so fortunate. On the Saturday of a moving weekend, the Master Carpenter went ahead to the next venue to check out the backstage facilities. After the Saturday night performance, two large trucks were packed with the company's effects, an operation called the 'get out'. With seven or eight complete sets and a hundred and sixty costume baskets, called 'skips', to carry into the lorries, plus forty boxes of props and orchestra parts, it was an operation needing meticulous organisation. The lorries were driven through the night to the next port of call, ready for the reverse operation, the 'get in', at 9am on the Sunday morning. The stage management team also needed to be in at that time, which meant a very early start on Sunday morning or, sometimes, a drive through the night if the next date was, as occasionally happened, over two hundred miles away.

Consideration had to be given to the storage of the sets for the operas not needed until later in the week, usually at the back of the 'scene dock'. The costume skips for the first two shows were placed in corridors as near to the wardrobe room as possible, the rest were stacked on top of each other, ready to be swapped round as necessary later in the week. Once everything was stowed in the theatre, the crew set about hanging the backcloths for the operas to be performed and, if there was time, laying the stage cloth. The base of the composite set for the opening show was put in position and that was it for the day. The aim was to finish by 6pm but, if things got behind, the crew stayed as long as necessary to complete the job. This was the routine every time the D'Oyly Carte moved on, so it was no wonder the technical staff were happy when they were in a town for two weeks. Better still was the three-month London season and four-week run in Manchester, when they actually had an occasional night off. How much harder it must have been for the technical staff in the 1950s, when the company transported everything by rail on a Sunday, which left much less time to prepare for Monday's first performance.

Perhaps the most daunting task on the Monday morning in a new venue fell to members of the wardrobe staff, who had the job of unpacking and preparing all the costumes for the opening show. However carefully they had been packed in the skips, each one needed attention to make sure it was ready to go before the audience. If, for example, *Pirates* was to be performed, there were sixteen ladies' chorus dresses, plus those for 'Mabel' and 'Edith', to be pressed, along with their second act nightdresses and dressing gowns, but at least the cotton bloomers, underskirts and crinolines didn't need ironing. When ready, the costumes were hung on rails and wheeled to the dressing rooms. Shoes were kept in white cotton drawstring bags with individual names written on them; hats and gloves were put in plastic bags and set out on the dressing tables. Thereafter, the care of a costume and its accessories was the responsibility of the performer. A really difficult job was ironing the large, striped skirt of the 'Ruth' costume, which was voluminous and extremely awkward to press, but it had to be done every time.

The men's costumes for *Pirates* were easier for the wardrobe staff to prepare, only needing the coloured cotton shirts and breeches worn by the pirates to be smartened up. But then, the odd crease would hardly matter to a bunch of scruffy pirates! The male principal costumes and police uniforms did not need too much pressing, which was just as well, given the amount of work required on the ladies' dresses. The opposite side of the coin was *Iolanthe*, with the ladies' fairy costumes needing very little work after unpacking, be they the old production's green ballet-style dresses, or the 1977 production's black and silver dresses. However, the robes worn by the peers were another matter, the heavy cloaks of velvet or satin requiring a good deal of pressing after they were taken out of the skip. To say they were cumbersome to manage on an ironing board is something of an understatement. Each of the operas presented different problems for the wardrobe staff and Shelagh Fawcett, who joined the company in 1976, has vivid memories of her arduous duties.

"I was contracted to look after the female chorus, which included dresses, underwear, crinolines, shoes, hats and gloves. Ironing was the biggest job, because there were no steam irons then, so the better you packed costumes away, the better it was when you got them out again. The easiest shows in that respect were *Pinafore* and *Mikado* (no costume changes in Act Two). The hardest show was *Patience*, the heavy woollen dresses and cloaks needed ironing several times under damp cloths. I remember we had to be really careful with the cloaks; they were lined and if you got the wool too damp, they would sag and look awful. Plus, there was a change and the Act Two costumes were hard to iron. Costumes were only cleaned once a year, during August, when there were no performances. Most theatres in the 1970s did not have laundries, or even a washing machine, so washing things like gloves, stockings, petticoats and bloomers was only done periodically. One job I hated was hand-washing white detachable collars from various costumes that were caked in make-up; it took a lot of rubbing to get them clean.

"The costumes travelled in large wicker skips, which were coded with different coloured bands around the sides. If I remember correctly, *Mikado* was red, *Pirates* was yellow, *Patience* green. The skips were stored, often several high, backstage and were very heavy. I felt sorry for the stage crew whose job it was to get them down for us. As we did a different show every night, there was the daily chore of packing the previous night's costumes away, storing the skips and bringing down the skips for that evening. Depending on the opera, there could be as many as a dozen to move on a daily basis. It was a treat when we were in a town for two weeks as we got Sundays off rather than travelling to the next venue, although that could sometimes be a disadvantage if the theatre facilities weren't brilliant. In Birmingham's Alexandra Theatre, the wardrobe was under the stage and any dancing on the stage above brought down a shower of dust that covered everything!"

At the same time as the wardrobe department was in full swing, things were equally busy on the stage. After a full day on Sunday, the technical crew had much to do on Monday morning. First priority was to put up the set and focus the lighting, a job which was managed between the company's staff and the resident stage crew of the theatre, under the supervision of the D'Oyly Carte Stage Manager. The second act set was built first, so that it could be lit, with some lamps needing to be manually adjusted, via a tall 'A' frame ladder, to pick out specific areas of the stage where important arias, or stage business were to be performed. That done, the second act set was taken down and the first act set built, for the same process of lighting to be repeated. It was a time-consuming process needing experienced professional technical staff. At least when finished, the first act set was ready for the evening show.

The general lighting then had to be plotted with the theatre technician operating the lighting system for the show, who needed to know what effects were required and when they happened. He also needed to be given warnings slightly ahead of any change of lighting state, known as 'cues', which would be 'called' to him in the lighting box by the

Stage Manager in the prompt corner as the performance progressed. The D'Oyly Carte's SM had every cue marked in a show libretto, the warning calls to the dressing rooms for the artistes' entrances and any pyrotechnics, such as those used in *The Sorcerer,* included. His job was to ensure the smooth running of every technical aspect of the show. In these days of computerised lighting systems, it is hard to imagine all the throwing of switches and levers needed to change the lights, but the company closed down before such a luxury became possible.

Another job to be done on the first day of a new date was sorting out the props for the show. The D'Oyly Carte always employed a Property Master, who was responsible for setting out a table in the wings which had on it all the props for the show to be performed. It was important that the singers and supernumeraries knew exactly where to find what they needed to take onto the stage without having to search around in the darkness. Larger items, like the halberds used by the warders in *Yeomen*, spears and banners for the guards in *Mikado*, and rifles used by the marines in *HMS Pinafore*, were placed against a wall near the table, so nobody had to hunt for them. The maintenance and repair of props was also down to the Property Master, who often had to spend time mending the fans used in *The Mikado*, when over-zealous twirling had caused the vanes to break. Some props were considered to be personal and were kept by the performers, who carried them in their theatre boxes. The fans came into this category, along with the spectacles, 'little list' and trick fans used by 'Ko-Ko' in *The Mikado*. In *Ruddigore*, two of the chorus ladies played fisher women and the opening of the show found them sitting on barrels either side of the stage working on pieces of embroidery, hardly an occupation one might have expected, but that was the D'Oyly Carte. These were personal props and Beti Lloyd-Jones worked on hers for more than twenty years, somehow managing to squeeze more and more designs on to the overcrowded piece of linen, most of them too vulgar to disclose.

It was essential that props were regularly checked and kept in good condition, any faults could lead to embarrassment on the stage, or be a distraction to the performer. In Act Two of *Pirates*, when the men sang 'With Cat-Like Tread', 'Samuel' had to enter carrying a canvas bag containing weapons to distribute amongst the pirates. It was tricky enough to sing whilst rummaging through the bag to find the item to match his next line; had anything been missing from the bag, his solo might have ended in chaos. A rather unusual task to fall to the props man was in the Anthony Besch production of *The Gondoliers*, which called for 'The Duke of Plaza Toro' to eat spaghetti while 'Don Alhambra' was singing 'I Stole the Prince'. The pasta was collected from a local restaurant and kept hot until needed, midway through Act One. Once the props man had piled it into a tureen, it was taken onto the stage by dapper waiter, and notorious wag, Jon Ellison, who often managed to add something revolting before he served it. John Reed got quite used to negotiating his fork round such delicacies as a glass eye, or obscenely-sculpted carrot, before having to eat the pasta. Ken Sandford, as 'The Don', soon learned not to look anywhere near the spaghetti whilst he was singing, because it was so distracting. At least Julia Goss, as 'Casilda', and Lyndsie Holland, as 'The Duchess', were able to cover their mirth behind fluttering fans.

Another busy person on Monday morning was the Wig Mistress, Heather Perkins, who had to unpack all the wigs from skips and get them to her room to dress for the evening performance, before carrying as many of the boxes as she could manage in one go to the dressing rooms. If she was lucky, they had been left in a good state and carefully packed by their wearers after the last performance. This was often not the case, so she had a lot to do, particularly on a *Pirates* night, when work was always required on unravelled ringlets. If she felt that a performer had not taken proper care with their wig, she had authority to take that person to task and remind them of their responsibility. The culprit usually didn't need telling twice!

With all the backstage personnel busily engaged, there were still a few more jobs to be completed under the supervision of the D'Oyly Carte Stage Manager before everything was ready for the show. One was the allocation of dressing rooms for everyone, be they principals, chorus, management, technical or music staff. Some theatres had rooms large enough to accommodate all sixteen male or female choristers, so all that was needed was a typed notice, 'Ladies of the Chorus', for example, to be affixed to the door. Other theatres had a number of smaller rooms for chorus, so the SM needed an awareness of friendships and who liked to sit with whom before he typed up the lists. In the early 1970s, there was a group of chorus men, which included Jeffrey

Cresswell, Jon Ellison, James Conroy-Ward, Barry Clark, David Porter, Jason Shute and John Broad, who were understudies and played small roles. They usually shared a separate room known as the 'Small Parts' room, or sat together if they were in a larger room. Their camaraderie and friendship was solid, to the point that, if one of them had to go on for a major role, one of the others took their interval mug of tea to the principal dressing room to see how they were getting on and offer encouragement. This tradition of a Small Parts room continued until the closure of the company. The ladies' chorus did not have an official equivalent, but the group known as 'The Royal Family' fell into the same category by default. Some half a dozen of the senior female choristers, led by Beti Lloyd-Jones and Anne Egglestone, liked to sit together and they were, mostly, understudies and small parters. If there were only small chorus dressing rooms, then the Stage Manager always knew to put the Royal Family into one of them. Membership of this exclusive set was by invitation only, and it was often a long time in coming.

In ideal circumstances, principals were given a dressing room to themselves to allow for individual preparation. This was not always possible, so knowing which of them were comfortable sharing was something the SM had to take into consideration when allocating rooms. For many years, John Reed and Kenneth Sandford rubbed along well when having to share but, if the truth is told, both would have preferred to be on their own. When Ken first joined the company in 1957, he had to share with Peter Pratt, which he found awkward. Their personalities were chalk and cheese and they did not really get on well but, as professionals, they put up with it. Size is not supposed to matter, but it certainly mattered to Lyndsie Holland at the Forum Theatre in Billingham, where the principal dressing rooms were ridiculously small and had obviously been designed by an architect who had never had to go on a stage. Lyndsie, John Reed and Ken Sandford were given a room to themselves, whilst other principals had to squash in together in a space barely big enough for two chairs. On an *Iolanthe* night, Lyndsie's costume was hung in her room, but the space was so confined that she had to put it on in the corridor. Once embedded in the voluminous 'Queen of the Fairies' crinoline, she was unable to get it back into her dressing room to sit down, so spent her time, when not on the stage, standing outside her 'cupboard'.

Principal dressing rooms provide very personal space, somewhere to be quiet and think; somewhere to warm up; somewhere private and somewhere to relax between entrances, or shows. In the D'Oyly Carte, the privacy of dressing rooms was strictly observed and everyone was expected to respect their colleagues. Barging into a dressing room without knocking was considered totally unacceptable behaviour, be it a principal or chorus room. The etiquette was to knock, say who it was, and wait to be told to go in. This may seem a statement of the obvious, but it was not unknown for music or production staff to think they had the right to go in at any time; after all, theatrical folk are supposed to be uninhibited, so what did it matter if ladies were standing in their underwear to be given production notes? Anyone showing such discourtesy to the performers was told in no uncertain terms to get out, and quite rightly, too! Sometimes, backstage visitors thought they could just walk into a dressing room without knocking and this really annoyed everyone. Chorus members had no option but to change in front of their colleagues, but that did not mean someone could burst in unannounced to witness them half-clothed. If a man needed to enter any of the ladies' rooms, he had to give them time to cover up before entering. The same applied for women entering the men's rooms although, I dare say, they didn't mind quite so much. In the modern world, many might think this reserve rather old-fashioned, but the D'Oyly Carte was old-fashioned and, maybe, it wasn't such a bad thing.

There was one last job to be done before the company was ready for its first performance of the run, the setting out of the orchestra pit. It was usual for the Music Director to tell the Stage Manager how he wanted the instrumentalists arranged, in spaces which varied from cramped to cavernous, depending on the size of the theatre. The stage crew then put out chairs and music stands as required, before the resident electrician tested the stand lights. The D'Oyly Carte carried its own conductor's stand, which had warning lights connected to the prompt corner to let him know when to start the overture and opening of the second act. Once the music was set out, the show was, technically, ready to go and the crew got a break until the evening performance. After such a demanding day for everyone backstage, the

126

whole process was repeated the following morning for the change of show. Costumes were removed from dressing rooms to be replaced by another freshly-pressed set; the set taken down, or 'struck,' to use the theatrical term, to be stored in the scene dock; the scenery for the next performance put up and lit in reverse order; more wigs dressed; props stored away and unpacked; ladders climbed to set special lights. It could have been worse, at least the dressing rooms and orchestra pit were organised. And so the week progressed until Saturday night, when everything had to be packed away and cleared from the theatre for the bandwagon to roll on to its next date. If the company was playing a two-week season, at least everyone got a well-earned day off on Sunday before the weekly routine started again.

Mention has yet to be made of the music department's working week, which had a rather different dynamic. For most of the thirty-nine years Isidore Godfrey was the D'Oyly Carte's Music Director, his week revolved around getting locally-recruited orchestras rehearsed for the shows. The company only employed a leader and one or two section leaders, so he had his hands full. Whatever town or city, his task on the first Monday afternoon at a new venue was to take his ad hoc bunch of musicians through the details of the Sullivan score for the evening's performance. With just three hours to accomplish this, it is no wonder there was no time to involve the performers and this was, very likely, the reason why Mr. Godfrey insisted everyone watch his stick like a hawk once the show was under way. If a soloist was not looking directly at him, it was not unknown for him to look over his shoulder in the direction of their gaze, a sarcastic reminder of who was in charge. This, combined with strictly enforced tempi, was not ideal for singers who would have preferred to react with the other performers on the stage, or take a different speed, but Isidore had to keep everything on a tight musical leash in fairness to the orchestra, which was playing the show on one rehearsal. The chorus, too, was expected to look directly at him at all times. It is no wonder the company was often accused of playing everything to the front.

Once she had begun to find her feet as principal soprano, Jean Hindmarsh was not afraid to ask Mr. Godfrey if she might sing something slightly differently, in a way that felt right for her. She remembers that he would listen to what she had to say, then tell her what he thought about her idea. Sometimes, after considering her point of view, he agreed with her and adjusted his conducting accordingly, but there were other times when he flatly refused to go her way. Jean found him approachable, but woe betide if you did your own thing in the middle of a show, when he would come down on you like a ton of bricks. The musical buck stopped at his door and he had to keep tight control, but he must have longed for the luxury of time to explore his musical options. If six or seven different shows were being performed during the date, he had to get the orchestra ready for each of them, using his limited rehearsal time to go through the main points, so it was important the players had good sight-reading skills. The standard of the instrumentalists varied considerably, but that was the lottery of hiring local musicians, many of whom were part-time players with day jobs. The same applied for the tours of North America, where Mr. Godfrey had to rely on the organisers to hire in an orchestra wherever they were appearing. Outside of the big cities, the quality of players was sometimes indifferent, when he had to make the best of a bad job. Once, in Saskatoon, the Canadian winter was bitter and chorus tenor, Glyn Adams, went into a shop to buy a warm coat. The gentleman who sold to him told him he would see him later that evening, as he was playing in the orchestra for the D'Oyly Carte season.

In the early 1960s, not long after of the expiry of the D'Oyly Carte's copyright on the Savoy Operas, the company took the historic decision to have its own orchestra, which radically changed the game for the music department. For Isidore Godfrey, it meant being able to audition and choose professional musicians, with plenty of time to mould them to his musical satisfaction. It was a huge change for the company, too, with new personalities becoming a feature of life on the road. Travelling with his own band gave Mr. Godfrey the opportunity to have rehearsals with the singers, a luxury rarely possible when picking up players in every town. It was a change for the better, releasing him from the wing-and-a-prayer pressure of getting the orchestra through a performance with just a few hours of preparation. It also gave him more free time to relax, vitally important when conducting so much, because it required physical fitness and stamina. However, old habits died hard and he remained a stickler for having the performers watch him at all times, something which frustrated Kenneth Sandford, who

128

Barbecue a la D'Oyly Carte, as some of the company's Tinkers' Club gather round for an impromptu 'fry up' in 1971. Included in the party are: Peggy Ann Jones with Judy (left), Royston Nash holding the frying pan, with John Reed next to him and John Broad, Peter Raper and Michael Tuckey.
Photograph courtesy of Trinity Mirror.

Mrs York Batley's afternoon tea party in Bournemouth in 1972. The lady herself, between Lyndsie Holland and Pauline Wales, top right.

The residents of 'Grotty 1A' in Newcastle: John Ayldon, James Conroy-Ward, Guy Matthews, Malcolm Coy and Anne Egglestone.

The infamous D'Oyly Carte Olympics, Saratoga Springs 1978.

Herbert Newby presents Patricia Leonard with her 'trophy', watched by Caroline Hudson, Michael Buchan and Heather Perkins.

The wedding of Vivian Tierney and Gareth Jones in New York in 1978.

The small-parters tea school. Left to right are: John Broad, James Conroy-Ward, Jeffrey Cresswell and Barry Clark, with Jon Ellison kneeling.

The Sydney fancy dress party in 1979. The birthday girls, Elizabeth Denham on the left and Susan Cochrane, with Patricia Leonard far left next to 'Dame Edna Everage', Kenneth Sandford, with John Coe-Roper far right.

Beti Lloyd-Jones' posh birthday party in Adelaide, 1979. She is surrounded by her admirers: Kenneth Sandford, James Conroy-Ward, Alan Spencer, Gordon Mackenzie, Peter Riley, Ken Robertson-Scott and Robert Crowe.

Outside the theatre in the Australian capital are Lorraine Daniels, Kenneth Sandford, Gordon Mackenzie, Beti Lloyd-Jones, Gareth Jones and Vivian Tierney.

A production meeting for the 1980 Last Night of the London season. Wilfred Judd and Leonard Osborn make notes, with David Mackie, Fraser Goulding and bassoonist, David Catchpole, discussing the music.

The daughters of 'Major-General Stanley' frollicking on Blackpool beach as part of a publicity event in 1981. Left to right are: Felicity Forrest, Margaret Lynn-Williams, Andrea Phillips, Jill Pert, Hélène Witcombe, Christine George, Beti Lloyd-Jones, Susan Cochrane and Roberta Morrell.

The company gathers for a bus ride through London to raise awareness of the plight of the D'Oyly Carte and to hand in a petition to the Arts Council.

The cast of 'HMS Pinafore' aboard Nelson's Flagship, HMS Victory, as part of the campaign to save the D'Oyly Carte. From bottom left to top left are: Roberta Morrell, Barbara Lilley, Patricia Leonard, Beti Lloyd-Jones, Margaret Lynn-Williams, Christine George, Guy Matthews, Thomas Scholey, Barry Clark, Clive Harré, James Conroy-Ward and Meston Reid.

once told me he longed to be able to look at his colleagues when singing to them, but Mr. Godfrey would not allow this. His successors were less demanding in this way, which allowed the singers to take more personal responsibility for their musical entrances and keeping in time with the orchestra.

On Isidore Godfrey's retirement in 1968, the appointment of James Walker as Musical Director brought a completely different style of conducting. A brilliant musician, he had a rather more 'laid back' approach and was not unknown to take a walk around a large pit during long sections of dialogue to chat with the musicians. Ken Sandford recalled occasions when principals were conscious that the next number was about to start and Jimmy Walker was nowhere to be seen, causing them to slow down their stage conversation until he realised and hurriedly clambered on to the box to start the music! After almost four decades of the genteel elegance of Isidore Godfrey, the rather earthy style of Australian James Walker was something of a culture shock to the company, but his talents as a musician were never in dispute. His short tenure saw Royston Nash appointed as his successor in 1971 and this led to important changes in the staffing of the orchestra. The need for economy drove most things in the D'Oyly Carte and Royston found the lack of brass players very frustrating, with the company paying only for one horn and one trombone, where Sullivan's scoring called for two of each, even three trombones in some of the later operas. He deemed the practice of representing the correct chording by using other instruments to be unsatisfactory and eventually persuaded the management to pay for the two extra players, along with more strings for *The Yeomen of the Guard*, something never managed by his predecessors. However, on the North American tours of 1976 and 1978, Royston encountered the same difficulties that Isidore Godfrey had faced on a weekly basis, as he told me.

"There was always a feeling of anticipation and excitement when it was announced that an American tour was being planned and so it was in 1976. My main concern was that in each city we visited, a local orchestra had been engaged and the quality of each group could vary considerably. Because of union agreements, we were not permitted to take our own players, although in 1978 I did get permission to include four of our section leaders. As I had minimal rehearsal time allotted, with one morning to cover the three operas being performed, the standard of the playing had to be high. I had four American players touring with me and the rest were local musicians. The opening night in Toronto was a disaster and I demanded extra rehearsal time for the orchestra. The management were not happy, but I managed to win them over. Playing such venues as The Kennedy Center in Washington DC and Lincoln Center in New York were great experiences and many other places were most enjoyable. In 1978, we had a scary situation on the Monday morning we arrived at The O'Keefe Centre in Toronto. We had been in Washington for a month, but on loading up for the move to Canada, the boxes of orchestral parts were overlooked. No one could get the parts to us for that evening's performance, let alone a rehearsal. There was one publisher in Toronto who just happened to have an old set of parts for *Iolanthe*, so that is what we had to go with. The parts were not marked with such things as encores and no cues at all, but we managed to survive."

Royston's words clearly demonstrate the perils of life on the road for a large opera company, but there were other difficulties to be overcome in the course of a working week and he, again, gives us a flavour of the different problems he encountered.

"Many of the pits in older theatres were not constructed for orchestras, but a group of some dozen or so musicians. There were a number of occasions when sections of the orchestra were outside the pit and sometimes played from the audience boxes to the right and left of the stage. There were often problems with the lighting and seating, none of which helped the balance of the sound. In Liverpool, on an opening night, there had been a traffic hold up due to an accident and four of our brass players were late arriving for *Mikado*. We managed to complete the overture, during which I was dreading what we could do about the opening of the first act, which has a brass fanfare. With that, the four players slipped into the pit, took up their trumpets and trombones and we immediately went into Act One. Musicians falling sick on tour was always a problem. Imagine what it was like trying to find a principal oboe at short notice in one of the smaller towns."

Another responsibility to fall to a D'Oyly Carte Musical Director was conducting recordings made by the company. These were usually done in London, where the Decca studios were located. As well as the usual weekly performances, the singers were called for extra rehearsals, supervised by the MD, to make sure the music was in tip-top condition before recording. A real bonus for the MD was having the opportunity to work with great orchestras like the Royal Philharmonic, which was favoured for most of the records, although The New Symphony Orchestra of London and the Orchestra of the Royal Opera House, Covent Garden, were sometimes used. It was an experience both exciting and intimidating for an MD used to a much smaller band of players, but it was also a rare chance to work with Sullivan's full orchestration. Doubtless, noses were put out of joint when Sir Malcolm Sargent was occasionally brought in to conduct some of the recordings, but he was a great name and it made good business sense to have him associated with a new release. It is interesting that some of the recordings made in the 1970s found the company's former Musical Director, James Walker, in the technical booth, where he worked for Decca after leaving the company.

The work of the music department did not fall solely on the shoulders of the Musical Director; he had two colleagues to share the load. The Assistant Musical Director was a vital member of the team, his other official title being Chorus Master. Deputising in the pit for his boss at least once a week, usually for a matinee, gave him the opportunity to hone his conducting skills, but this meant that singers and orchestra needed to be aware that tempi might be slightly different, requiring them to take extra care to listen and watch the stick. A classic tale from the mid-1970s concerns percussionist, Harry Smaile who, when questioned after a show by AMD, David Mackie, about his playing, told the bemused conductor that he felt the tempo was dragging, so he had decided to push it on a little! Fortunately, such initiative was not a common occurrence. Supervising the music at weekly understudy calls, or full company rehearsals, was another important duty of the AMD. Over the course of a long tour, musical detail could become sloppy, so it was up to him to keep things shipshape. With occasional forays into new arrangements and research, there was always much to do for the Assistant Musical Director.

The third member of the music staff was usually known as the 'music assistant' and this job meant dealing with everything that could not be covered by the Music Director and his deputy. In 1976, Paul

Seeley joined the D'Oyly Carte in this capacity and describes himself as the musical 'Lord High Everything Else'. As a repetiteur, he was often needed to teach the music to new recruits, as well as being required to play for some production rehearsals. Sometimes, he had to undertake score arranging and was very pleased that his version of the Welsh National Anthem was played when the company appeared at the New Theatre in Cardiff. Some of the operas had choruses which were sung from the wings; 'Over the Bright Blue Sea' from *HMS Pinafore*, 'Climbing Over Rocky Mountain' and 'A Rollicking Band of Pirates We' from *The Pirates of Penzance*, the Act Two opening of *Patience*, and it was Paul who conducted these, a job not quite as easy as one might think.

"This put pressure not so much on auditory skills in *Pinafore* and *Patience*, but on anticipatory skills, because if my beat came with what I heard, the singing would be a fraction behind the beat, and there were very few theatres where an off-stage conductor could actually see the conductor in the pit. Then there was the funeral bell in *Yeomen*, similarly testing anticipation." Another of Paul's important responsibilities was that of orchestra 'fixer' for the provincial tours, a time-consuming job which involved making sure there was always a full complement of players in the pit. When Fraser Goulding took over as Musical Director from Royston Nash in 1979, the playing standard of the orchestra was revolutionised by virtue of advertising orchestral vacancies in the Saturday edition of the *Daily Telegraph*, even though the company Business Manager, Gordon Mackenzie, was not happy about the expense this incurred. At this time, Paul's title was changed to 'orchestra manager', although this was a misnomer, as he had no executive authority. However, his skill in knowing how to acquire good replacement players in the smallest of towns was hugely impressive, often saving the day when the two men above him in the music department would have struggled.

"It was quite common for staff members such as myself and, of course, costumes and wigs people, to work a twelve-hour day if required. We were on fixed salaries with no overtime pay. I could be playing for a morning rehearsal, then go to the theatre to find a note with a message that someone in the orchestra was ill or incapacitated, and then it was up to me to find someone to deputise for the absentee, no matter how long it took. And not just anybody, it had to be someone technically reliable and with excellent sight-reading, ideally someone who regularly did extra work with a professional symphony orchestra. In places like Bournemouth, Birmingham and Manchester this was no problem. I memorised the office telephone numbers for the Hallé, CBSO, Northern Sinfonia, Bournemouth Symphony Orchestra, Opera North and anyone else I could think of. Other deputies came from conservatoires, but the lesser colleges of music rarely provided suitable people. Many names came from sources such as these and included prizewinners of the 'BBC Young Musicians Competition'."

The D'Oyly Carte's time-honoured tradition of recycling often saw Paul on the stage as a supernumerary, most frequently as the 'Sergeant of Marines' in *HMS Pinafore*, or as a guard 'clearing the rabble' in *The Yeomen of the Guard* and, less often, as one of the entourage of 'King Hildebrand' in *Princess Ida*. These appearances were unpaid and considered by the management to be a part of his job. If nothing else, Paul had plenty of variety in his working week and his talent for arranging music and re-scoring came in handy on several 'Last Night' performances in the late 70s and early 80s at Sadler's WellsTheatre, in collaboration with choreographer, Alan Spencer. The first of these was the 1920s 'flapper routine' for 'Climbing Over Rocky Mountain', from *The Pirates of Penzance*, which saw the ladies letting rip to Paul's imaginative reworking of the music and Alan's clever dance routine. It was highly successful, even if 'Miss Carte's young ladies' were a million miles away! Getting these routines ready required some official rehearsals, but much of the preparation was done in spare time, the dancing being practised in the voluntary dance classes held by Alan Spencer, when the chance to perform in a different style was eagerly seized, as Paul explains.

"While these were an opportunity for Alan and me to stretch our choreographic and musical imaginations, the main purpose was to demonstrate the versatility of chorus and orchestra at this critical time, to show that this was a company that could do anything. The orchestra members were certainly up for it and came forward with many suggestions, including the use of saxophones for example. My guiding principle in the re-orchestration was, as far as possible, to keep the vocal line unchanged except for varying the tempo, but to adapt the accompaniment to the chosen style. In contrast to this was the academic work undertaken by David Mackie and myself, not so much the odd article for the in-house journal, *The Savoyard*, but the rediscovery and recording of forgotten Sullivan works which was important to Royston Nash. My contribution, and I had to work through the night to complete it, was editing the *Marmion* overture. David did *The Zoo* and the *Victoria and Merrie England* ballet music."

It certainly seems that the lower down the pecking order in the music department, the more there was to do, the amount of work going on behind the musical scenes unknown to the performers, let alone the audiences. Despite his major contribution to the smooth running of the company, there was never a place on an overseas tour for the number three in the music department, although he had the consolation of knowing that his job would be kept open for the company's return.

The D'Oyly Carte was always the sum of its many parts and there was one other person quietly beavering away in the background on his weekly routine, the touring manager, the link between the workers and the Savoy Hill management. Over the years, the title for this job varied from Company Manager to Business Manager, but his workload remained much the same until the company closed.

In the 1950s, this post was held by Bruce Worsley, who had succeeded Alfred Nightingale. By all accounts, Mr. Worsley was something of a character, known by company members as 'The Group Captain', because he told everyone that he was the youngest RAF pilot in the First World War and the oldest in the Second World War. His rank and credentials were never confirmed, but everyone enjoyed his tales of derring-do, even if they did take them with a pinch of salt. He was a keen disciplinarian, who once told a stroppy Equity Deputy, Kenneth Sandford, "Damn it, Kenneth, Miss Carte provides the costumes, the scenery and the orchestra; all you have to do is go on the damned stage!" Although he seemed aloof, Peter Riley remembers that he could be considerate and understanding. When Worsley retired in the 1960s, he was replaced by Stanley Knight, then in 1970, the much recycled Herbert Newby became Business Manager, a post he held until his death in 1979.

There was always a second in command in the touring management team and, in the 1950s, this job was taken by David Palmer who, according to Cynthia Morey, was a pleasant man who managed to bridge the gap between the performers and management. This was no easy task given the D'Oyly Carte's preference, at that time, for keeping a distinct separation between the two sides of the company. By the 1970s, the feeling of 'them and us' was not so much in evidence, although due respect was always given to members of the management. Bert Newby's assistant through the 1970s was the popular Gordon Mackenzie, who had several spells in the chorus from 1954. A fine tenor, 'Mike' was always happy to give his Scottish songs at golf club receptions, where concerts were given in return for the playing facilities made available to company members. His reward for long service was being promoted to Business Manager when Bert Newby died. The final example of D'Oyly Carte recycling was Paul Seeley, who became assistant to Mike Mackenzie when he left the music staff after six years. Paul remembers the worst job he had was handing out the redundancy notices to his friends and colleagues in the company's final season at the Adelphi Theatre in 1982.

The duties undertaken in the touring management office were many and varied. The responsibility for placing adverts in local newspapers requesting accommodation for company members was a year-round job for the manager and his sidekick. Similarly, adverts for job vacancies needed to be put in the press. When auditions for singers were held in provincial theatres, it was common for the Business Manager to be on the panel. In any company but the D'Oyly Carte this might have seemed strange, but the recycling system meant that if they had been long-standing company performers, they were deemed qualified to comment on auditionees.

Minor disciplinary matters were dealt with by the touring manager without reference to Savoy Hill. If, for example, a performer was caught being late in getting to the theatre without good reason, or had shown a lack of professional behaviour during a performance, the miscreant might receive a letter warning them not to make the same mistake again, or be taken aside for a quiet word. This was usually sufficient admonishment in a company which prided itself on its professionalism. More serious matters, such as frequent absenteeism, being the worse for drink, or personal abuse of a colleague, member of the production or music staff, would be referred to the General

Manager in London, but this did not often happen. Letters from Savoy Hill would be considered as very serious and the equivalent to the modern-day written warning.

Notices detailing rehearsals for the following week were typed in the company office, as were those informing of any change of cast for a performance. In the days before mobile phones and e-mail, an understudy who had not popped into the theatre in the middle of the day ran the risk of coming in to find the dreaded notice proclaiming that they would be playing a principal role that night. Any communication to the full company from Savoy Hill came via the touring manager, but he was also there to deal with the company's Box Office takings and banking; to organise train calls and book transport; listen to the concerns of any member with a problem; collect passports prior to an overseas tour; be in evening dress in the foyer prior to a performance; entertain dignitaries in the bar or receive royalty at the theatre. But the most time-consuming job of the week in his office was the one for which everyone was truly grateful, the preparation and distribution of their wages!

CHAPTER SIX

"YOU'RE ON!"

The blood-chilling effect of those two words on the unsuspecting understudy arriving at the theatre for a quiet night in the chorus needed to be experienced to be believed. Before getting a chance to look at the notice board, some unsympathetic soul, who was already looking at the cast list, would be bound to gleefully shout, "You're on!" producing a lurch in the stomach of the shocked cover and reducing his or her legs to jelly. Even if an understudy got a few hours notice of having to go on, walking through the Stage Door was a lonely and, sometimes, scary moment. The responsibility of deputising for a principal performer in the great theatres of Britain and North America could be a petrifying experience, especially when going on for the first time but, in the D'Oyly Carte, the rewards could be great, often bringing elevation to principal status if the opportunity was seized to show the talent and temperament required to perform at the highest level. Many a young cover ended up starring in the prestigious company although, for some, shattered dreams remained in the chorus dressing room if stepping up a grade proved them wanting. However, the understudy system was a vital part of company life and most choristers jumped at the chance to show what they could do.

In the 1950s, the Savoy Hill management had the habit of swapping roles around amongst its principals, getting them to share certain parts, or removing roles from performers to give to newcomers, a practice which did not encourage a feeling of job security or satisfaction. It seemed as if a part was offered to anyone the company wanted to employ as an enticement for them to join, which did not go down well with the person stripped of the role. Although this chopping and changing was not popular within the company, it did mean that, with so many people knowing the parts, some of the principals were able to cover each other. On the surface of things, this seems to have been a sensible arrangement, but the system was not free from problems. Alan Styler and Jeffrey Skitch understudied each other in several of the baritone parts and Alan's widow, Vera Ryan, tells of an amusing incident that happened one evening when Alan deputised for Jeffrey.

"Alan had to have a front tooth removed as he had been in excruciating pain and the dentist put in a temporary one. The same night, Jeffrey Skitch was taken ill and Alan was summoned to take over 'Strephon'. We were chatting during the overture when Alan sneezed and Eileen Bruckshaw said that something had just flipped down the front of her dress. Alan pointed to the gap in his mouth! The front of the *Iolanthe* dresses were very low, so Eileen skipped round the stage until the offending tooth was recovered!" It can only be assumed that he managed to find a way of securing the false tooth in time for his first entrance. The same gap in Alan's front teeth caused him further problems when, according to Ralph Mason, the one-tooth denture that he later needed to wear, once shot out of his mouth halfway through the first verse of 'Giuseppe's Song', 'Rising Early in the Morning', in Act Two of *The Gondoliers*. With no little embarrassment, Alan had to pick it up between verses, turn upstage and shove it back in again!

Rather less comical was an acrimonious exchange between the Stage Director, 'Snookie' Fancourt, and principal baritone, Eric Thornton, when he was asked to go on as 'The Pirate King' for the indisposed Darrell Fancourt. With the fee for the performance obviously not agreed in writing, he was heard shouting in his dressing room, "In black and white, Snookie; black and bloody white!" He obviously got his way, because he went on but, according to Cynthia Morey, promptly forgot all the words to the 'Pirate King's Song'. If the payments for one principal going on for another were negotiable in the 1950s, in later years there was a sliding scale of set fees for understudies going on, depending on the size and importance of the role. Understudies were usually paid a slightly higher salary than the other choristers to reflect their extra responsibility. It is interesting that Alan Barrett remembers his wife, Mary Sansom, going on for 'Gianetta' in *The Gondoliers* when Jean Hindmarsh was unwell. Mary played the smaller soprano role of 'Fiametta', so she had to pay her understudy £1 from the £3 fee she received for going on for Jean.

Vera Ryan was very excited to be given the understudies to several of the soprano parts when Jean Hindmarsh became pregnant and left the company in 1960. She still laughs about the running joke amongst the ladies chorus whenever Bert Newby knocked on their door to announce that she was on. Everyone knew what she would say: "Has anyone got any toilet paper?" It is hard to imagine that anyone going on for an important part for the first time in the D'Oyly Carte did not feel almost paralysed by nerves, particularly if they were under-rehearsed, but it was the ability to control the stage fright that defined 'having the right temperament'. Being able to channel such negative energy into a confident and capable performance, when vocal technique was not compromised by understandable nervousness, was vital for any understudy. It was hard enough for experienced principals who suffered from pre-performance nerves, so how much more difficult for those who went on only occasionally? But some understudies coped better than others. In November of 1951, during her first tour with the company, Cynthia Morey got her opportunity to impress when she went on for a major role for the first time.

"It was about four o'clock one dreary wet afternoon when a knock came at the front door of my digs in St James Street, Newcastle. It was John Reed, with the message that Muriel Harding was ill and would not be singing in *Pirates* that evening, so I, as her understudy, would be playing 'Mabel'. My heart missed a beat or two when I heard this news but, I reasoned with myself, I knew the part really well and that would be a help. After the initial shock, a calm descended on me and I just got on with what I had to do, going to the theatre early; trying on my costume in case there were some minor alterations needed; fitting the wig and doing an extra special make-up. There was time to go through the duets with Neville Griffiths, who was playing 'Frederic', and time in the dressing room to check dialogue and moves. I did not go to Muriel's room to dress, but stayed in my place in the ladies' chorus room; the girls were all on in *Trial by Jury* first, which meant I had the place to myself for a while. The understudy dress for 'Mabel' was delightful, a crinoline in white satin trimmed with pale pink and apple green, with a fetching bonnet to match.

"When one is understudying, I think it is often better to be thrown on at short notice than to have a day or two to think about it. There isn't time to be nervous, you just have to get on and do the job. At all events, that seemed to be the case. The show went really well, I was greatly helped by all the other principals, particularly Neville, and almost before I knew it, the curtain fell to the customary enthusiastic applause. Everyone was very complimentary and I felt that I had made my mark. I have long since forgotten why it should have been John who informed me of this, perhaps the management were still trying to persuade Muriel to go on. After all, I was an unknown quantity; I had as yet played no small parts; no doubt the house was sold out, and Mabel is a very spectacular role; I might prove unequal to the occasion. I expect John overheard the deliberations and rushed round to warn me. It would be the sort of kind thing he would do."

That is exactly what happened. John, who had been with the company for only a couple of weeks, had been at a rehearsal when he heard the news about Muriel Harding and he felt it only fair that Cynthia should have as much warning as possible, going to the trouble of finding out where she was staying so he could let her know. No wonder they became such great friends; such acts of kindness are never forgotten. It was a pity he soon had to learn that not everyone showed such generosity of spirit. It was only a couple of weeks later when John had to go on for the first time in his capacity as understudy to Peter Pratt and it was a difficult start. The bathroom in his digs in Leeds leaving much to be desired, he decided to go to the theatre where he would at least be warm and there was plenty of hot water. As he arrived, he was met by the Stage Manager, Jerry Stephens, who told him that Peter Pratt was ill, so he would be playing 'Robin Oakapple' in *Ruddigore* that evening. Bundled straight off to rehearse without a wash and shave, all the hard work John had put into learning all his words and music paid off, because he coped well on his debut performance. His own words give invaluable advice to anyone finding themselves in the same situation: "All an understudy can do at a first performance is to say and sing the right words and be in the right place." But John had no time to enjoy the relief of getting through his debut, he was to play 'Ko-Ko' in *The Mikado* the following night.

After a run-through with the principals in the morning, John went to the theatre to check his costumes and props but found, to his dismay, there were no personal props for him to use; they had all been locked away. He had no option but to set about making the trick fans needed for the encores of 'Here's a How-de-do', grateful that he was good with his hands. He trudged off to Woolworths to buy a pair of thick-rimmed glasses, taking out the lenses to give him the 'comedy' spectacles which 'Ko-Ko' used to read the letter from 'The Mikado'. It was not ideal preparation and he made a vow that afternoon: if ever he became a principal, he would give his understudy all the help he needed and make sure he had access to all personal props.

About a year later, John had to go on for Peter Pratt as the 'Lord Chancellor' in *Iolanthe* at the Theatre Royal in Norwich, where the dressing rooms were shabby and lacking the most basic facilities. He knew that the principal room he was to use for the performance had been fitted with temporary extra lights because those provided were not adequate but, when he got there, he found that they had been removed and were nowhere to be found, making it impossible for him to put on the detailed character make-up required for the 'Lord Chancellor'. Director of Productions, Robin Gibson, was incredulous when he popped in to see John, unable to understand why anyone should have removed the lights. There was nothing for it but to return to the Small Parts room where he usually dressed. Likewise, when John was due to go on for his first 'Reginald Bunthorne' in *Patience* in Stratford-upon-Avon, he encountered another difficulty. Arriving to get ready for the performance, he found Peter Pratt's dressing room locked and the key missing. Fisher Morgan did not appear in the show, so the company manager offered John the use of his room, but he preferred to be in his own place in the chorus room to get ready for his debut in such an important role. Although John made no direct accusation, the implication of hindrance is clear. If so, such behaviour was most unusual in a company whose principals understood the vulnerability of their understudies going on with minimum rehearsal, or very little warning.

Mary Sansom once got just a few minutes' notice when she deputised for Jean Hindmarsh as 'Mabel'. Getting a message at the interval of *Pirates* that Jean could not continue, she hurried to get changed, but was not in time to make the opening of the second act. Realising that Mary was not ready, Jean stood next to Thomas Round, who was playing 'Frederic' until Mary was ready in the wings for the exchange to take place. Meanwhile, Tom was informing the 'Major-General' of his intent to lead the policemen in an attack on the pirates, finishing with the line, 'And then, dear Mabel, you will be mine', at which point he turned to find a different 'Mabel' facing him. An understudy having to go on mid-performance did not often happen, but there was a memorable occasion in a performance of *Ruddigore* in the 1950s which involved Leonard Osborn. A tall, athletic man, his first entrance as 'Richard Dauntless' was spectacular as he vaulted a rail at the back of the stage and ran down to join the ladies' chorus. Having effected this impressive feat on numerous occasions, he came to grief one night when his hand slipped on the rail, causing him to catch his foot and crash to the stage with sickening force. Scrambling to his feet, he somehow managed to get through his song, 'I Shipped D'you See' and the following energetic hornpipe as if nothing had happened, but those on stage that night remember the sweat rolling down his face and the agony in his eyes. In true show business tradition, he completed the scene before collapsing in the wings, having cracked an elbow and two ribs. His understudy, Frederick Sinden, quickly got changed from his chorus costume into a sailor outfit and completed the performance, also filling in for several weeks until Leonard's injuries had healed.

Another occasion which saw an understudy going on mid-performance once more involved Alan Styler filling in for a fellow principal. At London's Saville Theatre in 1968, Donald Adams, who was seldom off, informed the management that he did not feel well enough to perform as 'The Earl of Mountararat' in *Iolanthe*. His chorus understudy was also unwell and not in the theatre, so efforts were made to contact Alan to ask him to go on for Donald. He was eventually tracked down, via his wife, Vera Ryan, having a drink with his brother-in-law in a pub in North London, by which time Donald knew he would, at least, have to start the performance. Alan was concerned he had drunk a little too much to drive to the West End, so he was hurried into a taxi and arrived at the theatre at the interval. Meanwhile, legendary Wardrobe Mistress, Cis Blain, had managed to find a costume to fit him and Alan got ready to go on. The ailing Donald started the second act with very little voice left and managed to struggle through 'When Britain Really Ruled the Waves' before striding from the stage. During the applause to the song, Alan walked on to a very warm welcome from the audience and sang the customary encore! Peter Riley, the Stage Manager at the time, remembers asking Cis Blain how on earth she managed to find a costume to fit Alan at such short notice. She told him to take a look at the name tag sewn at the nape of the neck of the costume, which Peter did at the end of the show, where he was amazed to see the name of Henry Lytton. The beautiful velvet costume had lain at the bottom of a costume skip for many years, but Cis always knew it would come in handy one day. And Peter's assessment of Alan being thrown on for the part? "What a professional."

One person's loss is often another's gain and Peggy Ann Jones, to this day, enjoys a benefit of having deputised for Joyce Wright. In 1961, Joyce came down with a nasty illness which kept her off the stage for two weeks. Peggy, like her fellow choristers, was not paid very much and luxuries were unaffordable. In need of a watch, she had saved for a long time to buy one, but going on for Joyce for that length of time meant that the cheap watch she had her eye on was forgotten. Instead, she bought a gold Omega on the proceeds of her appearances, which she still wears some fifty-five years later. "It's great. I don't have to worry about getting a new battery for it, I just wind it up!" On a more serious note, Peggy looks back with gratitude at that two-week run as an invaluable experience; one which, she believes, was the springboard to her being made a principal when Joyce left the company. However, she admits that, without the help of all the principals who shepherded her through the performances, she would have struggled. Just a little bit of her feels that the beautiful wristwatch was a reward for all the times Joyce asked her to stand in the wings in case she was unable to continue, her delicate little cough suggesting she might be coming down with a cold.

The pressure of having to stand in for a popular principal was one of the most difficult things for an understudy to face. Sitting in the dressing room listening to the reaction of disappointment from an audience when it was announced that a leading artiste would not be appearing was a horrible feeling. Barry Clark remembers going on for his first 'Defendant' in *Trial by Jury* at the New Theatre in Cardiff in the mid-1970s. He heard the announcement made over the PA system: "At this afternoon's performance the part of the Defendant will be played by Barry Clark." The inevitable groan ensued, followed by a loud voice from the auditorium, "Who the hell's he?" That the audience felt let down when they had paid to see a favourite performer was understandable, but there was never any sympathy for the poor soul they did not want to see. Such was the lot of the understudy, but the best rose to the occasion and often surprised the audience with a sterling performance. The late, sadly-missed, Gareth Jones understudied many of the baritone roles in the 1970s before taking on several principal parts and proved himself very popular with audiences, but his first appearance as 'Pooh-Bah' in *The Mikado* found him in a state of trepidation. Sat trembling in the dressing room, the audible disappointment of the audience when it was announced that Kenneth Sandford was indisposed did nothing to alleviate the state of his nerves.

Having survived his first scene unscathed, Gareth proceeded to give John Reed, playing 'Ko-Ko', the same list of 'Pooh-Bah's' numerous titles he had presented to 'Nanki-Poo' in an earlier scene, both of which begin with 'First Lord of the Treasury'. The procession of jobs should have ended with 'Private Secretary', but Gareth found himself in the wrong place and ended with 'Lord Mayor, both acting and elect'. A measure of how much an understudy relied on the experience of the regular principals was evident in John's reply as he deftly retrieved the situation. "Lord Mayor would be very interesting, but suppose we say as Private Secretary?" thus getting the dialogue back on track. The D'Oyly Carte was that kind of company; the principals, with very few exceptions, were generous performers, who took care of those needing their help and support. Of course, it can be said that it was in their own interest to make sure they ran through scenes and offered advice before an understudy went on for the first time, but it was more about helping a newcomer to carry a good performance to the audience, something the production staff should have done, but seldom did.

There are countless examples of principals getting understudies out of a mess, but John Reed was a master at turning an awkward situation to good advantage, as Barry Clark discovered when he went on for the first time as an understudy at the King's Theatre in Glasgow. He had not long been given the cover to 'Richard Dauntless' in *Ruddigore* and had to go on at very short notice when principal tenor, Malcolm Williams, inexplicably failed to turn up.

"Jimmie Marsland anxiously asked if I knew it and I quickly told him I did, although I was actually far from sure I knew it thoroughly enough. He took me through the business and moves, including the dreaded hornpipe. 'Ooh, you should've seen Philip Potter dance the hornpipe, he was wonderful,' cooed Jimmie, setting me at ease. Eventually, John Reed turned up and we went through everything I had with him. He then took me to his dressing room where we went through lines and he made me up. 'You'll be fine,' he said. And I was, until I got tongue-tied with one of the interminable 'my 'eart it ups and it says, says it' speeches. I burbled on and on while John looked quizzically at me across the stage with a growing grin on his face. Eventually I ran out of steam and with his inimitable timing, John cocked his head to one side and said, 'Finished?' It brought the house down!

"I often found myself going on at extremely short notice, sometimes after the curtain had already gone up and I was in my chorus costume, as for a matinee of *Princess Ida* at the Alexandra Theatre in Birmingham. Geoff Shovelton had got the matinee days mixed up and failed to show. I was, almost literally, bundled on to fend for myself as best as I could as 'Cyril'. There were few cover calls for such a rarity as *Ida*. I was OK until we got to the point in Act Two when the trio of men had to don the women's robes. I had conscientiously watched this from the wings in a previous performance. Watching isn't doing, though, and I proceeded to get in the most frightful tangle trying to put the bloody robes on; inside out, upside down, back to front! The audience was in stitches, thinking it was all part of the fun, no doubt, but John Ayldon came to the rescue and eventually the show could continue."

If Barry experienced more hairy moments than most understudies, it was hardly surprising as he covered most of the major tenor roles. A fine actor, always respected by his colleagues for his classy delivery of dialogue, he was one of the unsung heroes of the D'Oyly Carte, a capable, reliable deputy who never let the side down. The same could be said of Howard Williamson, who understudied John Reed from 1967 to 1973. Carrying the burden of not being John Reed whenever he went on, he always acquitted himself with distinction according to his sister, Doreen 'Tweeny' Williamson, who joined the company in 1970 to follow in her big brother's footsteps. They always travelled together and Tweeny remembers an arduous journey from Cheshire, where both of them lived, to Edinburgh after they had been home for the weekend. Arriving at the theatre with little time to spare, Howard was horrified when he looked at the notice board and saw his name down to play 'John Wellington Wells' in *The Sorcerer*, a role he had never performed. Having only ever had the occasional understudy rehearsal and with no time to think about it, he got ready to go on, but later told his sister he needed to visit the bathroom several times before he went on! Tweeny watched him from the wings and thought he did brilliantly, despite his nerves, although she does admit to being a bit biased. How vital it was for the company to have such solid performers to maintain its standards when a principal went off.

Going on as an understudy could be a traumatic experience, but the opportunity to appear in a principal role often brought great pleasure. My own experience was limited to deputising for Beti Lloyd-Jones as 'Inez' in *The Gondoliers* whenever she went on as 'The Duchess of Plaza Toro', and the occasional appearance as 'Cousin Hebe' in *HMS Pinafore*, when Patricia Leonard was unwell. It was my debut as the latter that is one of my happiest D'Oyly Carte memories. Arriving at the Stage Door of London's Sadler's Wells Theatre for a Saturday matinee in 1976, I looked at the notice board and was shocked to see that I was on. Before I went to Trish's dressing room, I used the backstage telephone to let my parents know the news, promising to ring them after the first show to tell them how I had fared. I remember being nervous, but following John Reed onto the stage felt like having a big shield in front of me; who was going to notice me? I had to quickly learn the traditional 'lucky business' that John, being very superstitious, unfailingly observed in the wings before every performance. This included knocking on the wood of a scenery flat, touching our thumbs together then turning round and reciting little sayings to represent each tour venue in

146

chronological order. It was worse than learning lines! Thereafter, all I had to do was keep my front teeth in order for the sibilant 'and so do his sisters and his cousins and his aunts'. 'Hebe' is only a small principal role, the sort known in the business as 'a cough and a spit part', but I loved playing it and felt very proud to take a call with John at the end of the show.

As soon as the matinee was over, I went to the phone to let my parents know that I had acquitted myself reasonably well, but there was no reply. I tried several times before the second show, puzzled as to why nobody was answering. Not a little disappointed, I went back to the dressing room. A few minutes later, I was called to the Stage Door and there they were! My mother and father had always been supportive rather than pushy, but there was no way they were going to miss my big day. Dropping everything, they had picked up their best friends and the four of them jumped into Dad's car and dashed down to London from their home in West Bromwich. He was never very good at finding his way round big cities, so how he managed to get from the M1 motorway to Sadler's Wells Theatre before the days of satnav I will never know, but how good it was to have them there. They were so happy when we had a quick drink in the Harlequin after the show, but soon had to set off for the long drive back to the Midlands. It was a wonderful day for me.

In the 1950s and '60s, it was usual for the company to have second understudies, but the chances for them to go on were very few and far between. However, Pauline Wales, my predecessor as 'Cousin Hebe' twice-removed, once had to go on as a second cover at the traditional home of Gilbert and Sullivan, the Savoy Theatre in London. One evening, knowing that her understudy, Peggy Ann Jones, was ill, Joyce Wright asked Pauline who would go on as 'Phoebe' in *Yeomen* the next day if she, too, became unwell and Pauline told her, "Me". The following morning, she was summoned to the theatre and told that Miss Wright was not well enough to perform and, with Peggy Ann Jones not sufficiently recovered, she would be going on as 'Phoebe' that night. In only her second year with the company, she had learned the part, but had not even had a music rehearsal as second understudy and was horrified by the thought of being thrown on without any preparation. Pauline remembers spending all day going through her music, dialogue and moves with the only available pianist, William Cowley, a wardrobe assistant, who was asked to help out by working with her, although Music Director, Isidore Godfrey, kept an eye on things to make sure she knew how he would be conducting her music. As always, the principals rallied round, with Donald Adams and Kenneth Sandford being particularly helpful in going through their scenes with her.

Finding herself in a principal dressing room at the Savoy Theatre was very exciting for Pauline and she was most impressed to find that it had its own telephone. Whilst getting ready for the performance, she was startled when it rang. It was Joyce Wright to wish her all the best and ask what costume she would be wearing. She remembers the distinct chill in Joyce's voice when she found out that Pauline would be wearing her costume. Both being petite, it made no sense to alter Peggy Ann's understudy costume when Joyce's was a perfect fit. Her performance as 'Phoebe' went well and the only problem she faced was down to Ken Sandford. Her opening song at the spinning wheel, 'When Maiden Loves', was performed in front of a scenery flat which had a window cut into it. Flown in from a bar above the stage, it was usually quite secure, but when Ken entered behind the flat for their dialogue scene, he put his foot onto the 'window sill' as if to climb in and it collapsed around their ears! Pauline's warm and laid-back personality would have helped her in that unexpected debut, as it did through all of her distinguished D'Oyly Carte career.

Giving his time to Pauline that day certainly paid dividends for Will Cowley, because his excellent work was very much noticed by the management. Within a few months, he left his job as a wardrobe assistant and joined the music staff, becoming Assistant Musical Director in 1963. He had a reputation for being a huge help to any understudy going on, watching them at all times and giving clear leads, as if he knew how much they needed him. Will was one of the most successful examples of D'Oyly Carte recycling.

When John Dennison joined the company in 1956, he was given the second understudies to 'Pish-Tush' in *The Mikado*, 'The Counsel' in *Trial by Jury* and 'Strephon' in *Iolanthe*, roles played by Alan Styler. He would get no rehearsals, but was expected to know the roles. He never thought he would have to go on, but the occasion came when

148

both Alan and his understudy were indisposed, so an ill-prepared John had to replace them as 'Strephon'. Some sixty years later, he had just appeared in a production at the Opera House in Buxton, as part of the International Gilbert and Sullivan Festival, when he was approached by a very elderly man outside the Stage Door after the performance. The old soul shuffled up to him and announced, "I remember seeing you play 'Strephon' way back in the fifties." For John, who had spent most of his life in America, it felt as if the wheel had turned full circle.

A rather humiliating experience befell Michael Buchan when he had to go on for John Ayldon as 'Colonel Calverley' in *Patience*. Mike had understudied most of John's roles for several years and had been on for every one except the 'Colonel'. The two were great friends and often shared a joke about this, because it was John's favourite part and he always told Mike not to bother learning it as he would never be off. Unfortunately, Mike took John at his word, so he had the shock of his life when he got to the Grand Theatre in Leeds, at the start of a two-week run, to find that John had been taken ill and was likely to miss several shows. Mike remembers the opening show was *Mikado*, which was no problem as he had played the title role for John on many occasions. However, his stomach lurched when he realised that the Tuesday performance was *Patience*. As has been previously mentioned, understudy rehearsals for the least-performed operas were a rarity and Mike could not remember ever having attended more than two for *Patience*. Suffice it to say he was in something of a panic, with only a day to revise a part which contained one of W.S. Gilbert's wordiest songs.

Despite being an experienced understudy, Mike was horribly nervous as he waited in the wings whilst the Dragoon Guards marched round the stage and his fears about getting through the show proved well-founded. The swaggering entrance was easy enough and he started confidently with 'If you want a receipt for that popular mystery, known to the world as a Heavy Dragoon, take all the remarkable people in history, rattle them off to a popular tune', but that was it. Not another word of the two complicated verses passed his lips as he mumbled anything that came into his head to the accompaniment of the embarrassed sniggering coming from the chorus men behind him. He was amazed when the audience actually applauded at the end of the wordless song, but Mike knows it was more from sympathy than his humming of the tune. The rest of the show passed in a haze as he somehow got through dialogue and his second song, but it was a mortifying experience. He made sure he knew the part after that but, ironically, John never went off for *Patience* again. I asked Mike if he could remember his late wife, Patricia Leonard, having any understudy mishaps and, after some thought, he said, "No, she was always good." Nobody would argue with that.

A few years before Mike's memorable-for-all-the-wrong-reasons debut as 'Colonel Calverley', John Broad went on for the same role in unusual circumstances. John understudied many of the principal baritone parts and played several roles in his own right, but it was, understandably, something of a shock when he was told to go to the Alhambra Theatre in Bradford one morning early in the 1970s, where he was asked if he would go on for the 'Colonel' the following day, when it was not a part he covered. With John Ayldon unwell, his understudy, who will be spared identification, had been rehearsed to go on, but had struggled to cope with the demands of the part and went into meltdown, leaving the production staff in something of a predicament. They came to the conclusion that John was the man to save the day. Before he had time to realise what he had done, John found himself agreeing to help out, so he collected a score and libretto and returned to his caravan to get cracking. At least the management had the decency to give him the evening off.

The next morning, Will Cowley took him through the two difficult songs and sundry ensembles in Act One, plus the trio and quintet of Act Two, before Jimmie Marsland spent all afternoon teaching him the moves, whilst costumes were hastily altered to fit him. Before he knew it, he was standing in the wings wondering what the hell he was doing, but the intensive cramming paid off and he got through the numerous words of the first song without a mistake. Growing in confidence, he survived the performance without major mishap and was able to contemplate the unexpected appearance with a mixture of incredulity and relief. And his reward for taking on such a huge task? The gratitude of the management and a fee of less than £5!

John's wife, Rosalind Griffiths, had the misfortune to understudy Julia Goss as 'Rose Maybud' in *Ruddigore*, the ever-reliable Julia seldom being off. However, the unexpected happened one day and Ros got a message to say that Julia was unwell and would not be going on. Like all the understudies covering in a show that was not performed very often, she can only remember having a couple of rehearsals, but the indefatigable Jimmie Marsland rattled through the moves and walked her round the set. With a mixture of terror and excitement, she was leaving the stage to get ready, when Julia unexpectedly walked in and said she was feeling much better. To say that Ros was both dumbfounded and disappointed as she got into her chorus costume is something of an understatement, but she knew that a seasoned principal like Julia would not to go off unless absolutely necessary. Ros' luck wasn't much better when going on as 'Elsie Maynard' in *The Yeomen of the Guard*, the one part she had always wanted to play. Pamela Field had gone down with a heavy cold and Ros, unusually, had a couple of days notice that she would, at last, get her chance. On the morning of the performance, she woke up, to her horror, with the same streaming cold as Pam and had to go on unable to perform at her best. She is still indignant about it to this day.

The experiences of Peggy Ann Jones and Pauline Wales understudying 'Phoebe' are fascinating and yet another cover, Lorraine Daniels, has a tale to tell about going on for the first time, in the mid-1970s, in that most appealing of soubrette roles.

"Whilst we were playing Leeds, I had a meal in a cafe before the show. It took a lot longer than it should have done and I just managed to get into the theatre on the half-hour call. It was *The Yeomen of the Guard* and I would usually allow an hour before the start of this opera. As I climbed the stairs, I was greeted by Jimmie Marsland, who said, "You're on." My head went into a whirl, as it was my first time playing 'Phoebe'. Yes, 'Phoebe', the first person on stage! Trying to get ready was a real panic. The biggest challenge was the spinning wheel, because we never had a rehearsal with the wheel and it wasn't easy. Trying to use my feet; spinning the wheel; stopping it at the end of the first verse, only to start it again for the second. The only practice I had was during the overture. My opening song, 'When Maiden Loves' was interesting; there I was trying to work the spinning wheel and remember the words. Hence, I sang the second verse first and the first verse second, whilst the wheel was spinning backwards! What a start, but unless you knew the song, nobody could tell. I'm pleased to say that the rest of the performance went without a hitch and 'Phoebe' became one of my favourite parts but, after that, I made sure I could use a spinning wheel."

Going on for an established principal was never an easy task and James Conroy-Ward had more than his fair share of difficult moments understudying the 'patter' parts, the biggest of which was that he was not John Reed. He joined the company in 1973, as understudy to John, having previously been with The Royal Opera, where he was warned by a colleague, the former D'Oyly Carter, Clifford Parkes, that it was going to be a hell of a job. A lifelong fan of the company, James had landed his dream job and loved getting stuck into preparing the parts. From his earliest appearances, he had to deal with the pressure of audience disappointment when John was not well enough to perform, the collective groan from the auditorium, along with the grudging applause at the end of his songs, hardly filling him with self-confidence. But he knew how it worked and realised that it must have been the same for John when he had to go on for Peter Pratt.

The role he found the most difficult to learn was 'The Lord Chancellor' in *Iolanthe*, the 'Nightmare Song' giving them both many a sleepless night! Not long after he had joined the company, he was told he would be making his debut in the part at Eastbourne's Congress Theatre. He was in an understudy call at the time, so Director of Productions, Michael Heyland, sent everyone else home to concentrate on taking James through everything over and over again. Rehearsed within an inch of his life, all James wanted to do was quietly go over the 'Nightmare Song' and prepare for the performance in his own way. He remembers that I went back with him to his digs and took him through the tongue-twisting song in a way that made sense of the flow of the words, which helped far more than the 'do it again' approach to rehearsing. In fact, he got through it without a mistake that evening and never really worried about it again. It was more usual for Jimmie Marsland to take understudy calls and, if a cover had to go on, his calm approach and incomparable knowledge of the text, music and stage business got many an understudy through a show. James recalls having a conversation with Jeffrey Cresswell after Jeff had a similar experience. He, too, found the 'rehearse all day' approach before going on as an understudy left him exhausted even before he got on the stage. James' first appearance as 'John Wellington Wells' in *The Sorcerer* found him still being given instructions by the Director of Productions as the overture started. Such blanket coverage was not helpful; every performer needs quiet time before a performance and the chance to think about what they have to do.

In his early days as an understudy, James found the principals enormously helpful when he had to go on. On one occasion he told soprano, Julia Goss, that he hoped he would remember all the moves and she cheerfully told him not to worry because, if he was in the wrong place, she would work round him. Lyndsie Holland, on the other hand, found it much harder to improvise around an understudy and James often had to work with her. Any slight deviation from the business she was used to doing with John Reed seemed to discomfort her and he recalls her once slapping his hand away in their *Patience* duet, 'So Go To Him', then grabbing the other arm because that was the way she always did it with John. He is sure it was not meant unkindly but, after that, he was always careful to be spot on when working with her .

Two more memories of going on burn brightly in his memory and the first was his most difficult as an understudy. During the company's week-long visit to Rome in 1974, John Reed was not well enough to perform in *Iolanthe*, so James got ready to go on as the 'Lord Chancellor'. The tardiness of the Roman audiences getting to the theatre was a feature of the week; they drifted in to suit themselves and the curtain was held until they were in, resulting in some of the performances not starting until 9pm. It was nerve-racking enough having to go on for John, but the interminable wait for the show to go up really got to James as he sat for two hours not knowing when he would finally get on the stage. It was an experience he did not wish to repeat. The other incident was in Australia in 1979, when Australian Opera hosted a reception for the D'Oyly Carte in honour of its first visit to Sydney. Standing, drink in hand, taking in the magnificent view of the iconic harbour and bridge from inside the beautiful glass-walled foyer of the Opera House, he was dragged off to rehearse 'Ko-Ko' by Director of Productions, Leonard Osborn, as John Reed was ill. It was a part he had played many times and, just for once, he would have loved to enjoy the party and not bother with his 'Little List'.

If deputising for John Reed was hard, how much harder to replace him? When John left the company in 1979, James had very large shoes to fill and audience attitude to him was little short of hostile. It wasn't him, it would have been anyone who was not John Reed, but that didn't make it any easier. He had been accepted as 'Major-General Stanley' in *The Pirates of Penzance* for several seasons and Beti Lloyd-Jones always said he was the best in the role she had ever seen, but it was in the other parts that audiences were so unforgiving. When John took over from Peter Pratt, he had plenty of time to establish himself as the successor in the 'Grossmith' roles, but time was something the D'Oyly Carte could not give James. Kenneth Sandford was a great admirer of James Conroy-Ward and always believed that he would, eventually, have won over the audiences, but that we will never know.

In 1971, Kathryn Holding's debut as 'Pitti-Sing' in *The Mikado* came very early in the tour, so there had been little opportunity for understudy calls. Arriving at the theatre in Aberdeen to find her name on the cast list, she was thrown into a complete spin. Having had very little rehearsal for the part, it was a frightening moment, but Jimmie Marsland was on hand to talk her through a few of the points that worried her and that was it; she was on. She vividly remembers the wonderful support given to her by Ken Sandford and John Reed for their scenes together in the second act. Whispering to tell her what to do next, they seamlessly worked around her, their vast experience allowing them to do this without compromising their own performances. A somewhat less subtle approach to getting her through the show was offered by Michael Heyland and Jimmie Marsland who, Kate remembers, stood in the wings on either side of the stage shouting instructions to her. Whether or not these stereophonic directions corresponded is anyone's guess. The performance passed without any major problems, except for the one she encountered when she got back to the dressing room, shattered, but relieved to have survived. It was a fashion fad of the time to wear paper knickers and when her dresser helped take off the heavy kimono after the show, all that remained of them was the elastic round her waist and the top of her legs. Apart from the odd scrap of soggy paper stuck to her stomach, they had completely disintegrated, a measure of the perspiration emitted by a performer during a stressful show. At the time given away as a gimmick with bars of chocolate, these unmentionables were brought home in dozens by her father, who worked for a chocolate manufacturer, but Kate disposed of the disposables after that!

Kathryn was also 'thrown on' for her only appearance as 'Constance' in *The Sorcerer* at the Opera House in Manchester. Staying with her parents for the season, there was a problem with the telephone at the family home, so Kate did not learn she was on until she got to work on the half hour. Once again, she had to rely on Jimmie Marsland to give her some last-minute instructions and the help of the principals. With so little opportunity to rehearse the part, she had, like any good understudy, conscientiously watched from the wings when Linda Anne Hutchison played the role and, with 'Constance' being on the stage in the opening chorus, Kate knew, more or less, where to be. Peggy Ann Jones, as 'Mrs. Partlett', was a tower of strength in their scenes, talking her through as they went along, and John Broad was equally supportive as 'The Notary'. However, it was a scary experience and Kate was annoyed that the Director of Productions was nowhere to be seen before the show, tackling him about his absence at the first opportunity. As usual, everything was down to Jimmie and the principals. Kate makes the important point that going on so infrequently gave the understudies very little opportunity to consolidate their characterisations and gain experience, but that was the nature of the beast and it was the same for everyone, with the exception of the understudy to the contralto roles.

The 'dame' parts feature in all the full-length Savoy Operas, so it was a heavy workload for the principal contraltos. It was traditional for the D'Oyly Carte to have one understudy for all these roles, so having reliable covers to deputise was, therefore, extremely important for the company and, in particular, for the 'patter' men who worked so closely with them. During thirteen seasons, Beti Lloyd-Jones covered three principal contraltos, always performing with style, her assurance the result of having the opportunity to play the roles on a regular basis once the company decided to allow the principal a weekly night off. During her lengthy tenure, she got to play in the least-performed operas, giving her the chance to develop her own interpretations of all the characters over many years. It is extremely sad that she was relieved of the job in circumstances which do not reflect well on the D'Oyly Carte management. In 1977, she was replaced, amidst much secrecy, by Elizabeth Denham who, it was widely believed, had been approached to join the company as a chorister and understudy to the principal contralto, before Beti was informed that her services were no longer required. It was rumoured that Elizabeth was known to someone on the production team, but this cannot be verified. However, a member of the music staff at the time has confirmed that he was sworn to secrecy when he was sent to her home to coach her in the music before she joined. It is a measure of Beti's dignity that she accepted her demotion with good grace, returning to chorus duties to enjoy the tours of North America in 1978 and Australia and New Zealand in 1979 without responsibility. The popular Liz Denham was, herself, replaced by Jill Pert before the tour 'down under' and, like Beti, took it on the chin, going back to chorus duties and covering some smaller roles.

Jill covered the contralto roles until the company's closure in 1982 and recalls how difficult her first few weeks were when trying to learn all the chorus work at the same time as the roles she was covering. She knew she would be going on for Patricia Leonard as soon as the tour started, so it was a stressful time. She remembers being an ever-present at understudy calls, where Jimmie Marsland drilled her in the stage business, while Leonard Osborn, the Director of Productions, sat doing a crossword and smoking cigarettes as Jimmie did all the graft. But the difference between Jill and all the other understudies was that she knew when she was going on, because Patricia's nights off were scheduled into the tour dates. Her debut came at the Opera House in Manchester when she went on for 'Little Buttercup' in *HMS Pinafore*. Although she was fairly confident of her words, music and moves, she was grateful to receive advice from the principals to add some finesse to her performance. She was also happy to listen to the wise words generously given by Beti Lloyd-Jones to get her through that first show which, happily, passed without incident.

As the weeks went by, one debut followed another and Jill's main memories are of the help she was given by the principals, who freely gave their time to ensure she had the best possible chance of giving a rounded performance. For her first 'Ruth' in *Pirates*, Meston Reid volunteered to go through their first act dialogue and duet with her. When she told him to feel free to push her round the stage if necessary, he replied, "Don't worry, wherever you get to I'll come and find you." From then on, she always loved working with Meston in that dramatic scene and has never forgotten his kindness. Likewise, for her first 'Katisha', John Reed went over and above the call of duty. He offered to help her with dialogue and characterisation, so they met in a quiet corner of Eastbourne's Congress Theatre to run through the important second act scene between 'Ko-Ko' and 'Katisha'. Soaking up every point he made and feeling increasingly secure, she was in seventh heaven to be working so closely with one of the D'Oyly Carte greats. Before the show, John invited her to his dressing room and did her make-up, helping her understand the need to create an individual make-up design, rather than trying to copy what Patricia Leonard did. It was the start of a good friendship between the two.

It was to John she turned after a mortifying experience in New Zealand. Deputising for Patricia in *The Mikado*, she hurtled on for her first entrance 'Your Revels Cease', but the long train on her kimono caught on the edge of one of the platforms as she headed downstage, yanking her backwards and almost throttling her in the process! Completely thrown by her embarrassing entry, she could not think of her words, singing nonsense to the melody as she tried to keep in character with angry gestures towards Philip Potter, who was playing 'Nanki-Poo'. She can remember being cross with Philip, who had returned to the company for the tour down under to play the role he had made his own in the 1960s. With his back to the audience, he was in the perfect position to give her a prompt but, instead, he was grinning at her like a Cheshire cat. She eventually recovered her composure, but was more than glad when the first act curtain fell. Feeling completely humiliated, she rushed to John Reed's room in floods of tears, bemoaning her mishap. His long experience and a cup of tea soon worked wonders as he calmed her down with assurances that it was just one of those things that happened to every performer now and then.

Whichever of the principals went the extra mile to make sure she had the best chance of doing well as an understudy, Jill benefited from their experience and generosity of spirit. There were, of course, times when her appearances were not scheduled if Patricia Leonard was ill but, unlike all the other understudies, going on every week allowed her confidence to build and her characterisations to blossom. While

157

the other covers wrestled with the insecurity born of being under-rehearsed, she was reaping the benefits of regular performances and making the most of her opportunity. Her weekly outings were in sharp contrast with the sporadic performances of other understudies, who could go for months, or even years, between appearances. Going on so infrequently meant that they were more concerned with survival than character building. Those lucky enough to get a run of appearances found the experience invaluable, but such chances rarely came along.

When David Porter had to deputise for John Broad at short notice as the 'Lieutenant of the Tower' in *The Yeomen of the Guard*, John Reed's willingness to help got him into trouble. Having had only one rehearsal for the part, David asked John to go through their first act scene and John, as ever, was happy to oblige. Whilst going over the dialogue and moves on the set, they were discovered by Michael Heyland, who made it clear he was not happy about them being there as they had not asked permission to use the stage. David pointed out that he had asked John to go over the scene, but their impromptu rehearsal was cut short and John later told David that he had been given a ticking off for his involvement. This begs the question, why such a strong reaction? Was it because the head of the production staff should have been the one to instigate such necessary last-minute preparation?

In the 1975 centenary seasons at the Savoy Theatre and Royal Festival Hall, one of the highlights was the production of *Utopia Ltd.*, the first time it had been included in the D'Oyly Carte repertoire since its initial run in 1893. John Reed was cast as 'Scaphio' and David Porter was given the understudy. For several days before the show was due to be performed at The Royal Festival Hall, John had not been well and David realised he needed to put in plenty of work to get the part thoroughly learned in the event that John could not go on. He worked on the difficult dialogue late into the night, helped by his wife, Pamela Field, who was to play 'Princess Zara', and felt just about prepared to face the challenge. He told John not to worry if he was too poorly to go on, as he was ready if needed. David relates it was then that John told him he had been informed by the management that he was expected to go on under any circumstances. Admittedly, it was a prestigious season for the D'Oyly Carte and having one of its stars unavailable would prove a huge disappointment for audiences, but the pressure put on John to appear when ill was a step too far. Although far from well, John did go on for all the performances, but it couldn't have been much fun for him, or for David, who never knew whether or not he would have to deputise.

So, the job of the D'Oyly Carte understudy was never easy and often extremely difficult. In the days before there were telephones in digs or, as today, mobile phones and e-mail, contacting covers to give them advance warning of having to go on was often not possible, so they lost a few precious hours of time to prepare themselves. If they didn't go to the theatre every morning to check the notice board, they might have less than an hour's notice of being required to play a major role. Paid very little for the amount of responsibility they assumed, most accepted the less than ideal circumstances which preceded their appearances because it was a chance to shine, to make an impression. Ambition and self-confidence go hand in hand, but 'going on' in the D'Oyly Carte tested such character to the full. That the company could not afford to hold sufficient understudy rehearsals is understandable, so making the most of available time should have been of paramount importance. The input of Assistant Director, James Marsland, for the last sixteen years of the company, alongside the unstinting efforts of the principals, were the main reasons so many understudies acquitted themselves with distinction. However, Jimmie was a mechanic; he knew the nuts and bolts of the productions better than anyone, but he was not the man to help with dialogue or characterisation. Going back to the early 1950s and into the 1960s, production staff members such as Billy Morgan, Snookie Fancourt and Herbert Newby, taught stage business to understudies by rote, but rarely offered anything more. So where did this responsibility lie? Surely not with the principals, who had enough to do in sustaining their own performances for eleven months of the year? The title 'Director of Productions' suggests that those holding the number one job should have been the people to coach dialogue and develop characterisation but, with the possible exception of Robin Gibson, they never did. D'Oyly Carters of later years, to whom I have spoken, concur that Michael Heyland, Leonard Osborn and Wilfred Judd brought nothing to the table in terms of artistic guidance at a time when the company's productions were in need of fresh dramatic impetus.

Not one of the understudies whose stories are related in this chapter has been able to say that they received any help from the directors, nor did they seek it. In every case, it was the principals to whom they turned for the advice they needed to get them through their performances. In reality, it was the principals who directed the shows. There is a big difference between directing a production and teaching its stage business, but the D'Oyly Carte management never seemed to understand this distinction. A succession of people were employed who, however enthusiastic and conscientious, were not, it seems, capable of fulfilling the vital function of directing actors. Despite this unfortunate situation, many an understudy defied the odds and gave a first-class performance, or went on to become a leading performer, thanks to the experience so generously shared with them by the company's principals.

CHAPTER SEVEN

"YOU'RE OFF!"

Another two dreaded words to fill any performer with panic when they echoed around the backstage areas in search of the miscreant missing from the action. Being 'off', the theatrical term for not being on the stage for a scene when required is, next to forgetting words, a performer's worst nightmare. Most D'Oyly Carters, very occasionally, experienced the humiliation of missing an entrance, leaving colleagues to fill the gap on the stage and improvise until they eventually arrived. The absence of a principal for a few seconds can seem like an eternity to those left to cover, whilst the audience murmur and shuffle in their seats in embarrassed sympathy. Any live theatre performance, be it at the London Palladium or in the local village hall, is at the mercy of human error, accident, or unforeseen circumstance. Given that the D'Oyly Carte Opera Company gave around 380 performances every year, it is impossible to imagine that all of them passed without incident. There are many wonderful stories down the years of things going wrong, from missed entrances, forgotten lines, falls and costume malfunctions, to scenery collapsing. Every company performer will have experienced moments when the serene progress of a show was interrupted by horror, hiatus or hilarity. It has been impossible to include all of them here, but the following selection of disasters and dilemmas can be considered typical.

In the mid-1970s, the first act of a performance of *The Mikado* was in full swing when Michael Rayner, who was playing 'Pish-Tush', felt the need for a 'comfort break'. Unfortunately, he misjudged the time he needed to undo and refasten his cumbersome costume, struggling against time to be ready for his next entrance. With fingers becoming thumbs, his laborious efforts seemed to take forever and by the time he had finally managed to get dressed, 'Ko-Ko' and 'Pooh-Bah', John Reed and Kenneth Sandford respectively, were left high and dry in the dialogue prior to 'I Am So Proud'. As Mike raced from the toilet with the Stage Manager putting out calls and searching for him, the other two had no alternative but to make up a conversation until he arrived, each asking the other if they had seen 'Pish-Tush' because he was due to meet them for an important discussion. They looked into the wings for his arrival, commenting that they were sure he would turn up soon because they had seen him earlier, and all to the delight of the knowledgeable audience, who were loving watching two great D'Oyly Carte stars ad libbing suitable lines to bridge the lengthy delay. Eventually, an out-of-puff Mike rushed onto the stage to gasp out his line 'I am a bearer of a letter from His Majesty the Mikado', to which Ken Sandford drolly retorted, "Second class, obviously." The uproarious laughter greeting this delightful sarcasm at least gave Mike a chance to get his breath back. Although performers being 'off' was not something that happened often, when it did, it was memorable and *The Yeomen of the Guard* seemed to attract tardiness. Lorraine Daniels was a chorister when one such moment happened in the second act.

"We were in Bristol and our dressing room was right at the top of the theatre. I was busy washing my white show socks, because we were responsible for this job, when we heard a loud bang. I looked out of the window to see what it was and said it must be a car backfiring. Then, all of a sudden, we all realised it was the gun for the 'shot scene'! We ran like the clappers down all those stairs, very much out of breath. Unfortunately, we didn't make it on time and could only stand in the wings and watch the few people on the stage."

Even worse happened at the Eden Court Theatre in Inverness during

162

the company's tour of Scotland in 1980. A modern theatre built onto the rather grand Bishop's Palace, its dressing rooms were situated in the old part of the building, necessitating a lengthy walk to get to the stage. According to Christine George, the tannoy system was not working, so a call boy was being used to announce upcoming entrances, which he invariably did far too early. At the time, small portable televisions were popular in the chorus rooms and it was during a performance of *Yeomen* that the ladies were watching Suzanne Houlden's tiny black and white TV. So engrossed were they in a programme about a sex change operation that, when the call boy knocked on the door for 'Jack Point's entrance', they knew it was far too soon and continued to watch in fascination until someone mentioned that it had been a while since the call. The ensuing panic saw the chorus room empty amidst a clattering of chairs when they realised they might be off. As they tumbled down the stairs, Wig Mistress, Heather Perkins and Director of Productions, Wilfred Judd, were holding open the doors to the stage area so they didn't have to slow down.

Meanwhile, the only chorister who had not been in the dressing room (me) was in a state of near panic. Having been in conversation in the wings with James Conroy-Ward, who was playing 'Jack Point', it became clear that a solo appearance in 'Here's a Man of Jollity' was imminent. With no sign of the other choristers bar a couple of yeomen warders, James and Barbara Lilley, playing 'Elsie Maynard', stood either side of the stage ready to come on, looking very alarmed, whilst I lined up on my own behind James, dreading what was to come. The Stage Manager, amongst others, shouted for the chorus, but it was too late. The percussive introduction music to the scene began and the three of us had no option but to go on, with me trying to look like a baying mob! I can still visualise myself leaping around the stage, reacting with James and Barbara until the conductor, Fraser Goulding, whose eyes were out on stalks, brought me in and I sang on my own until the cavalry arrived. As bodies hurtled onto the stage from the nearest entrances, the numbers swelled until I was finally put out of my misery. Needless to say, the management was not impressed and there was an inquest after this unfortunate incident, but I will never forget the horrible experience of having to be a chorus of one; it certainly was a case of spreading myself too thinly.

Another unwitting solo chorister to carry a scene without his colleagues appeared in Act Two of *Princess Ida*, when the sword-wielding men's chorus rushed on for 'Walls and Fences Scaling, Promptly We Appear'. Out of the blue, a ramp collapsed leaving them floundering in the large gap in the set, but one small, agile figure managed to clamber up to his usual position atop a rock to find himself alone in the task of trying to frighten the ladies of Castle Adamant! With the rest of the men singing from the wings until they reorganised themselves, John Reed cut a solitary figure indeed as he sang in splendid isolation. I know how he must have felt.

In the early 1950s, during a performance of *Pirates*, a small group of chorus ladies, including Ceinwen Newby, Joyce Farrer and Cynthia Morey, was making its way underneath the stage of the Lyceum Theatre in Sheffield, to cross from one side to the other, when they heard the orchestra playing a beautiful melody which they didn't recognise. Commenting on how lovely it sounded, it dawned on them that it was the accompaniment to the end of the 'Major-General's' song, 'Sighing Softly to the River', which meant they were going to be late for their entrance in Act Two Finale. In a flurry of nightdresses and bloomers, they raced up to the stage and tried to slip on unnoticed, earning themselves a severe reprimand at the end of the show. Such instances of collective absence were rare, although there was once an awkward moment in *Iolanthe* when 'Strephon' summoned the fairies to his aid at the start of the first act finale and only six of the sixteen turned up! Most instances of 'being off' involved individuals and there are many examples of principals missing an entrance.

In 1961, Thomas Round took over the role of 'Richard Dauntless' in *Ruddigore*, playing opposite Mary Sansom as 'Rose Maybud'. As they waited in the wings before their entrance early in Act Two, it was her custom to ask Tom if he had remembered to put the union flag, which he used to wave over her head, in his pocket. According to Mary's husband, Alan Barrett, on one occasion when she did this, Tom realised he had left it in the dressing room and dashed off to get it just as the music heralding their arrival in the 'Murgatroyd' household was about to start. Mary had no alternative but to go on without Tom and sing the first verse for him, which involved some very quick thinking on her part as she swapped words round for it to make some kind of sense and sang: "Happily coupled are we, you see; you are a jolly Jack Tar, my star, and I am the fairest, the richest and rarest of innocent lasses by far, a star, of innocent lasses by far." Her invisible fiancee shot on just in time for her to sing the second verse to him, but it was a tricky moment for her. Mary's presence of mind shows how an experienced performer was able to salvage a difficult situation, when even the best had dropped a clanger.

Patricia Leonard was the consummate professional, commanding respect from all of her colleagues, but even she could be guilty of losing track of time, as Peter Lyon remembers only too well. Not long after he had taken over the role of 'Captain Corcoran' in 1979, he relates the story about a performance of *Pinafore* when Trish went missing.

"I had just finished the 'Captain's Song' and the chorus had exited. Expecting Trish to come for her recitative, 'Sir, You Are Sad', I adopted my worried look and waited. There was no sign of her, so I paraded around the stage checking ledges for dust and generally inspecting the deck. Conscious of my situation, the MD, Fraser Goulding, took matters into his own hands by deciding that I should do the second verse of the song again. After frantic whispered instructions to the orchestra and much rustling of music, they started the introduction and I was just about to sing when Trish rushed onto the stage. As the band ground to a halt, more rustling of pages turning finally led to Trish somehow being able to find her starting note for the recit, but it was an awkward moment to say the least and it felt like a lifetime."

There were other pitfalls for performers to negotiate, not the least of which was dealing with forgetting their words or, as it is known in the business, 'drying'. Something that happened to everyone on occasion, drying up was the stuff of nightmares and many an inexperienced D'Oyly Carte principal was grateful to get through a performance without paraphrasing or forgetting lines. At the other end of the scale, stalwarts of many years were careful not to take remembering their dialogue for granted, always going through the lines they had been saying for years before every performance. Sometimes, it was dealing with a colleague drying that caused problems and, with many of the D'Oyly Carte fans knowing all the words of a show by heart, principals could expect to be told of even the tiniest mistake outside the Stage Door at the end of a performance. Perhaps surprisingly, the

165

vast majority of performances passed without the slightest deviation from Gilbert's words, a tribute to the professionalism of the company's artistes. But there were, of course, a few exceptions.

Lyndsie Holland, like most of her colleagues, made the occasional blooper in her dialogue, but everyone on the stage knew when she had dried, because she started to click her fingers, an involuntary response to losing her words and the cue for someone to leap to her rescue. The most memorable example of this happened in the first act finale of *Iolanthe*, when she was playing the 'Queen of the Fairies'. Right in the middle of her list of threats to be heaped on the Peers when 'Strephon' went into Parliament, she completed the line 'He shall end the cherished rights you enjoy on Friday nights' and continued with the next 'He shall', then stopped dead, the fingers of her right hand immediately starting to click. It is likely that Lyndsie was the only person in the theatre who didn't know the next word, but although the principals standing nearest to her tried to give the word, she couldn't seem to latch on to it. Within seconds, the whole cast was trying to help her out and soon there was a whispered chorus of "Prick. Prick!" reverberating around the stage. It seemed like an age before she finally picked it up and was able to continue, by which time everyone was trying not to laugh about the unfortunate moment she had chosen to dry. Usually, when a performer forgot the words, an under-the-breath prompt from a colleague was all that was needed for them to get going again, a good turn that might be reciprocated at another time and all part of the job. Difficult to believe, maybe, but the D'Oyly Carte did not employ a 'prompt'. Considering that the Savoy Operas contain so much dialogue, it might have seemed logical, but it would have incurred extra expense for a company always operating on a shoestring budget. As ever, it was down to the hard-pressed principals to clear up any mess.

Some artistes were blessed with the facility to get themselves back on track when they forgot their words. One such was John Ayldon, a solid, reliable performer who seldom made a mistake, but when he did, it was always a cracker. The trick was that he never stopped talking or singing, he simply rambled around the words until he arrived back where he needed to be. All very commendable, but it usually left everyone else in fits of laughter. His most memorable gaffe occurred near the end of Act Two of *The Mikado*, when he accidentally substituted one word which changed the whole meaning of his line. Patricia Leonard, playing 'Katisha', rushed on to announce that she had just married 'Ko-Ko', and John, who was playing 'The Mikado', was supposed to reply, 'Oh, you've not been long about it'. Instead, he said, 'Oh, you've not been long at it.' It is hard to describe the instant effect this had on both cast and audience, but everyone immediately dissolved into giggles. John did not realise his mistake until told after the final curtain and had not been able to understand why everyone was trying not to laugh.

Another famous example of one of John's howlers happened in *HMS Pinafore*, when his variation on a theme left Clive Harré unable to continue. In the second act duet between 'Dick Deadeye' and 'Captain Corcoran', John, playing the rascally 'Deadeye', got the first line of the opening verse correct but, for no apparent reason, came up with a second line from out of the blue. He was supposed to sing: 'Kind Captain, I've important information, sing hey, the kind commander that you are, about a certain intimate relation, sing hey, the merry maiden and the tar.' Unaccountably, he sang: 'Kind Captain, I've important information, sing hey, the kind commander that you are, about a certain interfering fairy, sing hey, the merry maiden and the tar.' Unable to believe his ears, Clive tried not to laugh, but couldn't suppress his mirth and remembers being doubled over, unable to sing for the rest of the duet which, of course, started John laughing. Neither was very popular with the management after this debacle, but it certainly went down in D'Oyly Carte annals.

Why performers who have played a role many times sometimes stray from the text is hard to understand; perhaps it can be put down to a momentary lapse in concentration, tiredness or a distraction but, however professional the cast, an unexpected mistake can cause mayhem on the stage. Kenneth Sandford had been playing 'Sir Despard Murgatroyd' in *Ruddigore* for well over twenty years when he made a one word error that left the audience confused and the cast in hysterics. Striding menacingly to the centre of the back rostrum to disrupt the marriage of 'Robin Oakapple' and 'Rose Maybud' in the first act finale, he held up his hand and sang, 'Hold, bride and bridegroom, ere you wed each other, I claim young Strephon as my elder brother!' To his dying day he could never find an explanation for why he should have so unexpectedly picked out a name from *Iolanthe*, although he did admit that he had previously been teasing John about being too old to be called 'young Robin', so maybe it served him right. As may be imagined, the melodramatic moment was completely destroyed and the look on John Reed's face was priceless. It took quite some time for the cast to pull themselves together to continue without their shoulders shaking, but eye make-up certainly needed touching up at the interval.

One of the most famous D'Oyly Carte stories of all time involved an unintentional change of words, the culprit being Peggy Ann Jones, who was playing 'Lady Angela' in *Patience*. Ken Sandford, as 'Archibald Grosvenor', made his entrance in the first act finale and took his rather camp pose as the heartbroken poet, his appearance supposed to send the ladies into transports of delight. Peggy soon put an end to that when, instead of singing, 'But who is this, whose godlike grace proclaims he comes of noble race', she sang, 'But who is this, whose godlike grace proclaims he comes from outer space'! Barely able to believe what she had done, the cast members were in a dilemma, because they were supposed to repeat Peggy's line and, of course, some could not resist adding to her faux pas, although many were too convulsed with laughter to sing anything at all. But spare a thought for Ken Sandford trying to keep composed for his upcoming lines after an introduction like that. Even today, Peggy is at a loss to know why those words came out of her mouth, but does make the rather feeble excuse that, perhaps, it was because men had recently landed on the moon for the first time. However, she could not use such a reason to explain another hilarious mistake, this time in *The Mikado*. In the second act scene in which 'The Mikado' questions 'Ko-Ko', 'Pooh-Bah' and 'Pitti-Sing' as to why they have had his son executed, the three miscreants claim they didn't know who he was. Peggy was supposed to say, 'It wasn't written on his forehead, you know' but, for reasons known only to herself, instead said, 'It wasn't written on any part of his anatomy, you know', reducing the others to jelly and leaving John Reed almost incapable of getting out his next line.

Ralph Mason was another experienced performer to make a slip of the tongue which left the stage in uproar. Playing 'Ralph Rackstraw' in a performance of *HMS Pinafore*, he addressed John Ayldon as 'Dead

Dickeye'! On one occasion, when Kenneth Sandford was playing 'Dr. Daly' in *The Sorcerer*, he was bemoaning his lovelorn state, when he unaccountably said, 'I never remarked it before, but the youths of this village are very comely', when he should have used the words 'young maidens'. Perhaps it explained why the elderly vicar never got married! Patricia Leonard and John Ayldon, usually so reliable, once completely lost the plot in their *Yeomen* duet, 'Rapture, Rapture'. The tongue-twisting words, delivered at high speed, require great concentration and if words are missed, it is almost impossible for either performer to catch up. Neither was sure which of them made the first mistake but, once they had fallen off the wagon, try as they might, they found it impossible to pick up the words again. Both started to giggle and by the end of the duet, with the audience mystified, they were doubled up with laughter. It was a mortifying experience for two highly-professional performers and both were extremely embarrassed by their behaviour. It happened to the best in the D'Oyly Carte; the knowledge that the audience should never see performers helpless with laughter always fuelling the fire. Giggling quickly becomes hysteria, rendering an artiste incapable of continuing and this phenomenon is known as 'corpsing'.

During a London Last Night performance at Sadler's Wells Theatre in the 1970s, John Ayldon made his appearance as 'The Mikado' astride a large, white horse, much to the delight of the audience. Chatter in the dressing rooms prior to the show included speculation as to what would happen if the horse, unnerved by the noise and lights, had an accident. They were soon to find out, as the horse deposited a steaming mound in the middle of the stage. Of course, gales of laughter came from the audience, but the chorus, off the leash during such a fun show, were in fits and this got worse when Michael Rayner and Colin Wright rushed on with bucket and spade to clear up the mess. After several moments when everyone on the stage, John included, was absolutely helpless, he was eventually able to complete his song, but the hilarity returned when the chorus ladies, who had been kneeling across the front of the stage, got up to move to their next position, revealing a wet patch on the stagecloth indicating that one of them, who will not be named, had laughed so much that she, too, had not been able to control herself. Thereafter, the cloth bore the two stains of that memorable night!

Christene Palmer, as sensible and down-to-earth a performer as could ever be imagined, came to dread her entrance towards the end of the second act of *HMS Pinafore*, because she knew she would corpse at the antics of Jon Ellison. As the chorus of sailors, with herself as 'Little Buttercup' shepherding 'Josephine', crept onto the stage for 'Carefully on Tiptoe Stealing', Jon, as the 'Bosun', would wait for the tiny pause in the music after 'Captain Corcoran' had cracked his cat-o'-nine-tails, to create the sound of somebody breaking wind. The men then sang, 'Goodness me, why what was that?' to which 'Deadeye' replied, 'Silent be, it was the cat!' Christene fell apart every time he did this, having to turn her head upstage to cover her mirth. She knew it was going to happen; she was determined she would not laugh; it was silly and unprofessional, but she still got the giggles. Jon, of course, played on this because he knew how she would react, but he was always careful that the audience would never be aware of this 'in joke'. It must be remembered that having to perform the same shows scores of times every year could become very monotonous for the D'Oyly Carters, so subtle bits of fun were commonplace and very helpful in keeping shows fresh. Chorus bass, Mark Nelson, a notorious wag, always knew how to make Howard Williamson corpse. Howard was John Reed's understudy in the late 1960s and early 70s, but played 'The Judge' in *Trial by Jury* in his own right. Mark had the tedious, non-singing role of the 'Court Associate' in *Trial* and was seated at a desk directly beneath the judge's bench, from where he would take the opportunity to pass notes up to Howard, as if in some official capacity. The contents of these notes were invariably vulgar and guaranteed to make Howard corpse, but it was fortunate he had a newspaper as a prop, so he could disappear behind it until the paroxysm passed.

Sometimes, the jokes played between cast members bordered on infantile, but they were still a welcome diversion during a long week of eight performances. It took Meston Reid all his power of concentration not to corpse during one performance of *Pinafore*. Having just finished the dramatic first act duet with 'Josephine', in which the lowly sailor, 'Ralph Rackstraw', has his offer of undying love rejected by his captain's daughter, Meston was required to walk sadly upstage, before turning to sing, 'Can I survive this overbearing, or live a life of mad despairing'. One evening, his eye was drawn into the wings, where the chorus of sailors had dropped their trousers! It was rather more 'overbaring' than he would have liked, particularly just before having to sing a top b flat on the appropriate line, 'No, no, it's not to be expected.'

Even the doughty Kenneth Sandford was not averse to the occasional descent into schoolboy humour. In *The Sorcerer*, Ken, as 'Dr. Daly', along with 'Mrs. Partlet', Beti Lloyd-Jones, would stand in the wings during the first act duet between 'Sir Marmaduke' and 'Lady Sangazure', pulling faces at the chorus, who were 'frozen' in group poses, in the hope of getting them to laugh and break the freeze. Not that they needed much help with Michael Buchan around. He possessed the dubious talent of being able to move one eye independently of the other and took great delight, during the same scene, of sending an eyeball slowly from side to side whilst the other stayed still. If you were unlucky enough to be in the same group as him, you quickly learned never to look at him during the freezes for fear of starting to giggle.

I must confess to being responsible for John Reed corpsing during a scene in Act One of *The Mikado*. While 'Pooh-Bah' was in his speech complaining about having to say, 'How de do, little girls' to the 'Three Little Maids', the production required 'Ko-Ko' to move around the ladies' chorus giving each a peck on the cheek. When he got to me, I must have looked rather pained, because he quietly asked me what was the matter. My reply was forever etched in his memory. "Does packet soup give you wind?" John was, at first, taken aback, but soon dissolved into helpless laughter, my unexpected remark having caught him off guard. I certainly didn't intend to set him off, but he was so convulsed that Ken Sandford was left to fend for himself in the dialogue which should have included John. He never let me forget the 'packet soup moment' and often referred to it whenever we spoke after he had left the company. To an outsider, it may seem shocking that such mundane conversation should occur in the middle of a show, but whispered exchanges about all sorts of things were common and did not impair the quality of a performance. Company newcomer, Maggie Bourgein, recalls being appalled by some of her colleagues during her first *Pirates* matinee. Taking everything very seriously, she was acting her socks off at the feet of her pirate partner, when she overheard Beti

Lloyd-Jones, who was working next to her, ask John Broad if he had managed to get his car exhaust fixed. Having told her he had, she stretched her arms towards him in supplication and asked where he was going for tea! Maggie soon learned how it worked.

Another story in the windy category was, perhaps, the most unfortunate. In the second act finale of *The Yeomen of the Guard*, John Reed, as 'Jack Point', had just made his entrance for 'Oh, thoughtless crew, ye know not what ye do', with the assembled cast looking suitably sad. At the back of the stage, the phalanx of red-clad yeomen warders framed a spectacular scene. John always left a small, but highly emotional pause between 'Attend to me and shed a tear or two, for' and 'I have a song to sing-O'. With unbelievably bad timing, one of the yeomen, who will not be embarrassed here, found that exact moment to accidentally break wind. A second either side of that poignant gap in the music and it would have gone unnoticed, at least audibly, but everyone on the stage heard it and the effect was immediate. Of all the moments in the Savoy Operas not to have everyone shaking with laughter, that was it. Heads were bowed, or turned away from the audience, but the mass hysteria could not be stopped and poor John had to continue, not having a clue as to why everyone was laughing so much during the tragic ending of the opera.

My position on stage right saw me directly opposite John Ayldon, playing 'Sergeant Meryll' and over the years, we had traditionally shared many a quiet joke across the stage, but we dared not look at each other for fear of making matters worse. Chorus responses to John Reed's solo were almost non-existent and it was quite some time before everyone managed to control themselves for the final dramatic moment of the opera when 'Point' collapsed. Somehow, Barbara Lilley, playing 'Elsie' managed to sing her lines with John, but it was not easy with everyone around her trying to control their laughter. It will not be hard to believe that, after the final curtain, John was not best pleased and let everyone know it. He eventually saw the funny side of the incident and the culprit was, of course, mortified. Such an occurrence, however rare, may portray company members as unprofessional but, in reality, nothing was further from the truth. Down the years, there were many notorious pranksters in the D'Oyly Carte, but not one of them would deliberately undermine the work of a colleague. 'In jokes' remained exactly that and were never noticeable to the audience. However, there were times when something amusing occurred on the stage and the humorous moment was happily shared with the audience, such is the nature of live theatre, but no self-respecting performer would deliberately compromise the integrity of a show. Having said that, the unexpected sometimes happened when doing eight shows a week and unless corpsing has been experienced, it is impossible to explain how easy it is for hysteria to take hold, or how difficult it is to control.

Sometimes, it was members of the audience who inadvertently caused amusement or distraction for those in the middle of a performance. John Dennison remembers his wife, Barbra, upsetting two of the company's principals during the London winter season of 1956 at the Prince's Theatre on Shaftsbury Avenue. Over the Christmas period, the company presented a new production of *Patience* and Barbra, who was sitting on the second row of the stalls, wore a sparkling turquoise gown in honour of the occasion. This upset Leonard Osborn, who was playing the 'Duke of Dunstable' because, he complained, "The orchestra lights reflected off it in a most annoying manner." Not long after this, Fred Sinden, who was playing 'Mr. Box' in *Cox and Box*, noticed Barbra, who was sitting on the front row just to the left of conductor, Isidore Godfrey, but his reaction to her appearance was not one of annoyance, as he later told John. Barbra was unaware that her dress had ridden up to reveal her stocking tops, which Fred found very distracting, the tantalising sight on view every time he looked at the conductor! One thing the devoted fans on the front rows usually didn't realise was that they were clearly visible to those on the stage, so even something as innocent as the rustling of a bag of sweets being passed around, or a whispered conversation, could be very eye-catching for performers. But not, perhaps, as much as the sight of some know-all following the music in the score, looking to catch out someone missing a word, or turning a quaver into a crotchet.

A famous example of members of the audience causing distraction happened during a London season in the late 1950s, when Sir Winston Churchill attended a performance of *The Gondoliers* to celebrate his birthday. Accompanied by his great friend, Second World War hero, Field Marshall Montgomery, the illustrious guests were introduced to cast members at the interval before returning to their seats in the middle of the front row of the stalls. Just as Kenneth Sandford, who was playing 'Don Alhambra, started to sing 'There Lived a King', an usher walked to the end of the front row and passed a note along to the two distinguished visitors. Sir Winston, assuming it to be a summons back to the House of Commons for an important division, didn't bother to read it, but nudged his companion and the two of them got up to leave. The elderly Sir Winston's painfully slow exit was followed by every eye, including those on the stage, leaving Ken to wonder why he was bothering to sing at all. It was later mischievously suggested that the note was intended for the Field Marshall and contained the result of a football match in which he was interested.

It was not unknown for comments to be shouted out from the audience during a show and Pauline Wales tells of one such incident which happened when the company was on tour in Ireland in the 1960s. In the second act of a performance of *Iolanthe*, Donald Adams, who was playing 'The Earl of Mountararat', was worried about the possible reaction of Irish Republicans to the tone of his speech in which he asserts, 'If there is an institution in Great Britain which is not susceptible of any improvement at all, it is the House of Peers'. His concern proved well-founded. At the end of the line, when he was half expecting to be shot on the spot for such a controversial political statement, he was relieved that all he got for his heresy was a cry of, "Says you!" Pauline, who was playing 'Leila', remembers him muttering, "Could've been worse."

It may be difficult to believe, but the D'Oyly Carte Opera Company was so deemed to represent the essence of Britishness that it was twice targeted by the Irish Republican Army in the late 1970s. In two different London seasons at Sadler's Wells Theatre, performances were disrupted when warnings were given that bombs had been set in the theatre. Everyone knew the routine: the curtain was dropped without warning and the performers on the stage were told to immediately leave via the Stage Door, whilst an announcement was made over the tannoy for everyone to evacuate the backstage areas. Those lucky enough to be in the dressing rooms at least had the chance to grab coats, handbags and wallets before exiting the theatre, but the performers who were in the middle of a scene had to hurry out into the cold winter night in their costumes. The orchestra and technical staff also had to go as they were. With everyone assembled at the given meeting point in the street at the back of the theatre, a roll-call was taken to make sure nobody was still inside, whilst the audience was shepherded into Rosebery Avenue.

As may be imagined, it took some time for police officers to comb every inch of the theatre to make sure no bombs had been planted and for the incident to be declared a hoax, by which time an hour or so had passed before everyone was allowed back in for the performance to continue. Being resourceful D'Oyly Carters, the cast found a solution to waiting outside in the cold by piling into the two pubs near the Stage Door and those who had cash with them bought the drinks. One of the bomb scares interrupted a performance of *Princess Ida*, the costumes for which were designed by James Wade in 1954 and were gothically fanciful to say the least. The expressions of wonderment on the faces of the regular drinkers in the pubs at the invasion of so many weirdly-dressed people can be imagined and most must have thought they had drunk too much! Kenneth Sandford was rather annoyed to find that he had left his cigarettes in the dressing room when he hurried from the theatre. Luckily, there was a small shop a few yards from the pub, which crammed a wonderful array of provisions into a very small space and was a boon to many a D'Oyly Carter. Ken, in full 'King Hildebrand' regalia, sword, crown and all, popped in and had to laugh, because the genial owner didn't turn a hair as he enquired, "Twenty of the usual, Mr. Sandford?" Eventually, with the all-clear given, Stage Manager, Peter Riley, who knew where to find the cast, hauled everyone out. Audience members back in their seats, the performance continued from the point at which it had been suspended in Act Two. 'Hilarion', 'Florian' and 'Cyril', for the second time, climbed over the walls of Castle Adamant and furtively looked around to make sure they had entered the domain of 'Princess Ida' unobserved. Their first words caused yet another delay as the audience roared with laughter at the irony of the situation: 'Gently, gently, evidently we are safe so far'! It was a moment of pure theatre magic.

Seeing the comical side of a potentially life-threatening situation does not obscure the fact that the company took security very seriously; such hoaxes were common in public places in the 1970s, but the management repeatedly briefed its employees as to what they must do in the event of a bomb threat. But the day came when there really was a bomb and it exploded. The D'Oyly Carte was playing its annual season at the Opera House in Manchester and a Saturday evening performance of *Mikado* had just ended. As the cast was heading back to the dressing rooms, an enormous explosion rocked the building, shattering windows and filling the backstage areas with dust. John Reed, whose room was nearest the stage, had just started to take off his costume when the bomb went off and he vividly remembered a large shard of glass whistling past the end of his nose as the window crashed in around him. Panic set in as the cast raced to get changed, grab their belongings and get out of the theatre. A few fortunate people managed to leave in their cars before police sealed off the area for fear of a second bomb going off. I was one of those lucky ones and gratefully drove away from the scene after a nerveless young policeman had crawled under my car to make sure there was no explosive device underneath it. I was very scared and my legs were shaking so much that it was very difficult to engage the clutch, the car lurching away from the theatre as if powered by kangaroo petrol.

It was a frightening experience, so I was grateful for a stop at the first service area I came to on the M6 to have a cup of coffee and steady my nerves. Was I glad to see Patricia Leonard and Michael Buchan walk in soon after. Although we were partially deaf from the explosion, we compared notes on what had happened, before heading home to the Midlands for a welcome day off to recover from the shocking events in Manchester. It was a subdued company which convened on the following Monday, with everyone understandably nervous about going back to the theatre, but it was helpful for everyone to tell their own version of events surrounding the bomb going off. Some suffered damage to their cars; many were stranded for hours; two of the chorus ladies had been standing together on a half-landing when the explosion happened, one was blown down the stairs and the other up to the top of the flight. Nearly everyone suffered several days of slight hearing loss, but there was no doubt we got off lightly. We later learned that the bomb had been placed outside the Courts of Law across the street from the Opera House Stage Door and that was the target of the IRA bombers, rather than the D'Oyly Carte. However, very few who experienced that awful night will ever believe other than the IRA was trying to kill two birds with one stone.

Thankfully, most distractions or disruptions in a performance were not of such a serious nature and many were hugely funny. One favourite D'Oyly Carte anecdote tells of the time in the Act Two Finale of *The Gondoliers* when Beti Lloyd-Jones, playing 'Inez', was just about to reveal the name of the real 'King of Barataria'. It was a Saturday night and the wardrobe ladies, Cis Blain and Florrie Ewbank, were busy packing costumes in the fly gallery above the stage where the skips were stored. Beti had got as far as 'I called him son with pardonable slyness, his name …' when she made her usual dramatic pause before proclaiming the king's identity. At that very moment, a cry of "Flo!" rang out from on high before Beti could sing 'Luiz'. By the time she did complete the story, everyone on the stage was in fits of laughter and the rather odd name for a king was not lost on the audience. That was not the only amusing incident to happen to Beti as 'Inez'. She once started the recitative an octave too high and, being no soprano, ended up having to speak the name of the king.

Any live show can expect the unexpected and falling when on the stage is about as humiliating as it gets. In real life, a fall or stumble in public is embarrassing enough, but how much more so in front of an audience? Character credibility is hard to sustain when flat out on the stage, but it did occasionally happen to unlucky D'Oyly Carte performers. Barbara Lilley still feels the excruciating embarrassment of going flying during the second act finale of *Princess Ida*. Playing the title role, she was required to run up a flight of steps to a prominent position at the back of the stage and boldly defy the threats of 'King Hildebrand'. Although she lifted the front of her long gown, she still managed to miss her footing and went sprawling. With very little time before she had to sing, it was a scramble to regain composure and compromised dignity, but she has never forgotten the ignominy of that moment, which was not helped by the chuckles of her colleagues.

A well-known danger point for new recruits to the men's chorus was the entrance of the Dragoon Guards in Act One of *Patience*, the rumbustious military music needing them to enter at a quick march. Trained to keep their feet slightly apart in order to avoid locking their spurs, there was still the occasional mishap when a newcomer forgot the instruction, particularly when having to move in circular formation around the stage. One poor chap, resplendent in his scarlet tunic and shining, plumed helmet, proudly marched on and immediately caught his spurs together. They were locked solid, so he had nowhere to go but flat on his face, leaving the men following behind either piled on top of him, or struggling to jump over his prone figure. He finally managed to get to his feet and take his place in the line, but how terrible he must have felt. His consolation had to be that, although everyone in the company knew who had caused the pile-up, the large moustache he sported and the helmet pulled down to the bridge of his nose at least meant nobody in the audience knew the identity of the Dragoon lying in a heap on the stage. It was a favourite pastime of Wig Mistress, Heather Perkins, to stand in the wings and watch the new recruits trying to keep their spurs apart and she certainly got value for money that night.

Another performer to take a tumble was Kenneth Sandford, but his fall did not take place on the stage. During the D'Oyly Carte's final visit to the Theatre Royal in Norwich in 1981, Ken was playing 'Wilfred Shadbolt' to Lorraine Daniels' 'Phoebe' in *The Yeomen of the Guard*. As usual, he built up a head of speed when chasing her off the stage after she had slapped his face in the dialogue scene with 'Sergeant Meryll' late in the second act. Ken always slowed his momentum by running, hands outstretched, into the theatre wall in the wings but on this occasion, the wall turned out to be an emergency exit. Crashing into it, the doors flew open and he fell headlong into a large puddle of rain water in a car park! With only a couple of minutes before he had to re-enter, Lorraine hauled him to his feet and dusted him down as best she could, just in time for them to go on for the Act Two Finale. The audience, not to say most of his colleagues, must have wondered why he had gone off bone dry and immediately come back on soaking wet. It was one of Ken's fondest memories and he dined out on the story for many years.

Scenery, such an integral part of any live theatre performance, was occasionally the cause of problems for cast members and there are several amusing stories relating to parts of the set collapsing, luckily, without causing injury to those on the stage. In the 1950s, the second act of *Pirates*, which is set in a ruined chapel, had just got under way when one of the free-standing columns towards the back of the stage toppled over, narrowly missing the ladies of the chorus grouped around the 'Major-General', played by Peter Pratt. Realising that it was blocking the entrance soon to be used by the 'Sergeant of Police' and his trusty cohorts, Peter whispered to the girls to get it off the stage, so the audience was treated to the hilarious sight of two slips of girls each putting one end of the enormous 'masonry' pillar under their arm and marching into the wings with it! Apparently, the stage-hands didn't hurry to relieve them of their burden because they thought it was part of the stage business. Cynthia Morey recalls that during the later scene, in which the 'Pirate King' and 'Ruth' were supposed to hide from 'Frederic' behind two of the columns, Daryll Fancourt went to his usual place of concealment behind the missing piece of scenery and stood in full view of the audience. Rather than finding somewhere else to hide, the habit of over thirty years must have kicked in, because he made no attempt to use his initiative and give the moment credibility. Doubtless, the audience saw the funny side of it, but it was astonishing that such an experienced principal did not think to hide behind a flat, or even 'Ruth', played by Ann Drummond- Grant, who was behind another pillar.

Also in the 1950s, during a season at Oxford, Alan Barrett remembers the weather turning very hot so, during a performance of *The Gondoliers*, the Stage Manager made the decision to open all the doors under the stage to create a flow of cool air. Unfortunately, just as the 'Cachuca' was about to be danced in the second act, a breeze got up, causing the beautiful black and white checked stagecloth to inflate like a balloon, leaving the helpless cast trying to dance on what resembled an impromptu trampoline! Some twenty years later, three chorus tenors found themselves in something of a scenery pickle, as Edwin Rolles explains.

"I remember a performance of *Ruddigore* when, I imagine, apprentice stage-hands must have assembled the set. In Act Two, when the ghosts appear, Jeff Cresswell, Barry Clark and I could not get the doors of the picture frames to open and, when we eventually did, they almost fell off their hinges with a terrible banging noise. During the whole time we were onstage, the three of us had to hold up the scenery for fear of it crashing down on us. Goodness knows what the audience must have thought!"

That was bad enough, but one must feel sympathy for Alan Spencer who, along with Michael Buchan, was a guard to 'Katisha' in *The Mikado*. During one performance, Alan ran on for the finale of Act One followed by Mike, when two four-foot platforms, which were built side by side, split apart and Alan disappeared down the gap between them! Fortunately, there was enough room for Mike and Patricia Leonard, as 'Katisha', to skirt around the yawning chasm and rush down to the front of the stage. Meanwhile, poor Alan managed to clamber out, but his hat had gone in one direction and his wig in another, whilst his spear, which had bounced off one of the platforms, had broken in two. As Mike stood taking solo guard duties, Alan collected together his bits and pieces and resumed his place holding just the shaft of the spear, not a little embarrassed by what had happened. Mike remembers them exchanging a quick glance, which was enough to send both of them into fits of laughter, along with the rest of the cast, who could not believe what had just happened. Throughout the pandemonium, the supremely professional Trish Leonard kept in character and did her best to restore credibility to the drama against all the odds. Mike says that, at one point, she turned upstage and glared at her two quivering guards with a deadly expression, setting them off again, to the point where Mike had to run from the stage in danger of having an accident, leaving 'Katisha' in the charge of a dishevelled minder with no point on his spear! Even relating the story, Mike was howling with laughter and rating it his favourite D'Oyly Carte memory although, as the next story shows, he and Alan seemed to attract trouble when put together.

The company was playing a season in Leeds, the Grand Theatre having a backstage bar which attracted the chorus during any lengthy breaks in the performance. Accessed by a narrow spiral staircase, it was a pleasant place to sit and had a tannoy to alert them to their next entrance. For some reason, a small group of chorus men, which included Alan, Mike, Barry Clark and Edwin Rolles, missed the call for 'The Mikado's Entrance' whilst enjoying a chat and a quiet pint. When they heard the familiar music drifting from the speaker on the wall, there was panic, but it took them an age to negotiate the twisting staircase at the top of the building, as well as the several flights of regular stairs below it. By the time they reached the stage, the rest of the chorus was lustily singing, minus two tenors. John Ayldon and Patricia Leonard, as 'The Mikado' and 'Katisha', had to make their appearance without two of their retinue, who eventually made an entrance carrying the royal banners long after John and Trish were seated. Eddie Rolles and Barry Clark managed to sidle into position, downstage right, but Eddie had not been able to find his wig in the rush for the stage, so he was sporting a tall hat that was far too big without the false hair to pad it out. Throughout the scene, it slipped, wobbled and waved about as Eddie did his best to adjust his head position to keep the hat from slipping down over his face, or falling off, much to the amusement of Mike and Alan, who had a bird's-eye view of his dilemma from their position at the back of the stage. Doubtless, they were all a little more careful the next time they popped up to the bar for a swift half.

Almost losing a hat was one of the more minor examples of 'costume malfunction' that beset many a D'Oyly Carte performer. There is much to think about during the course of a show, but costume problems are the last thing a performer expects. If, however, something untoward does happen, it can be distracting at best and, at worst, disastrous. There are lots of stories of elastic in bloomers breaking during *Pirates*, the simplest solution being to step out of them and chuck them offstage. On a couple of occasions, bloomers which had been thrown in the general direction of the wings failed to clear the scenery rocks and, much to everyone's amusement, lodged there waving like a flag of surrender until the interval, but these were minor matters which caused little more than amusement for cast and audience. Some moments of costume embarrassment were self-inflicted as Susan Jackson remembers only too well.

During a performance of *Ruddigore*, in which she was playing 'Rose Maybud', she went on for the first act 'apple' scene with 'Mad Margaret' and wondered why Peggy Ann Jones was staring at her costume with some confusion. It was then that she realised she was wearing the wedding dress she was supposed to wear for Act One Finale. Why she had made such a mistake and changed too soon, she had no idea, but it certainly made for interesting improvisation as she told Peggy that she thought an apple might make her feel better and that she had one, but couldn't find it! Susie remembers that the expression on Peggy's face was a picture as she made up a few words in response, before getting the dialogue back on track when she asked her the very apt question: 'Tell me, are you mad?'

According to Norman Wilfred Wright, chorus tenor, David Rayson, once made a big blunder when he managed to spill red wine on his white gondolier's trousers. Rather than face the terrifying wrath of Wardrobe Mistress, Flo Ewbank, he decided to go on for the first act wearing a pair of white *Iolanthe* tights which, he thought, would do the job. Unfortunately, his shirt was not long enough to cover his modesty, so he spent the first act hiding behind bits of scenery or handy cast members. He then took the trousers home to wash and press, so that Flo would never find out what he had done!

One of John Broad's favourite disaster moments happened to his pal, Howard Williamson, in the second act of *Ruddigore*. Howard was dressed in the red costume of a cardinal, which was featured in one of the portraits in the ancestral gallery. At the end of the 'ghost scene', the men had to move upstage in the direction of their frames, but Howard's cassock was very long and he began to 'walk up' the front of it as he went. By the time he was near his frame, he could hardly move and the last attempt to mount the small step in front of it proved fatal. Unable to lift the costume away from his feet, he fell and crashed through the door of his portrait, ending up flat out with just his shoes protruding onto the stage! John reckons it was one of the funniest things he has ever seen and it certainly goes to show that managing a full-length costume is never easy.

Audiences rarely appreciate how difficult, awkward and cumbersome theatrical costumes can be, or how long it can take for a costume to fit comfortably into a performance. Getting used to the physical restrictions some costumes present, particularly for ladies, is something professional performers deal with on a regular basis and it can take time to become used to working when swathed in period costume. The D'Oyly Carte Opera Company, quite rightly, prided itself on the authenticity of its costumes; everything, including undergarments for the ladies, was correct for the period and learning to manage crinolines, bustles and bone stays was something every new company lady had to do. The Osbert Lancaster costumes for the 1971 production of *The Sorcerer* were gloriously colourful, but some of the ladies' dresses were very uncomfortable and inhibited easy movement. The outfits for the three old women, for example, had a corset built into the crinoline, over which was a thick woollen dress, topped off by a large shawl, also made of wool, so kicking up heels was a tricky, not to say hot and bothersome, task. If it was bad enough wearing them on the stage, imagine having to visit the toilet when encumbered by such garments.

The voluminous blue and white-striped dress worn by 'Aline' in Act One needed an enormous crinoline underneath it which stuck out at the sides and caused problems for every incumbent of the role because, once dressed, a visit to the loo was a nightmare. On her return to the company in February of 1982, Pamela Field was very nervous before her debut in the part and was unable to put off the need to go to the loo before she went on. Unfortunately, after managing to lift the huge costume, returning the crinoline to its proper position proved impossible and her struggles resulted in it twisting ninety degrees, with the side panniers sticking out front and back as if she was in a pantomime horse costume! Running out of time before her first entrance, she looked in vain for someone to help and it was only by the skin of her teeth that she managed to right the crin in time to go on. It was an experience she found very unnerving. Her predecessor as 'Aline', Barbara Lilley, developed a technique for getting round the problem by entering the toilet cubicle sideways before lifting the crin, then reversing the process on the way out. If only audiences had known what went on behind the scenes in the cause of art, theatrical magic would have been non-existent.

Similarly, wearing a full suit of armour was not easy, so a visit to the bathroom prior to getting dressed was essential for the three sons of 'King Gama' in *Princess Ida*. Having put on the mock chain mail suits in the dressing room, the boys put on the armour in the wings, where each set was laid out on a blanket, to be strapped on by their dressers one piece at a time, hopefully without loud clanking noises. The metal suits were very heavy to wear, so it was a source of much amusement to company members that two of the 'three hulking brothers' were played for some years by lightweights, Jon Ellison and James Conroy-Ward.

Iolanthe was prone to more than its fair share of costume malfunctions, particularly in the 1977 Queen's Silver Jubilee production. Bruno Santini's controversial black and silver fairy dresses were made from a thin material covered in prickly silver lurex thread, which acted as a magnet for any nether garment hung over the back of a chair in the dressing room and there are several instances of bras making unscheduled appearances. In one of the earliest performances of the new production, the 'Queen of the Fairies', Patricia Leonard, emulated her great forbear, Ann Drummond-Grant, by making her first entrance with such a garment hanging from her wings. Trish was unaware of this and did not notice the bra being deftly removed by the nearest fairy and spirited offstage. In the same production, the title role was played by Lorraine Daniels, whose first entrance brought her downstage over a wooden bridge. The beautiful, sparkling turquoise cloak she had to wear frequently got caught as she made her way to the front and on one occasion, she heard the smothered giggles of the chorus fairies behind her, who were the first to spot the wire coat hanger adorning the back of the long cloak. Fortunately, 'Celia', played by Suzanne O'Keeffe and 'Leila', Hélène Witcombe, were required to take the cloak into the wings, so they were able to take the coat hanger with it.

Santini's designs may have been striking and imaginative, but they were certainly not user-friendly. The dresses had individually designed decorations of silver balls, leaves and flowers around the neckline of the bodice which were horribly uncomfortable and scratchy, as were the matching chokers worn at the neck. The latter, secured with velcro, had a tendency to fall off at any given moment, but the most irritating bit of the glittering costume was the synthetic black wig, set solid with silver spray paint and topped with a spiky crown. Madeleine 'Caroline' Hudson and Patricia Anne Bennett once came to grief during the opening chorus, their crowns locking together as they danced round at the front of the stage. Much pulling, tugging and swearing under the breath did little to separate the pair, who resembled a couple of battling stags! They eventually prised themselves apart as the other fairies continued to dance around them. Patricia, who played 'Fleta', certainly had her share of problems in that production. On another occasion, she managed to kick off both of her silver shoes whilst dancing, to reveal two big toes protruding through holes in her socks. Maybe the audience did not notice, but it certainly made the fairies giggle. Thereafter, the cheap shoes were fitted with silver elastic to stop them flying off. Given the company's history of having the finest quality costumes, it is unlikely that the dresses made for the fairies in the Santini production would have lasted more than a few seasons and, sadly, that is all they were needed to do.

Having to face the wrath of the Wardrobe Mistress if a costume was accidentally damaged was something that every company member dreaded; a ticking off from the likes of Cis Blain or Flo Ewbank was to be avoided at all costs. Kenneth Sandford, despite his stature in the D'Oyly Carte, was not a little scared of the fearsome Flo and too embarrassed to mention that, during a performance of *Iolanthe*, he had put the bearskin helmet he wore as 'Private Willis' on its stand too close to the bulbs around the mirror in his dressing room. Oblivious to this until he smelled burning, Ken used nail scissors to cut out the singed fur and trimmed the surrounding area in the hope that the result of his carelessness would not be noticed! He must have done a good job, because he wore the slimmer version without comment until the day the company closed.

Sometimes, costume problems were not so much down to mishap as to the physical appearance of the wearer. One tenor understudy to 'Frederic', in *Pirates*, was a rather portly chap and, although the costume fitted him, he looked rather ridiculous in the part of a romantic young pirate, with all the ladies feeling embarrassed for him rather than swooning over his beauty. This begs the question, why was he given the cover in the first place? Principal contralto, Gillian Knight, was a tall, slim young woman of twenty-four when she joined the company in 1959 and not the ideal build for the 'dame' roles, as she explains.

"There were, of course, obvious difficulties to overcome. I was eight stone thirteen pounds and had to be padded all over for forty-eight weeks of the year. That worked for the body, but the long neck and thin arms were a problem. When we went to the USA, I remember one reviewer saying that, as 'Little Buttercup', I looked just like Popeye's girlfriend, Olive Oyl. So true. People might not know that the design of the 'Fairy Queen' costume changed during my time and long sleeves were added." One might well ask why someone so young, slim and pretty should be chosen by the D'Oyly Carte management to replace Ann Drummond-Grant in the 'old lady' roles when she did not have the right physical attributes? The answer is, she was available at short notice to replace the ailing Ann but, more importantly, she had a magnificent voice.

Of all the potential problems that could befall the unsuspecting performer, being carried off the stage in the middle of a scene applies, probably uniquely, to Pamela Field. Unusually for the D'Oyly Carte, supernumeraries, remembered by company members to be Shakespearean actors, had been recruited to play guards to the 'Lieutenant of the Tower' in *The Yeomen of the Guard* at Stratford-upon-Avon. Pam was playing 'Elsie Maynard' and had been tussling with the angry citizens after her Act One duet with 'Jack Point', when the 'Lieutenant' came on to investigate the rumpus. At his instruction to clear the chorus from the stage, the supers, whose rehearsal time had been minimal to non-existent, included Pam and one of them started to roughly steer her towards the wings. Her plea to be unhanded, as she had to stay on for dialogue, fell on deaf ears; the more she protested, the more he thought she was acting and responded by upping his own performance, finally bundling her offstage in Oscar-winning style. There was only a slight delay before she could extricate herself from his grip to get back on for the next scene with the 'Lieutenant', but Pam recalls it being a strange experience.

Things going wrong during a performance were, on rare occasions, due to a problem behind the scenes and performers needed to be inventive enough to cope with anything thrown at them. At the beginning of one performance of *Pirates*, the curtain stuck a few feet into its ascent, leaving the audience with a great view of the pirates' legs as they rollicked around the stage. Jon Ellison, playing 'Samuel', decided the best thing he could do was to duck down, poke his head under the curtain and sing his solo bent almost double. In true 'the show must go on' fashion, the cast continued as if nothing had happened until the problem was fixed and the curtain finally ascended to an ironic cheer from the audience. 'Elli' was notorious as a prankster, but he was, in truth, a great professional. Despite the awful things he sometimes added to the spaghetti for John Reed to find, he was excellent at adapting to an unexpected situation. Peter Riley recalls an occasion in *Gondoliers* when the company's Props Master went out to collect hot pasta from a local Italian restaurant and came back far too late for it to be of any use. One of the stage crew generously volunteered his stale ham sandwich to the cause and Peter put it into the spaghetti tureen for Elli, as the waiter, to take on. With great panache, he went to John Reed, removed the lid with a flourish and waited whist a taken-aback John held up the dog-eared delicacy. There followed an improvised routine during which John angrily rejected the offending sandwich and Elli feigned offence as he was waved away. For the next few minutes, Reedy, who should have been munching pasta, had to make up suitable business until Ken Sandford, as 'Don Alhambra', had finished his song.

A few years later, the same Props Master caused another problem in the spaghetti scene. One of the white wrought iron chairs set around the cafe table had become rather wonky, so he tried to stabilise it with wire. Embarrassingly, the not inconsiderable frame of Kenneth Sandford proved too much for the repaired chair, which collapsed under him. Ken instinctively reached forward to grab the table to stop himself falling to the floor, but this sent the tureen of pasta flying, its contents spilling across the stage. Guy Matthews, who had inherited the role of the waiter when Jon Ellison left the company in 1979, remembers Jimmie Marsland, in something of a flap in the wings, saying, "You're the only one who can go on; get a brush and clean it up." Guy did as he was told, sweeping up the strands of spaghetti as the scene progressed around him, finally exiting to a round of applause from an appreciative audience. Neither of these mishaps were great disasters, but they provide an illustration of the adaptability of D'Oyly Carte performers when called upon to save a scene if something went wrong.

The causes of unexpected chaos on the D'Oyly Carte stage were many and varied and they left a wonderful array of personal stories, but there is one which stands out as the ultimate in the embarrassment stakes. In the late 1970s, Stage Manager, Ken Robertson-Scott, played the role of the 'Headsman' in *The Yeomen of the Guard*. Tall and strongly-built, he was ideally cast as the executioner ready to dispatch 'Colonel Fairfax' in the first act finale. After processing solemnly to the block with the axe held in front of his masked face, Ken was required to swing it menacingly back and forth before slamming the sharp tip hard down into the block, a position to be held until the curtain fell at the end of the act. After convincingly carrying out this duty for scores of performances, the day came when, to his utter dismay, he swung the axe, aimed it at the block, but missed, resulting in it slipping from his grasp and careering down to the front of the stage, where it stopped just short of 'Elsie Maynard'. Our macho hero's immediate reaction was to cover his face with his hands as if he was about to burst into tears! His next move was to retrieve the recalcitrant axe and return to his position, but it was too late, the credibility of the dramatic moment had gone and the cast found it impossible to contain their mirth. Poor Ken! It was such a long time to have to stand and contemplate his wish for the stage to open up and swallow him. Naturally, everyone felt for him, but it took a long time for him to get over such excruciating embarrassment. He remembers dreading the next *Yeomen* and doing the same thing again, but he was fine after that. He can now laugh about it and is only too happy to relate the story of his extraordinary humiliation. Given the number of potential banana skins for performers during the course of a show, it says much about the professionalism of the D'Oyly Carte artistes that the vast majority of them passed without a hitch.

CHAPTER EIGHT

BY ROYAL COMMAND

The yearly routine of the D'Oyly Carte Opera Company was predictable and, sometimes, lacking in variety for its performers, so any diversion from the norm, such as an overseas tour, making a recording, or taking part in a performance attended by royalty, was always welcome to keep everyone motivated. From the earliest times of the company, the popularity of the Savoy Operas was not lost on the monarchy; Gilbert and Sullivan was hugely popular across every social class, from the poorest folk to the Royal Family. Everyone loved to whistle Sullivan's popular tunes and chuckle at Gilbert's cutting satire, so much so that, in 1891, Queen Victoria requested two Royal Command performances, *The Gondoliers* at Windsor Castle and *The Mikado* at Balmoral. Following the performance at Windsor, the Queen made an entry in her personal diary.

"The music, which I know and am fond of, is quite charming throughout and was well acted and sung ... Afterwards, I spoke to Mr. D'Oyly Carte and complimented him. We then went to the Drawing

Room, into which all the company came... Everybody was much pleased."

In 1975, during the company's centenary season at its spiritual home, the Savoy Theatre in London, Her Majesty, Queen Elizabeth II, was scheduled to attend a performance of *The Gondoliers*, a fitting honour for the D'Oyly Carte to top off the celebrations to mark its one hundred years presenting the Savoy Operas of Gilbert and Sullivan. Unfortunately, just before the show, it was announced that she was indisposed, much to the great disappointment of the company, The Duke of Edinburgh instead being accompanied by their son, Prince Andrew. Her Majesty did, however, attend a performance of the new production of *Iolanthe* at Sadler's Wells Theatre during her Silver Jubilee celebrations in 1977, the premiere of which had been attended by The Duke of Gloucester. Such occasions always brought great excitement for the company, particularly the principals, who knew they were likely to be introduced to the royal party. The protocol for deciding who would be included in the line-up for presentation started with a list being submitted to Buckingham Palace for consideration, as Peter Riley explains.

"The D'Oyly Carte management would send along the names of those they wished to be presented after the performance and wait for a response. If there were, for example, twenty names on the list, they would expect a counter offer acceptable to the Palace. I remember the list of names Savoy Hill submitted for consideration for the Queen's visit to the Savoy Theatre in the company's centenary season. Seeing such people as the London Wardrobe Mistress, the assistant to Albert Truelove and Secretary to Frederic Lloyd included, I felt it was management heavy and made my opinion known. I pointed out that the royal visitors would wish to meet the performers rather than second tier managerial staff and suggested that two representatives from the male and two from the female chorus should be included. I was told that behind-the-scenes staff all played their part in the performance and were worthy of presentation, but I didn't agree." As it turned out, the chorus was allowed to line the backstage staircases and got a bird's-eye view of the royal party leaving after the performance of *The Gondoliers*, but the disappointment of the Queen not being well enough to attend was keenly felt by all.

During his twenty-five-year D'Oyly Carte career, principal baritone, Kenneth Sandford, was presented to members of the Royal Family on many occasions, but there was one encounter which stuck in his memory, when the teenaged Prince Charles asked him a question to which he got an answer that left him bemused. It was at a time when the young Prince was interested in the theatre and, after he had attended a company performance, he complimented Ken on his make-up, which seemed to fascinate him. He then asked Ken what he used to remove the greasepaint. When Ken replied, "Trex, Sir" the Prince looked blank and eventually said, "What's Trex?" Trying to explain to a future king, who had probably never seen the inside of a kitchen, that it was a cooking fat used to make pastry was an unusual experience, to say the least, and it was received with: "I see, that's ... er, absolutely fascinating." Ever the thrifty Yorkshireman, Ken did not mention that it was cheaper than buying Crowe's Cremine, the make-up remover of choice. When Prince Charles was even younger he made a visit to the Savoy Theatre to see *The Mikado*, which Gillian Knight remembers with much amusement.

"The Prince was around eleven years old when he came to see us in *Mikado*. After the show, he asked to go backstage to meet John Reed, who was playing 'Ko-Ko'. In John's dressing room, he asked if 'Katisha' was really that ugly and John must have asked him if he'd like to find out, so I was asked to go to John's room. Because I was still very young, my make-up was heavy and rather fearsome to help cover my age. It was a very relieved young prince who met me without all the greasepaint, but I do recall him blushing when he saw my youthful appearance!"

Sometimes, members of the Royal Family made a private visit to see the D'Oyly Carte, when there was no official recognition of their presence. Princess Alice of Athlone was occasionally known to attend performances in London, always paying for her tickets. Commoners might imagine such low-key trips to the theatre were a welcome change from the inevitable formalities required during official visits. HRH Queen Elizabeth, the Queen Mother, was a personal friend of the famous rose growers, Alec and Anne Cocker, who lived near Aberdeen and she formally attended a performance with them at His Majesty's Theatre in the Granite City during a company tour of Scotland in the 1970s. Although appearing in the Court Circular as an official engagement, the atmosphere was relaxed and the performance must have seemed like a pleasant evening out with friends for the Queen Mother, after which she attended a party hosted by the Cockers, to which the cast was also invited. For them, it was such events, however infrequent, that relieved the inevitable tedium of eight performances every week when away from home. However, such royal encounters paled into insignificance when it was announced to the company that the Queen had commanded a performance of *HMS Pinafore* to be given at Windsor Castle on Thursday, June 16th, 1977, as part of her Silver Jubilee celebrations. The feverish excitement was almost tangible and dressing room conversation was of little else, although the logistics of making it happen passed them by; that onerous responsibility was to fall squarely on the shoulders of Peter Riley.

The first Peter knew about it was when he received a phone call from Joan Robertson, the secretary to the company's General Manager, Frederic Lloyd, while the company was playing in Wolverhampton. This, in itself, was unusual and he was intrigued when she asked him what he had planned for the following day. He told her that he would be doing his usual jobs, supervising set construction and lighting. His curiosity was further piqued when she said, "Oh no you won't. You will be going to the highest castle in the land." Catching on to her cryptic humour, he responded with, "But that's Windsor, where the court is." Obviously enjoying playing him along, Joan then told him he must be at The Savoy Hotel at 8.30am the following morning ready to be taken to Windsor Castle and that all would be explained when he got there. Not knowing what to make of all this, Peter rang the railway station and found that, by taking a very early train, he could be in London in time for his appointment. On arrival at The Savoy, he was met by Frederic Lloyd and Sir James Hanson, one of the D'Oyly Carte Trustees, and they were immediately whisked off in Sir James' Rolls Royce, to be waved through the gates of the castle with no question asked as to the nature of their business. They were expected. Much later on, Peter learned that another company trustee, the former Prime Minister, Sir Harold Wilson, in conjunction with Sir James, had been instrumental in the invitation for the company to give the Royal Command Performance.

Once they were seated in the office of Sir Peter Ashmore, the Master of the Royal Household, all became clear to Peter when he was told that Her Majesty wished the company to give a performance of one of the operas at the castle. Introduced by Freddy Lloyd as the man with the technical know-how, Peter, still reeling from the shock, ventured to ask where in the castle the performance would be staged. He was immediately escorted by Major Nash, the Superintendent of the Castle and Head of Works and Maintenance, to the Waterloo Chamber. The historic room, resplendent with huge portraits, crystal chandeliers and Grinling Gibbons carvings left him open-mouthed and struggling to take in his surroundings, but on the long walk back to the Master of the Household's office, Peter's professional instincts kicked in. The first thing that became apparent to him was that there were only two shows that could be considered, *HMS Pinafore* and *Patience*. If a stage was going to be built in such a restricted space, there would be no way that scenery could be stored ready to change for a second act, so a standing set was the only option. *The Sorcerer* was not a contender, because its set was far too big. Explaining this to Sir Peter Ashmore, he was politely, but firmly, told that it was not so much what the D'Oyly Carte was prepared to do but, rather, what the Queen wanted them to do. Peter's response was to ask a favour: "Do you think you could possibly try and persuade Her Majesty that she would like us to do *HMS Pinafore*?" The Master's diplomatic skills must have been something special because, a few days later, much to his relief, Peter got a phone call to say that the Queen would very much like the company to perform *HMS Pinafore*.

That decision made, there was no time to be lost. The logistics of making such a prestigious performance happen in just a few weeks would involve a huge amount of planning, from getting a stage constructed; hiring drapes and lighting; planning transport for every aspect of the operation; contracting specialist firms and booking accommodation, to liaising between the Savoy Hill management and The Master of the Household. At least the scenery was not going to be a problem. After the filming of *Pinafore* for television in 1973, Peter offered ATV, the company which produced the film, £250 for the set which it had specially built. A replica of the D'Oyly Carte's usual set, it was slightly smaller and would be ideal for the restricted stage area

193

in the Waterloo Chamber, so Peter buying it proved to be a stroke of genius: he always thought it might come in handy one day!

The most important thing on the technical side was the building of a stage and false proscenium to house the set, but Sir James Hanson seemed to have the answer. As owner of Trident Television, he promised Peter the services of the company's set builders and carpenters; in fact, anything he needed to get the job done. However, when Peter met Trident's Master Carpenter at Windsor, he was in for a shock: there was no way Sir James' man would take the risk of damaging any of the priceless artefacts in the Waterloo Chamber and that was that. Back to square one, Peter contacted the BBC and received the same response. Other contacts also proved fruitless. By now getting concerned, he was flicking through the pages of an old trade catalogue, when he came across a company called Showex, whose advert bellowed out: "We build anything anywhere!" Wasting no time, he rang them.

"Can you build a stage inside Windsor Castle? Are you insured? Can you meet me at Windsor tomorrow morning at nine?" All questions answered in the affirmative, Peter felt they were worth a try and his trust was not misplaced. The following morning, after Peter had sought authority for them to be admitted, two Showex surveyors met Peter at the castle and they were confident of doing a good job, with only one real concern, the safety of the priceless portraits adorning the walls at the end of the chamber where the stage would be built. With scaffolding poles swinging around, there was danger of the paintings being damaged. They asked if it would be possible for them to be taken down, so Peter consulted the Master of the Household and was told that the frames could not be moved, but the canvases could be taken out. Later on, as the portraits were removed for set construction, Peter had the shock of his life when he saw pantomime characters painted underneath! Cinderella, Prince Charming, Aladdin and Dick Whittington, amongst others, stared down on the delighted crew. Painted for the young princesses, Elizabeth and Margaret, on the instruction of their father, King George VI, they made a fine setting for the Royal Family's Christmas pantomimes and the great works of art they replaced were kept safely stored away during the Second World War.

With the construction of the stage and false proscenium in hand, Peter turned his attention to organising the drapes and a curtain track, called a 'traveller', a simple system allowing the smooth in-and-out action of the curtains. The D'Oyly Carte did not own anything suitable, so he made several enquiries and settled on a company called Rex Howard Ltd., based in West London. However, Howards required the drapes, curtain track, legs and borders they were supplying to be insured, which Peter had to arrange through a specialist theatrical insurer and that was another job ticked off the lengthy list of things to do. He knew that the usual *HMS Pinafore* backcloth was too large for Windsor and remembered that, in the company's London stores, there was a cloth that would be ideal. Exactly the same as the one the company normally used, except for its length, the shorter version would perfectly fit the set to be used at Windsor. A phone call to Jim Murray in the stores was all that was needed to get both set and cloth sorted out, although Jim was more than a little apprehensive about the logistics of the operation as can be seen in the following short extract of a letter to him from Peter.

"I shall be down next week and we can discuss things in greater detail then, so don't panic yet! It may not be as bad as it looks; this is why I want to see you and talk about it in detail." Only the ship's wheel, hatch and binnacle would need to be taken from Brighton, where the company would be appearing, to Windsor. Getting them back in time for the company to perform the same show at the Theatre Royal the following night would be another matter, but the same applied to costumes, wigs and props, which would have to be prepared in advance to go on a special van two days ahead of the performance. Transport to and from Brighton for everyone involved in the Royal Command Performance was another of the complicated tasks to be organised. A firm called Limebourne Ltd. in Battersea was Peter's final choice, because its coaches were equipped with radio communication, which would be important in the event of an emergency. Two coaches were hired to carry the seventy-seven company members involved in the performance. The first, carrying the staff would leave at 1.30pm, giving time for the setting out of costumes, wigs and props. The cast and orchestra would leave two hours later. That, of course, was on the day of the performance; transporting the necessary workers between Windsor and the stores in South London to load and unload the set would be carried out the day before and reversed the day after the performance. Precise timing would be essential, so Peter drew up a schedule, making sure that it was passed on to the Castle authorities, along with all relevant vehicle registration numbers. There was one more important technical consideration; the performance could not go ahead without proper lighting and Peter brought in his friend, Robin Barnes, to organise this. Robin owned a theatrical lighting business, so he was the ideal man to set up the construction of a lighting rig and bring in all the necessary lamps and cabling.

It being impossible for Peter to deal with every detail of the operation, Sir James Hanson promised practical help, which came in the form of Kenneth Osborne, one of Sir James' associates in the Hanson Trust, who provided invaluable assistance in taking responsibility for everything other than the theatrical side of the performance, including public relations, the press and outside guests, in liaison with Sir Peter Ashmore. Another matter to be addressed was the cancellation of the scheduled Brighton performance, which had to be squared with the manager of the Theatre Royal and financial compensation agreed. All correspondence concerning the Royal Command Performance was circulated between The Master of the Queen's Household, Peter Riley, the D'Oyly Carte's General Manager, Frederic Lloyd, and Kenneth Osborne, so everyone knew what was happening. One thing that quickly became clear was the cost of mounting such a huge operation and discussions with Sir Peter Ashmore helped establish who was to pay for what, as may be seen in an extract from a letter to Peter Riley and Frederic Lloyd from Kenneth Osborne.

"It was agreed that all the catering costs including the cast and supporting staff would be the responsibility of Her Majesty. The cost of the stage assembly and payment of the cast and other support requirements would be to the D'Oyly Carte Opera Company." It is interesting that, in the same letter, Osborne comments on the Queen's opinion of the upcoming performance.

"Sir Peter Ashmore emphasized HM considered a command performance as her own private and personal party, but Sir Peter did agree that the Palace Press Office would prepare a special release in order to assist the D'Oyly Carte, in particular, for its 1978 tour of North America."

Sir James Hanson, who was a wealthy businessman, had generously offered to personally cover all the costs which fell to the D'Oyly Carte but, obviously, Peter needed to account for every penny to be spent, a task which needed a great deal of paperwork, as if he hadn't got enough to do! An itemised account for the cost of getting the scenery from the London stores to Windsor and back had to include meal costs, gratuities, fuel for vans, telephone calls, labour and Peter's own motoring expenses at 10 pence a mile. All this came to £722.25. Coaches to get the cast and staff to Windsor would cost £314; Robin Barnes quotation for providing the lighting rig, lamps and cabling and running the lighting console during the performance was £922 plus VAT at 8%. Showex quoted £2,600 plus VAT to 'supply, erect and finally dismantle Showex materials to form scaffolding, including protection to floor and carpet with hardboard'. Another expense was the accommodation required for cast and staff, so Peter used the D'Oyly Carte's connections with The Savoy Hotel to facilitate this, the Reception Manager, Mr. Versolato, being delegated to find a suitable hotel. In one of the many round robin letters to keep everyone informed of costing, Peter explains the arrangements.

"The accommodation for the company is not going to cost as much as I thought, as over half the company have decided to travel back to Brighton after the supper. Mr. Versolato has secured rooms for us at the Post House Hotel at Heathrow. He has obtained special rates of £18 for a twin-bedded room, £12 for a single room and these rates include bed, breakfast, service and VAT. The total cost should amount to £438, plus about £100 for our own staff requirements." However, with the company members not due back at the hotel until after 1am, Peter had to make special arrangements for a late breakfast at 10am. He was also expected to negotiate a complimentary suite for Frederic Lloyd and his wife. The financial outlay to cover every aspect of the Royal Command Performance was in excess of £10,000 and one can only wonder what it might cost nearly forty years later, but Peter had consistently advised his colleagues that only the best of everything should be considered for such a prestigious occasion.

Peter drew up a minute-by-minute schedule for the four days requiring the company to be at Windsor. A work of art in itself, it details the comings and goings between Savoy Hill, Brighton, Windsor, South London and Heathrow. It is worthy of reproduction to illustrate just how much work he put in to ensure a successful outcome to the operation.

PETER RILEY

Proposed schedule for Royal Command Performance

Contact addresses:-

        1. Windsor Castle,Windsor,Berkshire,SL4 1NJ.
           Tel.(from London) 95-68286
           Tel.(STD 07535) - 68286.

        2. The Post House Hotel,Sipson Road,West Drayton,Middlesex.
           Tel. 01-759-2323 (Telex 934280)

Tuesday,14th.June.

07.00.	Depart Brighton
09.00.	Arrive Windsor Castle
12.00.	Winston Hornby collect PR at Windsor and drive to Stores to collect crew
13.15.	Depart Stores
14.15.	Arrive Windsor with crew
14.30.	Commence get-in of scenery,wardrobe,props. and effects.
17.00.	Winston Hornby return crew to Stores.
	PR drive to Post House and check in.
17.45.	Meeting with Rodney Darwin at Post House re arrangements for Company check-in etc..
20.00.	Return to Windsor and observe progress of SHOWEX(SGB)
21.30.	Return to Post House

Wednesday,15th.June

07.00.	Depart Post House for Windsor.
07.30.	Arrive Windsor Castle.
09.00.	JBE arrive and get-in equipment.
	At Windsor all morning.
14.00.	Winston Hornby collect PR at Windsor and drive to Savoy.
15.30.	Depart Savoy - drive to Stores and collect crew.
16.00.	Depart Stores.
17.30.	Arrive Windsor - crew commence fit-up of drapes and set.
22.00.	Winston Hornby return crew to Stores.
	JBE continue fit-up - focus and light - all night session .

Thursday,16th.June

09.00.   Crew and Winston Hornby on stand-by for any alterations.

11.00.   Full technical run-through with JBE - run cues etc..

12.00.   Free for technical work.

15.30.   1st.company coach arrives - all staff on this coach - lay-out Wardrobe,pit,props.etc.

          Brief all staff on layout, and discuss operation of the performance.

17.30.   2nd. company coach arrives.

18.30.   Full Company assemble in the Waterloo Chamber for a briefing session.

18.45..   Rehearsal with company and orchestra.

20.00.   Refreshments provided by HM for everyone, prior to changing and making-up.

21.00.   Company and Orchestra change and make-up.

21.30.   Guests take their seats - orchestra file into pit.

21.40.   Royston Nash takes his place in the pit.

21.45.   The Queen enters - national anthem is played when she reaches her seat, performance commences.

22.35.   Interval - 3 minutes.

22.38.   Act 2 commences.

23.18.   Performance ends.

          Artists and staff being presented assemble in order outside the presentation chamber, in the Garter Throne Room.

23.25.   Presentations.

          Rest of company change during presentations.

23.40.   Supper commences.

Friday,17th.June

00.01.   Winston Hornby collect crew from Stores.

01.00.   Crew arrive Windsor-commence de-rig - strike set & all drapes.

02.00.   Radcliffe van in position for loading scenery - only Brighton scenery on this van.

10.30.   THEATRE ROYAL CREW unload van; van returns to Windsor.

14.00.   Crew load ATV set and drapes onto Radcliffe Van - drapes unload at Rex Howard, and scenery at Stores.

15.00.   Winston Hornby return crew to Stores.

          Showex de-rig.

Her Majesty having invited many distinguished guests, including prominent politicians and ambassadors, to join the extended Royal Family for the performance, security was going to be of vital importance. As mentioned earlier, the Irish Republican Army was in full cry in the 1970s and acts of terrorism were all too frequent, with Royalty and senior politicians a top target, as the Royal Family was to find out some two years later when one of their own, Earl Mountbatten of Burma, was murdered by the IRA. How poignant that he was to attend the D'Oyly Carte's Royal Command performance assured that measures would have been taken to ensure the safety of all the Queen's guests. A list of everyone who would be at the castle for the performance, right down to the coach driver bringing the company to Windsor, was required to be submitted to Sir Peter Ashmore before being passed on to the relevant authorities. Names, home addresses and length of service to the D'Oyly Carte were duly sent, but nobody involved had the slightest idea of the vetting process which, according to Peter, saw each individual involved checked out at the very highest level. With two hundred high profile guests due to attend the performance, no stone was left unturned to ensure their safety. Happily, all D'Oyly Carte personnel passed muster, but it is interesting that four company members, who had appeared as witnesses in court cases, were scrutinised with extra care.

It must be said that the timing of the Royal Command Performance was better suited to the Royal Family than the D'Oyly Carte. The day before the show, the Waterloo Chamber would be in use for a Garter Ceremony, so the company was left with just twenty-eight hours to make everything happen and Peter Riley knew full well that the Showex construction team, as well as the company's own technical staff, would have to work through the night if everything was to be ready in time. Hardly a straightforward build, Peter remembers he and the Showex foreman setting it up together in situ, on the basis of 'Let's see how we can do this'. The D'Oyly Carte's Master Carpenter, Paul Godman, would be responsible for overseeing the building of the set once the stage and false proscenium were constructed. One problem they encountered was how to get the backcloth into the chamber without causing damage. After much discussion it was decided the safest way to achieve this was to pass it in through an outside window.

Peter recalls an amusing encounter at around 2am, when the banging and hammering were going at full tilt. The unexpected appearance of Her Majesty and the Duke of Edinburgh caused work to cease and looks of amazement on the faces of the crew when the Prince enquired, "What's going on?" Peter explained that they were getting everything ready for the performance of HMS *Pinafore* the following evening. Having expressed interest in the nitty-gritty of the proceedings, Prince Philip then said, "Are they looking after you properly?" Peter assured him that the staff were taking very good care of them, whereupon the royal visitors marched out without another word. Having returned from an official engagement in the small hours, Peter concludes that the Queen and Prince Philip must have seen the lights in the Waterloo Chamber and heard all the noise, so had decided to investigate the cause of the din. It can only be hoped that the royal sleeping quarters were far enough away from the commotion to assure them of a good night's sleep!

Through the long and busy morning of June 16th, refreshments were provided to keep the exhausted workers going. By mid-afternoon, the D'Oyly Carte's wardrobe staff had arrived on the first coach to leave Brighton, along with the Wig Mistress, Property Master and all other staff, their effects having been brought to the castle two days earlier. The Garter Throne Room, situated near the Waterloo Chamber, had been turned into an extremely impressive dressing room, with beautiful screens separating male and female cast members. The recently-laid carpet, which had cost a fortune, was covered with sheets of plastic to protect it from the D'Oyly Carte horde. Rails were brought in so that costumes could be hung up ready for the performers. The orchestra was allocated a room nearby and the conductor, Royston Nash, would change with them. Trays of food and drink regularly appeared, brought in by footmen in full livery and this led to one of the best-remembered quotes from that glorious occasion. Props man, John Sammett, gawking at the finely-dressed flunkies was heard to say, "It's posh 'ere, innit? They cut the crusts off the sandwiches."

Given the frighteningly short time frame for such a complex operation it was, perhaps, inevitable that there would be a hitch, and it was a big one at that. The curtains had been hung on the traveller track but refused to open and close without jamming. Closer inspection revealed a problem with the mechanism, but it was not easy to fix and the start of the performance was too close for comfort. Frantic efforts were made to solve the problem, with a dinner-jacketed Peter Riley on top of the scaffolding trying to push the curtains along by hand in an effort to free the movement of the track. In the nick of time, the crew were fairly confident of having sorted out the problem, but Peter kept his fingers and toes crossed at the beginning and end of each act. Fortunately, the curtains opened and closed smoothly, avoiding any embarrassment, but it was a close call.

Elsewhere in the Waterloo Chamber, a covering had to be laid to protect the beautiful flooring from any damage that might be caused by the two hundred chairs needed for the Queen's guests, while a platform about a foot high was placed halfway back from the stage to seat the senior members of the Royal Family, giving them, of course, the best seats in the house. Fortunately for the company, the £2,000 cost for this fell to her Majesty. Florists were busy with the magnificent flower arrangements which separated the orchestra from the first row of the audience. Music stands were placed, their lights checked and music set out. By 5.30pm, the second coach had disgorged the excited cast and orchestra members, who had an hour to organise themselves in the dressing rooms before a briefing and short rehearsal. Ken Robertson-Scott remembers having to tell the company that they could not smoke in the state rooms, but they could go to the servants' bar if they wanted to have a cigarette. It was essential to have a rehearsal, because the restricted space on the set meant that some entrances and exits had to be changed. The company's Director of Productions, Leonard Osborn, oversaw the repositioning of the cast to allow for the smaller working area on the stage. A break for refreshments brought the time to get ready for the show at 8.45pm and excitement was at fever pitch.

Barbara Lilley, who was playing 'Josephine', says she was more excited than nervous, but regretted that, without her glasses, she was not going to be able to see any of the Royal Family. She also recalls the acoustics being dreadful, like singing under a blanket. Those of us in the chorus had the opportunity to glance out at the audience, but could see nothing. Suzanne O'Keeffe describes the blackness of the auditorium as "a dark void". Usually, from the stage, it is possible to make out people in the audience, but the restricted lighting over the Waterloo

Chamber made this impossible, something of a disappointment to say the least. With no overture, an interval of just three minutes and the Entr'acte cut, the performance of *HMS Pinafore* passed quickly with no mishaps and was over all too soon. It is fair to say that the response of the audience was polite rather than wildly enthusiastic: perhaps the presence of Queen Elizabeth and her family was too intimidating to encourage cheering!

After the final curtain call it was time for the presentations, but for the chorus, it was a case of being surplus to requirements. We were told to return to the dressing room. The agreed list of people to be presented to Her Majesty did not include any chorus representation, whilst D'Oyly Carte principals not taking part in the show were invited to meet the Royal Family. James Conroy-Ward, Geoffrey Shovelton, Jane Metcalfe and Julia Goss were amongst them, but Kenneth Sandford had chosen to stay at home to spend time with his family. Whereas the choristers understood that it was impossible for everyone to be presented, the disappointment of missing out was terrible. Surely it would have been right to include us in some way? It could have been arranged for us to be in the background to watch the proceedings. Going back to the dressing room to get changed without as much as a glimpse of the royal party felt like a collective slap in the face bordering on insult, the atmosphere only lightened by the amusing sight of flunkies bringing in valuable antique china jugs and bowls of hot water so we could get washed. Not being considered worthy of presentation that night spawned the acronym 'JBC', 'Just bloody chorus', which prevailed to the closure of the company.

For those lucky enough to meet the Royal Family, it was a wonderful moment. Dame Bridget D'Oyly Carte was, of course, there and she presented Her Majesty with a gold toast rack engraved with the company crest as a memento of the occasion. The D'Oyly Carte Trustees were present, including Sir James Hanson and Sir Harold Wilson, as was General Manager, Frederic Lloyd and his wife. In fact, all of the company's top brass were selected for presentation. Herbert Newby, the Business Manager was included, as was the Wig Mistress, Heather Perkins. Wardrobe Master and Mistress, John and Vera Carnegie were, quite rightly, included. Leonard Osborn, Jimmie Marsland and Royston Nash were presented along with the principals. Standing outside was Bert Newby's assistant, Gordon MacKenzie, a company stalwart of some twenty years, whose omission made him upset and angry when Savoy Hill staff had been included. What should have been the experience of a lifetime proved a bitter disappointment for those who felt that their contributions were not considered important enough for them to be in the same room as the Queen. It can be argued that such a slight was not intended, but that was how it felt at the time and it still rankles all these years later.

Inside the Grand Reception Room, John Ayldon was at the head of the presentation line and Guy Matthews, who was in the chorus, clearly remembers John telling him that Princess Margaret was making her way in singing 'For He Is An Englishman' at the top of her voice and then Prince Charles, at a nod from the Queen, leading her out again! Michael Buchan admits to having been very nervous about being presented and when asked by Prince Philip which part he had played, became rather garrulous, rambling on about being 'The Carpenter' and that the set would not have been built without him! Looking back, Mike still feels the embarrassment of making an idiot of himself and, in particular, catching the look the Queen cast in his direction. Her Majesty, of course, met everyone she had to, after which there was a general circulation, but Barbara Lilley says the Queen Mother was the star of the show, moving around the room to chat easily with as many people as possible, even addressing John Ayldon as 'Dickie Deadeye'. A vision in her pale lemon evening gown and glittering tiara, she charmed everyone. Peter Riley was standing next to Jimmie Marsland and he can remember Jimmie, who was always ready for a good natter, having a lengthy conversation with her as they had previously met at the Cockers' party in Aberdeen. Their chat went on for some time, so the Queen, who was waiting to leave the room, had to give her a less than subtle hint that she and Prince Philip needed to go. Both Barbara Lilley and James Conroy-Ward remember Her Majesty heading for the door before turning to say something along the lines of, "Come along, Mummy, these people will be wanting their supper." At this prompt, the Queen Mother got the message and trooped out, along with the rest of the Royal Family. That was the signal for the show principals to head back to the dressing room to get changed. A little before midnight, the company convened in the Yellow Drawing Room for a sit-down supper, where they enjoyed the same food and wines served to Her Majesty and her guests a few hours earlier. As luck would have it, I kept the menu card, along with a tiny box of matches from the table, stamped with 'ER', as souvenirs of the day.

MENU

Consommé Philadelphia

Dinde à la Crème
Salades

Lemon Posset
Biscuits

Jeudi, le 16 juin, 1977 WINDSOR CASTLE

Soon, that remarkable day for the D'Oyly Carte Opera Company was over, the cast and orchestra heading back to Brighton, or to the Post House Hotel at Heathrow. But, for Peter Riley, architect of the whole operation, supervising the process of removing all traces of *HMS Pinafore* from Windsor Castle began immediately, the 'get out' of the set, drapes and costumes commencing as soon as the crew had arrived from the London stores at 1am. Understandably, it was a somewhat jaded company that turned up for the performance of *Pinafore* at the Theatre Royal in Brighton the following evening. It was particularly hard for the technical crew, wardrobe and wigs personnel, who had not had much sleep. The contrast in the venues, with less than twenty-four hours between the two shows, could not have been greater but, as ever, the professionalism of the singers and orchestra kicked in to ensure the Brighton audience was given nothing less than a first-class performance.

As for master tactician, Peter Riley, who should have been able to look back with pride and satisfaction on a job well done, there was an unexpected extra duty to perform to tie up the loose ends of the Windsor adventure. A couple of days after the performance, he received a phone call from Sir Peter Ashmore who, with some embarrassment, informed him that cutlery used at the after-show supper had gone missing and must be returned. Peter was shocked to be told that a number of gold teaspoons, several knives and forks and a cruet had been taken as mementos. He was mortified, but his profuse apologies were accepted by the phlegmatic Sir Peter, who had, very likely, seen it all before. Given instructions as to how to get the missing items back to Her Majesty, Peter decided on a moratorium, putting up a notice stating that anyone who had taken a piece of cutlery could put it in the box he would place on a skip outside Bert Newby's office. If everything was returned, no further action would be taken. His faith was not misplaced; the guilty parties did as they were asked and Peter was able to take all the cutlery back to Buckingham Palace. Arriving at the trade entrance, he was met by a man with a smug expression. "Ah, Mister Riley returning the stolen cutlery, I presume." Asking how it would be taken back to Windsor, he was told that it would be sent on the milk train! It was a rather unedifying end to the Royal Command proceedings, but it can only be supposed that those who had been tempted to own something from Windsor Castle did not mean any harm. Several people think they remember one of the teaspoons making an unscheduled appearance in *Pinafore* the night after the Windsor show, presented to Meston Reid, who was playing 'Ralph Rackstraw', as a 'tip' during the second act finale. True or apocryphal, it makes a good story which sums up that famous, bitter-sweet royal occasion.

CHAPTER NINE

THE D'OYLY CARTE AT PLAY

It is often said that show business life is glamorous and sometimes that is true, but for D'Oyly Carte folk, their working lives revolved around the grinding monotony of year-round touring performing the same operas over and over again. It was, therefore, essential for them to have interests to keep them sane, as was the chance to socialise away from the theatre. Inevitably, overseas tours provided more opportunity for having fun, but on home soil, everyone found something to do to entertain themselves in their limited free time, be it of a sporting nature, a handicraft, or something more cerebral.

From the 1950s to the closure of the company in 1982, golf was a favourite pastime for many D'Oyly Carters and being a member of a famous opera company opened golf club doors. In towns and cities in which the company was appearing, the golfers were often allowed to play for free in return for giving a short G&S concert at the end of the season, when they were joined by the non-golfers, who bolstered the number of singers and enjoyed a free supper for their troubles. It was mainly the men of the company who played, although Mary

Sansom, Peggy Ann Jones, Beti Lloyd-Jones and Patricia Leonard were known to wield a mean driver. Peggy and Beti often played together when they were on tour in the UK, although they seldom played in America. In his younger days, jack of all D'Oyly Carte trades, Herbert Newby, loved playing golf and even though his health declined in the 1970s, his clubs were carried on the company lorry to the day he died in 1979. Thomas Round was another keen golfer and, at the ripe old age of a hundred, can recall how playing alongside Peter Pratt always made him chuckle. Peter was competitive by nature and took his golf seriously, whereas his colleagues enjoyed a leisurely round and didn't mind who won. Tom relates that Peter would get a little impatient with anyone lagging behind and chivvy them along when they were chatting. He would hit his ball and immediately move off after it, at what Tom describes as a "funny little trot". He never walked, always anxious to be on to his next shot whilst the others dawdled behind. After so many years, just talking about this quirky side to Peter Pratt made Tom laugh aloud.

Tennis was a great passion for John Dennison and during the summer months of 1957, he made up a foursome with Anne Sessions, Joseph Riordan and Jean 'Tilly' Barrington. They were the only regular tennis players, but many of the company men enjoyed playing cricket. The D'Oyly Carte boasted its own team which played occasional matches during the 1950s and '60s, the bags containing their bats and pads always carried alongside costumes and sets on the company train. Kenneth Sandford, Herbert Newby, Norman Meadmore, Peter Pratt and Donald Adams were stalwarts of the side, with choristers forming the rest of the team, John Banks being the most accomplished player of these. Leonard Osborn usually served as umpire. Ever the proud Yorkshireman, Ken Sandford considered himself the team's answer to the great Yorkshire and England fast bowler, Fred Trueman, but as the following interesting extract from the Gilbert and Sullivan Journal of May 1960 shows, his efforts did not merit a mention.

"During the present season, the D'Oyly Carte cricket team has arranged matches in Bristol, Oxford, Belfast, Dublin, Liverpool and Brentwood. Although the 1959 season was not memorable for matches won, it was nevertheless very successful, both from the sporting and social angles. There was a glorious afternoon's cricket against Brighton

College when, despite a fine 52 knocked up by Peter Pratt (the highest score in the book by a D'Oyly Carte player) and Glynne Thomas taking 5 wickets for 32, the team lost by 1 wicket. Another exciting finish was against Magdalen College Cygnets, when the clock forced a draw with only 2 runs needed to win. The star performer of that game was, undoubtedly, John Banks, who took 7 wickets for 23 runs, including the only D'Oyly Carte hat-trick ever remembered. Other enjoyable matches were played in Bristol, Bournemouth and Exeter, where the team played on the Devon County ground against the cathedral choristers. The season ended with a very pleasant match against a Brentwood School XI. Altogether, six matches were played last season, of which two were won, three lost and one drawn. Norman Meadmore headed the batting with an average of 20.8, followed by Peter Pratt with 15."

Before Jennifer Toye was promoted to principal soprano in 1960, she took advantage of the leisure time she had in her years as a chorister and small-part player to indulge her passion for horse riding. She loved the exhilaration of galloping along the flat sands at Whitley Bay whenever the company was in Newcastle-upon-Tyne and tried to find nearby stables wherever the tour took the company. After meeting Julian Bream at a D'Oyly Carte function, she invited the world-famous classical guitarist to join her and some friends for a ride in the New Forest. But there were many other pastimes she enjoyed, too.

"One memory that sticks in my mind were the trips to Bristol Zoo. We were always there in the spring and the blossoms in the gardens of the zoo were spectacular. John Fryatt took reams of movies there. We would spend the whole day walking round the gardens and looking at the marvellous animals. We picnicked in the grounds, or went on to the Clifton Downs. Bristol was a huge favourite, but most cities had places of interest to visit. Afternoons were sometimes spent using a free pass to the cinema, then going off to the Kardomah, or some other cafe, for tea before the show. Mornings with the girls involved having coffee or, in the days of the big department stores in Manchester, Leeds and other places, the girls would be invited to a fashion show in the times when there was an in-store catwalk and all the models smiled and danced their way through the show. We were tempted by some of the outfits, but they were invariably out of our league. Marshall and Snelgrove, now defunct, used to put on great shows. We took studios to play the piano, or practise singing anything other than G&S. In London and New York, I managed to catch a lot of matinees and saw Broadway performances of *Camelot, My Fair Lady, The Sound of Music* and many others. In Los Angeles, we were taken round the Fox Studios. It was a fantastic time for us."

Whilst some company members favoured sporting pursuits, others found less energetic pastimes to fill their leisure hours and tenor chorister, Edwin Rolles, was quite ingenious in finding ways to entertain himself in the free time permitted by eight shows every week. Apart from indulging himself in his love of visiting historic buildings, he found time to form a small vocal group, The Savoy Barber Shop Quartet, in which he featured alongside fellow tenor, Kevin West, chorus baritone, Patrick Wilkes and second trumpet in the Carte orchestra, Alan Wilson who, according to Eddie, had a rich bass voice. They appeared at many after-show functions as well as singing in churches and at weddings. Not content with that, Eddie, who was a qualified music teacher, successfully coached chorus bass, Paul Waite through his Associate of the London College of Music diploma and orchestra member, Chris Blood, with his Associate of the Royal College of Music teaching qualification. It must be said that such laudable pursuits were not the norm, most company members preferring something less challenging to fill their off-duty hours.

As a young man, James Conroy-Ward, like Jenny Toye, had always enjoyed horse riding, but his D'Oyly Carte contract, unlike in earlier times, strictly ruled out such an activity, along with skiing and ice skating, so his equestrian prowess had to be put on hold during his time with the company. Anyone discovered to have flouted this rule would be deemed to be in breach of contract and ran the risk of dismissal. Such activities were considered too dangerous; the management, understandably, did not wish to lose its performers for weeks on end with broken limbs, so less risky hobbies were the order of the day. Many people enjoyed going to the cinema in the afternoons. Equity members just had to show their union card to gain free admission, so going to see a film was a popular way to relax. There was a great rush to see *The Exorcist* on its release in the 1970s, the iconic horror movie proving a topic of conversation in the dressing rooms as everyone relived being scared to death. Less terrifying hobbies such as reading, cooking, doing crosswords and needlework were popular and, in the early 1970s, soprano Marjorie Williams was famous in the dressing room for her prowess with knitting needles, seemingly able to produce a sweater for herself, or her husband, Colin Wright, in a couple of days. Not so successful in this pursuit was contralto understudy, Alice Hynd, who, after getting fed up of writing letters during the interminable Sunday train calls of the 1950s, decided to knit a delicate evening shawl, which required the finest of wool and some five hundred stitches on the needles. Needing to count them at regular intervals, Alice got very frustrated by almost getting there, when someone would burst into the compartment for a chat and she would have to start all over again. It did not take many journeys for the shawl to disappear never to be seen again. An unusual hobby for bass, George Cook, was making fans for *The Mikado*, an interest which turned into a business after he left the company, when he provided sets of fans for many an amateur G&S production.

My great interest was photography and I particularly enjoyed shooting the glorious scenery of Scotland when tours took us north of the border. My first company tour of North America in 1976 was so different from anything I had previously experienced, that I was never without my camera to record the exciting sights of the vibrant cities we played and the beautiful, varied landscapes of the huge continent we criss-crossed over five months. By the end of the 1978 American tour, I had amassed hundreds of slides which constituted a photographic record of the company at work and play from Massachusetts to California. My passion for capturing everything I saw continued through the 1979 tour of Australia and New Zealand. Because slide transparencies deteriorate very little, I can still look back on those wonderful days some thirty-seven years later as if it were yesterday. From publicity cruises around the harbours of San Francisco and Sydney, to the informal parties we held to keep our spirits high when so far from home, my trusty camera captured it all and the memories are there whenever I want to look back on those incredible times. Principal tenor, Geoffrey Shovelton, was also a keen photographer and we often enjoyed friendly competition as to whose shots were best.

Kenneth Sandford, who had studied at The Royal College of Art in London, always had his easel and oils in the back of the car and took every available opportunity to paint when out on tour. He was an accomplished portrait painter and many a company member sat for him on a rainy afternoon although, when the weather was fine, he would often be out and about painting landscapes. Towards the end of the D'Oyly Carte, Ken had an exhibition at Sadler's Wells Theatre in London, selling many of his works. He often received commissions and his portrayal of scenes from the Savoy Operas as seen from the wings, or the auditorium, were extremely popular with those anxious to have an original Sandford hanging on their wall. Even on an overseas tour, Ken always had a sketch pad with him and when the company played seasons at the Opera House in Central City, Colorado, he managed to squeeze an easel and brushes into his luggage. The luxury of time to paint was restricted to tour dates, because whilst living at home during London seasons, family responsibilities were the order of the day and there was always a long list of jobs to do around the house, not to mention spending precious time with his two children. However, during week-long runs of *Pirates* and *Pinafore*, shows he was not in, he still found a little time to work on his latest canvas. He was not the only one to dabble in oils. Cynthia Morey and John Reed were always game to try different creative pursuits and Cynthia had a rather embarrassing moment as a result of one of their forays into the world of art.

"John and myself were enthusiastic about oil painting. My large and rather awful nude woman wasn't dry to pack for the train call one Sunday, so I had to carry the canvas in full view of everyone!" It is noted that Cynthia gives no indication as to the identity of the subject and it can only be hoped that nobody on the train recognised themselves. John Reed's passion for all things creative took a rather silly turn when he was sharing digs in Edinburgh with Peggy Ann Jones, as she explains.

"We were a bit bored, so I went out and bought some modelling clay. John and I spent a fortnight filling our free time making models of all sorts of things, most of them bad and many of them very vulgar. We had a great time laughing at each other's efforts and were rather sad to throw them all away when we moved on to the next date." But Peggy's main interest was in crochet, which she describes as the perfect touring hobby, requiring only a hook and string, which she often used to make lacy tops. Having been introduced to crocheting by one of the ladies in the company in the 1960s, it has been a lifelong interest, which she still pursues with enthusiasm. She also loved making clothes and when she toured in her caravan, had a hand-held sewing machine to run up dresses at a fraction of the cost of buying them. Even when away on American tours, Peggy could never resist buying colourful material to hand-stitch simple tops and shift dresses. Inspired by the deep, vibrant colours of California, which she found thrillingly different from the drab shades back at home, she was never happier than when she was making brightly-coloured clothes which reflected this love. During one American tour, Valerie Masterson, who was expecting a baby, complained that none of her evening dresses fitted her any more. Without further ado, Peggy went out to buy a length of velvet, measured Valerie and handmade a gown to last her through the receptions on the tour which required formal dress. To quote Gillian Knight: "Every company needed a Peggy Ann Jones." Such was the camaraderie within the company.

D'Oyly Carters loved parties and there are many memorable instances of the company coming together to socialise. Given that they were thrown into each others' company for six days of every week, and seven when they had to travel together, or were on overseas tours, it is remarkable that they so often chose to play together. The hardship of being away from home for so much of the year cannot be stressed enough, so being part of a large, surrogate family was essential to fill the void. It was much easier to party when on tour abroad, because everyone was, usually, billeted in the same place. After many an American performance, there were gatherings in hotel rooms, when drinks and snacks were brought in to pass a merry couple of hours before bedtime. In the 1950s and '60s, the ever-popular Alan Styler was always in great demand, keeping everyone entertained with his never-ending supply of side-splitting, usually very rude, stories. The need for after-show relaxation often led to a restaurant or bar, but after one New York performance at the Uris Theatre during the 1976 tour, the drinks left everyone feeling on top of the world. In one of the ladies' dressing rooms, some bright spark suggested a race to the top of the Empire State Building, the last at the bar having to pay for the drinks. The crazy idea appealed and the news quickly spread to the other dressing rooms, leading to a rushed exodus and jostling for taxis outside the Stage Door. Even though the bar at the top of the iconic skyscraper stayed open late, they only just made it, but it was well-worth the dash to witness the skyline of Manhattan lit up at night. Such spontaneity was typical and many great company parties happened off the cuff.

If North America seemed far from home, how much more so Australia and New Zealand? The unique 1979 tour, however exciting, was hard for company members, most of whom had been on the lengthy tour of North America the previous year. On the other side of the world for five months, the need for companionship was greater than ever, so every opportunity was taken to go on sightseeing trips, celebrate special occasions and get together after shows. It would have been unlikely for the whole company to be bosom buddies with everyone else, so groups of particularly close friends tended to stick together. This did not mean cliques or factions but, rather, it was sensible to spend time with those with whom one felt totally comfortable. Nevertheless, many trips were arranged for all the company and one of them brought great disappointment. On the middle Sunday of the two-week season in Auckland, a bus was hired to take everyone to visit the famous volcanic hot springs and geysers at Rotorua. Unfortunately, the heavy rain that had drenched the city for two days caused a landslip which blocked the road just a few miles from the world-famous site, forcing the bus to turn back. So near, yet so far, it was a very miserable group which went back to the hotel to contemplate missing out on seeing one of the great wonders of the natural world.

That sad experience was very much in the mind of a small group of Carters when the company moved on to Christchurch. The fabulous scenery of the South Island was not to be missed and, as the company was only playing a one-week season, a weekday was chosen to see the Canterbury plains and Southern Alps from the air. A six-seater Piper plane (and pilot!) was hired from Mount Cook Airlines to carry Jane Stanford, Kenneth Sandford, James Conroy-Ward, Bryan Secombe, and myself on the flight of a lifetime. On as glorious a clear winter's day as could be imagined, the bucolic pastures of the plains quickly gave way to the grandeur of snow-capped mountains as our little plane bobbed and weaved in and out of the peaks and over glaciers, culminating in a circuit around the majestic summit of Mount Cook. Jane can remember the pilot saying he would drop the plane's wings to give us a better view and somebody telling him to leave them where they were! It was bumpy and scary at times, but unbelievably exciting, a trip never to be forgotten. And all because we were privileged to be on tour with the D'Oyly Carte Opera Company, paid to travel the world bringing G&S to its many fans whilst we had fun. How lucky we were.

In relating the stories of company parties and excursions, it would be wrong to give the impression that D'Oyly Carters did far too much partying. In reality, they were professionals fully aware of their responsibilities and the need to be at their best for each of the eight weekly shows. There had to be a balance between work and play, but in Gillian Knight's case, the balance fell heavily on the side of work. During the six years she spent with the company, she was contracted to do every performance and that left little time for leisure activities. Her main priority was to rest as much as possible and keep in good health to be able to perform at her best in every show. Having to do so many performances every week was a test of vocal stamina and the need to look after herself was essential, so going out after a performance was something that happened only occasionally, usually for an official reception. As she points out, she was newly-married to Property Master, Trevor Morrison, so being with him was all she needed. Even though their work schedules were very different, they went home together, so she was happy. Gillian's predecessor, Ann Drummond-Grant, and Peter Pratt were others who appeared in every performance, so their main concern was rest, not play. In John Reed's autobiography, he contrasts the lot of those principals on the 1955 American tour, who rarely got a night off, with the relatively carefree members of the chorus.

"I was to realise on subsequent American tours that this first one, when I was only a chorister and understudy, was the most enjoyable of all. I would always go over the opera to be played the next night just in case I had to go on for Peter, but that was all. I was free to go sightseeing, stay up late at parties and generally have a good time whereas, in the future, although I did not know it at the time, this sort of thing would not be possible."

It must not be forgotten that between 1950 and 1968, some of the tours took place during the harsh months of the North American winter,

216

so sightseeing very much depended on the weather and also how long the company was appearing in a place. In those days, it was not unusual for there to be only two or three days played in smaller cities before moving on, so the chance for leisure time was very restricted as everyone was busy packing, travelling and unpacking again. Christmas on these tours meant spending the festive season thousands of miles from home and family, so celebrations were what everyone made of them. A few people were lucky enough to spend Christmas Day with friends made on previous tours; some of the better-paid principals flew their families over for the holiday, but the majority mucked in together to make sure they had something to celebrate, although it was not so easy for spouses and children back at home without a missing parent or partner. Cards and presents could be posted, but it was not the same.

The principals had to be very conscientious, so free time activities for them when on overseas tours were, usually, saved for weekends; Saturday nights and Sundays were the time to let hair down and party, or go on excursions. Even though individual responsibility was less for the chorus, the need to conduct themselves in a professional manner was always kept in mind even when temptation was put under their noses. The programme book for the tour of Australia and New Zealand was sponsored by Benson and Hedges, its large, glossy cover being the same gold colour as the cigarette packets and it contained a full-page advert for the famous brand, which were liberally handed out to the company's many smokers. The tobacco company held a reception after the opening performance at every date of the tour, which company members were expected to attend. With champagne flowing, it would have been easy to have too much to drink, but most people were sensible and limited themselves to a glass or two. In fact, by the end of the five-month tour, everyone was sick of the sight of champagne!

Although there was much of interest to see and do in many of the towns on a British tour, the sights and sounds of big North American cities were infinitely more exciting, so sightseeing was hugely popular amongst the company members when it came to filling leisure time. In the early spring of 1976, the Carte was playing a season in Toronto and, on a free Sunday, cast members were invited by the local Gilbert and Sullivan Society to visit Niagara Falls. Meeting in the lobby of the

King Edward Hotel, we were randomly allocated to car drivers who would host us for the day. James Conroy-Ward and I were placed in the hands of British-born couple, Gareth Jacobs and Elizabeth Thomson, who drove us to the falls and entertained us in fine style. Luck or fate, I don't know, but that day saw the beginning of a friendship which has not only endured, but also become stronger in the ensuing forty years and I count them among my dearest friends, whom I am now able to visit at their home just outside Edinburgh. The forging of such lifelong friendships was not uncommon on an American tour, when hospitality shown often led to close associations which the intervening Atlantic Ocean did not diminish.

During the American tour of '78, which saw the company play four cities in California, the opportunity to enjoy the fine weather and luxury of hotel swimming pools was not to be missed, the company gathering every afternoon to swim and relax in the sunshine becoming a feature of a very happy few weeks. Despite the urge to linger around the pool, the evening performance was never far from mind so, at around 4 o'clock, there was a general dispersal to rest and prepare for going to work. In San Francisco, the chance to tour Alcatraz prison was considered a must, as was travelling by cable car to Fisherman's Wharf for lunch at Tarantino's. San Diego's famous zoo was a popular haunt and it was just a short trip across the border into Mexico to visit Tijuana. Disneyland and Universal Studios proved enormously popular in Los Angeles, particularly as some of the company had family visiting for two weeks. With the Hollywood Bowl just down the road from the motel which housed the company for its season at the Greek Theatre, there was plenty of entertainment to be had. The highlight of the Californian leg of the tour was a publicity cruise around San Francisco harbour in celebration of the centenary of *HMS Pinafore*. Officially a work engagement, it was so exciting that everyone remembers it as a wonderful day out. Appropriately decked out in *Pinafore* costumes, the company boarded a 19th century schooner to sail around the infamous prison island of Alcatraz and under the Golden Gate Bridge. Luckily, it was a gloriously sunny day and there was not a trace of the chilly fog that so often shrouded the bay. Accompanied by the fire boat of the San Francisco Fire Department firing its plumes of water high into the air and the city's Coastguard helicopter hovering just above the water, it was a spectacular sight which gave the press launch ample photo opportunities. It is unlikely that anyone aboard will ever forget such an amazing experience.

After a wonderful few weeks, it was a down-beat company that reluctantly left California to move on to Colorado, but the hotel in Denver again boasted a pool, so the swimming routine continued, much to everyone's delight. However, the high spot of the week was a trip to the legendary Central City, scene of the hugely successful D'Oyly Carte seasons of 1955 and 1968, which spawned the many amazing stories related by those who were lucky enough to be in the company at the time. It was great fun for those of us too young to have been on the earlier tours to see the place that held such a special place in D'Oyly Carte history. Everyone had a fantastic day, despite the fact that Ken Sandford got a small group of his colleagues lost on the walking trails outside the town. Anxious to show them the places where he had spent many happy hours painting, he couldn't remember the way back to town, resulting in them missing the bus back to Denver and having to hitch a lift in a passing truck!

I paid the price for putting pleasure before work when trying to cram in as much sightseeing as possible during the week we were in Colorado. Whilst on a visit to Universal Studios a couple of weeks before the Denver season, I had chatted over lunch with a couple from the city who said they would love to show me the sights when the company came to town. Contacting them when we arrived, they arranged to pick me up at the Stage Door of the theatre to take me on a trip to the top of Mount Evans. It was June, so the road up to the summit was open, although it was odd to be in a sun dress and sandals with snow piled up at the side of the road, but it was a fantastic drive and I could only marvel at the scenery as we climbed to over 14,000 feet to have lunch at the cafe so high up in the Rocky Mountains. I can remember feeling light-headed at such altitude, as if I had drunk too much, but thought little of it. With the long drive back down to Denver, there was just time for my friends to drop me back at the theatre for the performance of *Pinafore*, in which I was to play 'Cousin Hebe'. I was fine during the first act, but when I started singing in the second act finale, I began to feel faint and nauseous. John Reed, who was playing 'Sir Joseph Porter', sensed I was not well and kept a tight grip on my arm, even pinching me to keep me alert. Somehow, I got through to the end of the show before collapsing, to be diagnosed with a mild case of altitude sickness!

Having never before been higher than the top of Mount Snowdon in Wales, going from 6,000 feet to 14,000 feet and back in just a few hours really disagreed with me, but twenty-four hours complete rest saw me restored to good health and I learned a valuable lesson that day: however tempting it might be to cram in as much as possible when on an overseas tour, work had to come first. It is worth mentioning again that it took most D'Oyly Carte performers a day or two to acclimatise to singing at over a mile up, when breath control was compromised. John Reed, in particular, found delivering patter songs at altitude left him breathless and sometimes in need of the oxygen available in the wings. We all found that dancing left us out of puff, but by the end of the week, we had forgotten about it as our bodies naturally adjusted to being in the Mile High City.

Performing at high altitude in Denver was an interesting experience for the D'Oyly Carters who had not been in the company for the seasons at the Central City Opera House, which was even higher up in the Rockies at 8,000 feet. In 1955, Cynthia Morey loved her time during the company's first season there, but remembers how difficult it was to breathe, especially when singing, never feeling quite at ease at such dizzy heights. However, her description of the social side of the season sums up everything that was so special about the town and its surrounds.

"Our season at Central City Opera House was an experience I shall never forget. The location was unique, the scenery spectacularly beautiful and the friendliness of the local people exceptional. Many were the invitations to parties, from family gatherings in friends' homes to opulent occasions at luxurious ranches. We rode up mountain trails on dubious hired horses, lurching dangerously in bucket saddles; picnicked by rapids; climbed up to craggy viewpoints. We visited ghost towns long since deserted by disillusioned fortune hunters disappointed in their search for gold. And all around us the splendour of the Rockies stretched away into the purple distance." Happily for such intrepid adventurers, D'Oyly Carte contracts of those days were not so strict when it came to potentially dangerous pursuits.

Invitations from wealthy people anxious to enjoy the prestige of hosting a world-famous opera company were common during American tours and, in both 1976 and '78, Mr and Mrs J. Gerald Mayer invited everyone to their home on Cape Cod on the middle Sunday of the Boston season. A bus was hired to take the company some seventy miles north to the elegant beach-side home of the Mayers, where lunch was served and cocktails freely flowed. During the afternoon, everyone lazed on the private beach, or took trips aboard Mr Mayer's yacht and the glorious day out concluded with dinner at a local seafood restaurant. Little more than a wooden shack on stilts built out into the sea, it served delicious, freshly-caught clams and lobsters which rounded off a fantastic day before the jolly drive back to Boston.

In Washington DC on the '78 tour, the company was invited to a party thrown by long-time Gilbert and Sullivan fans from Texas, Overton Shellmire and his wife, Suzette, who had become great friends of the company after they got to know Ralph Mason and Anne Sessions on a tour in the 1960s. Overton's influence stretched to borrowing the Mayflower Hotel apartment belonging to one of President Gerald Ford's senior aides. It was a very swish affair, so suitably up-market transport to the hotel was arranged in the form of a fleet of White House limousines. Everyone had been informed that cars would take us to the hotel, so we assembled outside the Kennedy Center after the performance, amusing ourselves by speculating as to which celebrities or VIPs inside the theatre complex were expecting to be whisked away in the line of black limos parked outside the Opera House. To say we were astonished when we found out they were for us is an understatement, but it can be supposed that the crowd of people gathering to see which famous people would be leaving in the limos must have felt very cheated when we piled into the luxurious cars. The party that followed was spectacular, the food and drink of the finest quality, giving me my first experience of Wild Turkey bourbon.

During the Washington season two years earlier, formal invitations to cast, staff and management were received to attend a party at the British Embassy hosted by the Ambassador, Sir Peter Ramsbotham, in honour of the bicentenary celebrations. Attended by Frederic Lloyd, Dame Bridget D'Oyly Carte and Sir Harold Wilson, who had flown over for the occasion, it was a chance for everyone to dress up and enjoy the plush surroundings. The principals not appearing in the show that evening gave a concert and everyone else arrived after the performance. Before dinner, trays of cocktails were taken round by waiters and Wig Mistress, Heather Perkins, chose one which she tried, but didn't like. Spotting the floral decoration in the centre of her table, she craftily poured the drink into it and went off in search of something more to her taste. She thought nothing more about it until after the main course of the meal, when a waiter, with a flourish, removed the flower arrangement from the top of the flower pot to reveal the dessert. The look of astonishment on his face was matched by the one of horror on Heather's as they surveyed the liquid sloshing round on top of the pudding. Needless to say, she was mortified. Everyone else, of course, was helpless with laughter. It was later rumoured that someone had stubbed out a cigarette in another of the flowery pudding pots. It certainly was a memorable evening, topped off by the amusing incident that Ken Robertson-Scott remembers. On the bus going back to their hotels, the Company Manager, Herbert Newby, got very cross with the well-fed and watered company, who were so rowdy that the driver found it difficult to concentrate and reversed into a tree!

Seeing the sights on days off sometimes required research as to how best to get there, so a few of the Carters decided that the easiest, if not the cheapest, way to get to see Virginia's famed Blue Ridge Mountains, was to hire a chauffeur-driven stretch limousine for their day out from Washington DC in 1976. The group, which included Heather Perkins, Jane Metcalfe, Barbara Lilley and James Conroy-Ward, set off in style on a fine day to enjoy the magnificent scenery. Stopping whenever they wanted to take photographs or get something to eat, the convenience of sightseeing in luxury was worth the expense and much better than hiring a car or going by bus. Also that day, they had time to visit the awe-inspiring Luray Caverns, which boasted spectacular rock formations, stalagmites and stalactites. While they were off enjoying themselves, their driver dozed in the limo before returning them to Washington.

On the tour of Australia and New Zealand, apart from the all-too-regular first-night receptions, there were no formal functions to attend, but there were lots of impromptu gatherings and trips to keep everyone entertained. Days out to wildlife reserves were very popular, where the chance to cuddle a koala and stroke a kangaroo, or in the case of Meston Reid, wrap a huge python around his neck, made the subject of many a photograph. Cars were hired to take trips and the free Sunday of the Brisbane season saw an exodus to the beaches of the Sunshine coast, a couple of hours drive north of the city. Even though it was the Australian winter, the Queensland weather was like a summer day back home, so sunbathing and swimming in the warm Pacific proved a wonderful way to spend a day off. Local Aussies, who were dressed for cold weather, thought we were totally barmy to be lying on the beach in swimming costumes, but what did we care? It was great fun to spend free time with friends and enjoy being on the other side of the world. On another day out from Brisbane to see the strangely-shaped Glass House Mountains, Kenneth Sandford, John Coe-Roper and Elizabeth Denham got lost, eventually finding their way back to Brisbane in the dark. During the three-week Sydney season, it was a trip to the Blue Mountains, whilst in Perth, a memorable wine tasting cruise along the Swan River started sensibly enough, but ended with the Carters not a little tipsy. A lingering memory of a drive into the outback of Western Australia, is a photograph of the ever-dapper James Conroy-Ward posing by a car on a dusty dirt road sporting a smart jacket, collar and tie, with a flower in his buttonhole!

By a strange coincidence, almost twelve months to the day after the company had sailed round San Francisco harbour, arrangements were made for a cruise around the iconic Sydney Harbour and it proved equally memorable. On this occasion, it was a private party, company members being invited to join James Hardy aboard his ocean-going yacht after a champagne and smoked oyster reception on the quayside. Again suitably attired in *Pinafore* costumes, everyone had a wonderful time taking in the stunning vistas. With the owner, himself, at the wheel, it was an exhilarating experience as everyone spontaneously sang their way through the show and cheered when several sailor hats ended up in the water. Jim Hardy, a lover of Gilbert and Sullivan, was a seasoned yachtsman who had competed in many international ocean races, often alongside the former British Prime Minister, Sir Edward Heath. He also owned a vineyard which produced the wines now so popular around the world. He certainly gave the D'Oyly Carters the experience of a lifetime and anyone on board that day who now buys a bottle of Hardy's wine cannot fail to raise a glass to the memory of that wonderful occasion.

Another highlight on the social side of the tour was the chance to attend a dress rehearsal of the Australian Opera Company's production of Mozart's *Don Giovanni* in Melbourne, which starred the great Dame Joan Sutherland and the American baritone, James Morris in the title role. Performing Gilbert and Sullivan every day masked the fact that the vast majority of D'Oyly Carte performers were trained classical singers, so the opportunity to indulge their love of grand opera was a welcome change. Ken Sandford, who had always cherished an ambition to sing in opera, was enthralled by the performance of James Morris, who had the sensational voice, looks and theatrical charisma required for the part. It is no exaggeration to say that the Carte ladies were drooling over him! James was thrilled when he heard that members of the D'Oyly Carte were in at the dress rehearsal because, as a youngster, he had grown up listening to D'Oyly Carte recordings and was a huge fan of Kenneth Sandford. Needless to say, the two were delighted to meet and the following evening, James was to be found sitting cross-legged on the floor in the wings for a performance of *The Mikado*, watching his childhood hero playing 'Pooh-Bah'. Their mutual admiration brought great pleasure to both men.

A few days before the *Don Giovanni* rehearsal, James Conroy-Ward was sitting in the foyer of an up-market hotel following his favourite pursuit, a nice afternoon tea, when he saw Dame Joan sweep in with a retinue in tow. He had met her during his time with The Royal Opera, when they appeared in the same opera but, as she headed in his direction, he felt reticent about speaking to her in case she did not remember him. He need not have worried. As she went past, she suddenly stopped and turned to look at him. "Bloody hell, it's Jim Ward!" The ensuing conversation explained what he was doing in Melbourne and James was thrilled that the great diva was happy to chat as if they were old friends. The chance meeting made his tour.

It being the company's first tour down under, promoting performances was key to the success of the tour, so principals were expected to do television appearances and radio interviews whenever the management dictated. An accepted part of the job, they could sometimes be a nuisance, an intrusion into precious free time, but they could also be fun. The 'Three Little Maids' were in great demand, singing their famous trio on television shows in almost every city on the tour. Definitely falling into the fun category was the radio interview Ken Sandford did for a small radio station in New Zealand, when it immediately became apparent to him that the young presenter asking the questions had no idea about Gilbert and Sullivan or the D'Oyly Carte Opera Company. Ken struggled valiantly to make some sense of the interview, doing his best to plug the tour and trying not to smile at the naïve questions put to him, but he was rendered almost speechless when asked, "What are Gilbert and Sullivan doing now?" After a moment's thought, Ken cleverly remembered Gilbert's famous quote and countered with, "Decomposing"!

The wonderful experiences available to D'Oyly Carters on overseas tours were the pay off for having to spend so much time away from home, but despite the sightseeing trips and parties, nobody lost sight of the fact that they had a job to do. Most days revolved around the usual routine of life on the road, finding somewhere to eat; buying groceries and cooking when in self-catering accommodation; looking for laundrettes and dry cleaners; going to rehearsals and, of course, performing eight shows a week. The touring life was not for everyone; the demands of constant travel and separation from family proved too much for some, who lasted only a year or so with the company, but for those with the temperament to cope with the rigours of an itinerant lifestyle, their reward was being paid to see the world.

Back in the UK, opportunities for socialising were less frequent because people were more scattered, either staying in digs on their own, sharing with one or two others, or living at home. For those who did not live in London, there were always parties to enjoy during the Christmas season and Alan Barrett tells of one that stands out in his memory in the late 1950s. He and his wife, Mary Sansom, had rented a house for the London season and had plenty of room to entertain, so lots of company members were invited to their New Year's Eve party.

"I remember Tom Round being there with his wife, Alice. Tommy was not a great drinker, but Alice did not approve of him having alcohol and watched him like a hawk when they were at parties. That night I gave him a large gin and tonic, which he hid behind a curtain, returning to take a crafty swig every now and then, while he chatted to everyone in sight of Alice with a mineral water in his hand. I replenished his glass when necessary, so he did actually get to toast in the New Year." One can only hope Alice did not notice the smell of booze on his breath on their way home!

Beti Lloyd-Jones was another who loved to throw a good party at New Year and I, to my shame, was found clinging to a lamppost outside her flat during one of these sedate occasions and I still don't know why. On one New Year's Eve early in the 1970s, a company fancy dress party was held in the opera rehearsal room at the top of Sadler's Wells Theatre. Nobody can now remember who came up with the idea, but there was food and drink aplenty and everyone pushed the boat out when it came to costumes. The fantastic array of colourful and imaginative outfits was topped by John Reed's appearance as an Elizabethan nobleman and Beti Lloyd-Jones, who turned out as a Bunny Girl, fishnet stockings and all. Jon Ellison, dressed in a mini-skirt, wig and high heels, complete with large false bosom, sported a beauty contest sash proclaiming him to be 'Miss D'Oyly Carte'. He had the shock of his life when he came face to face with the real thing, having been told she would not be attending! The fact that the festive season was so short for everyone in the company meant that a lot of seasonal spirit was crammed into a very short time. Theatre folk have always had to work unsocial hours, so performances at holiday times were a part of the job that had to be accepted. It was usual for the company to give a matinee on Christmas Eve, before everyone left to enjoy Christmas Day with family or friends, returning on Boxing Day for two shows. On New Year's Eve, the end of the evening's performance featured the singing of 'Auld Lang Syne', but there was no other concession to end of year celebrations.

From the earliest times of the company, the build-up to Christmas was taken very seriously, with everyone getting into the spirit of things. In the 1950s and '60s, wherever the company was playing, Carters who could not afford to buy them, made their own festive decorations for digs and theatre. In the 1970s, dressing rooms at London's Sadler's Wells Theatre were festooned with balloons and tinsel, cards were put up around mirrors, gifts exchanged and in the chorus rooms on Christmas Eve, a few sherries consumed. By 5.30pm, those travelling home by car were on their way, sometimes driving for many hours just to be with their families for a few precious hours. There were always a few people who could not get home and they were usually scooped up by those who lived in London, or by others who were also forced to spend Christmas in their digs. The D'Oyly Carte family was there to supply mutual support and make sure nobody was alone on Christmas Day. However reluctant everyone was to come in for the Boxing Day matinee, they made the most of things and tried to create a festive atmosphere in the dressing rooms, with wine, mince pies and turkey sandwiches aplenty for the break between shows. But it was the company's final London season, at the Adelphi Theatre, that saw a truly madcap idea for a party between the shows on December 26th, 1981. Maybe it was because it was to be the final D'Oyly Carte Christmas that the scheme was hatched in the ladies' chorus room for a proper festive meal.

Many of the principal dressing rooms at the Adelphi were much bigger than those at the Wells and the ones nearest the stage were the 'star' rooms with lots of space. As Christmas fell during a week-long run of *The Pirates of Penzance*, Ken Sandford was lucky enough to have several days off, leaving his dressing room temptingly empty. It has been impossible for anyone involved to remember who originally came up with the idea for having turkey curry, cold meats, salads, trifle, Christmas cake and mince pies in Ken's room, but we do know that Beti Lloyd-Jones volunteered to make the curry in her large electric frying pan. A list was drawn as to who was providing what for the meal, not forgetting glasses, plates and cutlery and everyone went away for Christmas looking forward, for once, to coming back on Boxing Day.

Making an early start on the curry before the matinee, Beti plugged in her frying pan in Ken's dressing room, coming back at regular intervals during the show to give the large amount of spicy mixture a stir, whilst everyone else brought in their contributions until the room was full of festive fare. Unfortunately, keeping the door closed failed to stop the aroma of the curry from seeping into the stage area and auditorium, so it was lucky nobody had let slip to the management the plans for the highly irregular between-shows shindig. Complaints from the audience at the interval about the pungent smell wafting around the theatre left the Stage Management team bemused as to the source of the cooking smells and we certainly didn't enlighten them! We got away with it and, between the shows, everyone squeezed in to enjoy a great meal together. It was such fun and so typical of the D'Oyly Carters ability to create something out of nothing. The epitaph to that crazy afternoon came a few days later, when Ken Sandford arrived back to work completely at a loss as to why his dressing room smelled like an Indian restaurant and his costumes reeked of curry! Of course, he eventually found out what had gone on in his absence, his only complaint being that he had not been there to join in the festivities.

Out in the provinces, particularly when the weather was fine, if there was a chance of having some fun, the resourceful company members would take it, sometimes in the most unlikely of places. The Sunderland Empire was usually played every other year in the autumn and a chance conversation led to, probably, the craziest of all the D'Oyly Carte parties of the 1970s. John Ayldon and Guy Matthews were staying with a delightful elderly couple, who happened to mention how fond they were of the North Sea coastline between Sunderland and Newcastle-upon-Tyne, in particular, the spectacular rock formation at Marsden Bay, known as Marsden Grotto, some ten miles up the coast. Guy can't now remember whether it was he or John who came up with the idea of a beach barbecue but, when they visited the spot, it seemed an ideal place to hold a party. They thought it all out, then put up a notice in the theatre to see if there was sufficient interest to make it work. The response to the mad idea of having a party on the beach at midnight was very enthusiastic, so John and Guy went ahead with the planning. They decided it had to be held on a *Gondoliers* night, when John was not performing, so that he could collect wood and build a fire in the daytime, then organise the food and get the fire going during the evening before everyone arrived after the show. It occurred to them that it was important to advise the police of the party plan, hoping there would be no objection. Whatever the local constabulary thought about the strange idea, they must have put it down to having eccentric theatricals in town, because they were quite happy for the unusual gathering to go ahead, even volunteering to be around to keep an eye on proceedings and ward off any gatecrashers.

Although it was October, the weather gods looked down kindly on the late-night frolics, because it didn't rain and was not too cold. The procession down the steep cliff path by torchlight was precarious and great care was taken not to drop the numerous bottles of wine and beer being carried down to the beach. John had been there for some time to get the fire going and bring out the burgers and sausages, which he had concealed in a cave earlier in the day. With the flames leaping and crackling to illuminate the beach and the sound of the waves breaking on the sand, it was a magical scene. Hot food, a few drinks and good company made it a special D'Oyly Carte occasion which lasted well into the small hours. With the blue lights of the police car flashing on the cliff above, the gathering was secure and everyone had great fun. So successful was this madcap al fresco party, that it was repeated on the company's next visit to Sunderland, the second gathering being best-remembered for orchestra leader, Ivan Fox, being spotted wading out into the sea still wearing his dinner jacket! He was in up to his waist by the time he was persuaded to come out. Why he had done this was known only to himself, but it can fairly be assumed that alcohol played its part in his decision to take a fully-clothed midnight dip.

A rather more sedate pursuit favoured by many of the company was the boat trip on the Norfolk Broads whenever the company played a two-week season in Norwich. Hiring small motor cruisers to spend a Sunday pottering around the peaceful waterways was always popular with those unable to get home for the weekend. After a brief training session on how to steer the boats and abide by waterway etiquette, a small flotilla of D'Oyly Carte craft, laden with picnic baskets and ample supplies of alcoholic refreshment, set off to enjoy the gentle pace of a day on the water. On one occasion, James Conroy-Ward, ever the picture of sartorial elegance, donned an eye-catching matching shirt and shorts combination which, with his Major-General's monocle affixed, gave him the air of an aristocrat at leisure. During another cruise, there was an amusing incident involving one of the ladies of the chorus, who found herself desperately in need of a toilet whilst a long way from the nearest facilities. At a loss as to what she could do to avoid a disaster, it was suggested that the boat be drawn up to the edge of the water where the bank was low, so that she could easily scramble to the top and, with the aid of a strategically-placed golf umbrella, take relief out of sight of her colleagues. Unfortunately, so anxious was she to make sure she could not be seen from the boat, that she failed to notice the group of highly-amused fishermen sitting on the opposite bank until it was too late!

Late in the 1970s, John Ayldon, Guy Matthews, Ken Robertson-Scott and Thomas Scholey formed a fine dining group as something to do on Sundays out on tour when they could not get home. Researching the most expensive restaurants within a twenty-mile radius of the town in which the company was appearing, they elected to spend their hard-earned wages on lavish meals and fine wines. Regardless of what they ordered, the bill was always equally split. None of them had the family commitments which precluded many others in the company from such treats and the boys thoroughly enjoyed their gastronomic pastime. In 1980, another group was formed, this one having the intention of taking off pounds, rather than piling them on. The D'Oyly Carte Diet Club, aka 'The DCDC', had several members anxious to lose weight, including Beti Lloyd-Jones, Bruce Graham, Heather Perkins, Paul Seeley, John Ayldon and Thomas Scholey. Because joining a group such as Weight Watchers was impossible when travelling all over the country, they decided to set up their own dieting club and the results were impressive. Meeting in the theatre every Saturday at 1pm, the weekly weigh-in was preceded by desperate last-minute visits to the loo to get rid of a few more ounces before hitting the scales. The club had its own song, sung to the tune of a famous old television advert for the hot drink, 'Ovaltine', the rendition of which could be heard echoing around the backstage areas. Whoever had lost the most weight was dubbed dieter of the week and given a badge, whilst the person to have lost the least, or worse, put on weight, was given a ceramic pig to put on their place in the dressing room for the following seven days. The money collected at each weekly meeting was saved up to pay for them to have an occasional slap-up meal together. The camaraderie and mutual support within the group continued until the company closed and all its members lost a significant amount of weight. It was a perfect example of the Carters ability to both work and play together.

The social event that, perhaps, best summed up the genteel nature of the D'Oyly Carte Opera Company was the traditional afternoon visit to the home of Mrs. York-Batley whenever the company appeared in Bournemouth. The widow of a theatre chaplain, she continued to entertain members of touring companies long after her husband, who had initiated these gatherings, had died. Through the 1960s and '70s, many folk in the touring theatre business went to one of Mrs. York

Batley's parties, which always followed the same rather quaint format. If the weather was fine, everyone was expected to play croquet on the large lawn, but if it was raining, parlour games were organised before tea was served. The menu never varied; it was pots of tea, boiled eggs with bread and butter, followed by cake. A group photograph of the guests was taken to add to the York-Batley album, which was always on display, and it was interesting to see the many famous theatre folk who had experienced this unique theatrical tradition. Alan Spencer was able to look at photos of a party he had attended there when he was on tour with *The Black and White Minstrel Show* before he joined the Carte. One might reasonably wonder why anyone would want to spend an afternoon in this way when there was an evening performance to consider, but these parties were always well-attended by company members, who enjoyed the predictable, if slightly eccentric, nature of the afternoon's entertainment.

It is unlikely that there was never an instance of a company performer putting pleasure before work, but the professionalism of D'Oyly Carters was rarely in question. The physical and psychological demands of travelling away from home for forty-eight weeks of every year, combined with performing eight shows a week, should not be underestimated. Such a schedule called for fitness, stamina and self-discipline, the daily performance always being the priority. Within these restrictions, the need for relaxation was vital for both personal and company morale. The attractions so readily available on overseas tours paint a picture of a glamorous lifestyle filled with sightseeing and parties, but socialising and leisure activities were sensibly fitted in with work commitments and never at the expense of performances. A good balance of work and play is essential in any job and although being with the D'Oyly Carte Opera Company offered opportunities to see the world and have a wonderful time, this was just a bonus which offset the hardship of life lived out of a suitcase.

CHAPTER TEN

LEADING FROM BEHIND

Having thus far detailed how the D'Oyly Carte Opera Company functioned from the point of view of its artistes, backstage staff, music department and touring management, it must be explained that everything associated with the company's operation was dictated by the decisions of the London management. Until 1961, the running of the company had been a family affair, starting with the founder, Richard D'Oyly Carte, who was followed by his son, Rupert, and finally, Rupert's daughter, Bridget. All three took personal responsibility for the running of the family's main business interests, The Savoy Hotel and the D'Oyly Carte Opera Company. It has been well-documented that Bridget felt ill-qualified to run the opera company and was less than enthusiastic about Gilbert and Sullivan as a young woman. However, the accidental death of her younger brother, Michael, in 1932, and the failure of her short, childless marriage meant she was the last of the family line, so she felt an obligation to continue the work started by her grandfather. This she did her best to sustain, often at the expense of her real interests. On the death of her father in 1948, the opera company was hers alone until 1961, when the expiry of the copyright on performing Gilbert and Sullivan forced a rethink in order to protect the future of the company in the face of expected competition from other professional opera companies which, for the first time, were able to mount their own productions of the Savoy Operas. It was then that she founded the D'Oyly Carte Opera Trust to oversee the company's interests, becoming one of its Trustees. She donated all of the company's scenery, costumes and other effects to the Trust and put in a substantial sum of her own money to help get it under way. She also formed Bridget D'Oyly Carte Ltd. to run the company's day-to-day affairs, appointing herself as Managing Director.

Miss Carte's true interests lay in interior design, in which she had trained, and child welfare, although she worked as assistant to her father in running The Savoy Hotel from 1933, where she took great interest in the redesign of many of its rooms. She also gained experience in the running of the opera company, but finding herself with sole responsibility for the D'Oyly Carte business empire must have been a daunting prospect. In 1949, she was considered to have made a serious error of judgement, which caused problems within the opera company, when she appointed a former member, Eleanor Evans, better known as 'Snookie', as Director of Productions. The wife of the company's famed bass, Darrell Fancourt, she had been a chorister and small-part player between 1921 and 1945, but her experience of playing principal roles was limited, so her dictatorial manner and temperamental nature upset many of the company's experienced performers. According to Cynthia Morey, who had joined the company in 1951, many of her colleagues were of the opinion that Snookie was the main reason for the exodus from the company that year, which saw the departure of several principals, including the revered patter man, Martyn Green, and principal contralto, Ella Halman, as well as numerous choristers. Green, in particular, was scathing about her appointment. A total of twenty-seven people left the company at the end of The Festival of Britain Season at the Savoy Theatre.

It has not been possible to ascertain why Miss Carte chose to put Snookie Fancourt in charge of productions but, if it was on recommendation, she may not have been knowledgeable enough about stagecraft to realise that employing someone without the necessary experience of working with established leading performers was not a good idea. Martyn Green wrote to Miss Carte to express his dismay at what he considered to be such an unsuitable appointment, to no avail. Given that Green and the other principals had to work closely with Darrell Fancourt when there was such a general dislike of Snookie, one wonders what the atmosphere between them was like. Even after she left the company when her husband retired in 1953, she was brought back to coach new principals for several years, as Kenneth Sandford never forgot. When he joined in 1957, he considered many of the things she instructed him to do to be nonsensical and completely against the nature of an actor. On politely questioning some of her instructions, he was told to get on with it as that was the way things were done in the D'Oyly Carte. It is possible that Miss Carte did not recognise the fact that Snookie was something of a liability, but it is equally possible that she did not like her decision-making being brought into question, continuing to employ Snookie to make the point that she could do as she pleased with her own company. That we shall never know. Her next major appointment was far more successful with the choice of Frederic Lloyd to succeed Alfred Nightingale as General Manager in September of 1951. Lloyd had been a director of The Festival of Britain, so it is not unlikely that he was recommended to Miss Carte, or that she had met him during the festival. His credentials for the job were excellent; he had worked for some years in arts administration and was knowledgable about music and theatre. She would come to rely heavily on Lloyd for the day-to-day running of the D'Oyly Carte until the company closed in 1982.

As to Bridget D'Oyly Carte the person, it is fair to say that she was something of an enigma as far as most of the company members were concerned. The choristers rarely saw her, let alone had a conversation with her, and it is unlikely that she knew any of them by name, with the possible exception of long-standing members such as Jon Ellison and Beti Lloyd-Jones. She was thought of as a remote figure living in splendour in The Savoy Hotel, who was seen only at an occasional official function, or costume parade. The principals got to know her slightly better, but there was always a stiff formality when she was around and she referred to most of them as 'Mister' or 'Miss', particularly in the early days of her reign, when old-fashioned etiquette was expected at all times. She was a little more at ease with the artistes who had worked for her company for many years, getting to know them well enough to feel she could use their Christian names. But the truth was that she was extremely shy and hardly the charismatic personality that might be expected at the head of a theatrical company which presented comic operas.

Her love of design led to a passion for the company's costumes and settings, it probably being true to say that she was more interested in the look of the company than in the quality of its onstage artistry. Right from the time she took over from her father, she kept productions looking fresh by commissioning new sets and costumes for the operas, mainly from Peter Goffin, whose work she very much admired. She also used James Wade to redesign *Princess Ida* in 1954; Luciana Arrighi and John Stoddart for *The Gondoliers* in 1968; Osbert Lancaster for *The Sorcerer* in 1971 and Bruno Santini for *Iolanthe* in 1977. She was fanatical about costume detail and seemed to miss nothing. Whenever she attended a performance, any little deviation from what she considered to be correct was dutifully noted down by her secretary, Albert Truelove, to be addressed as soon as possible. On one occasion, Jon Ellison and Mark Nelson swapped their *Iolanthe* coronets for a better fit, but she noticed the change, because the coronets did not match the insignia on the cloaks the two men were wearing. Whether it was the slightly askew position of the buttercups attached to Christene Palmer's 'Little Buttercup' bonnet in *HMS Pinafore*, as she remembers once happening, or hair peeping out from underneath a lady's wimple in *Princess Ida*, she spotted it and action was taken. Peter Riley is convinced that money was always made available for costumes when other areas would have benefited from an injection of cash.

Sometimes, when the company was playing a London season, Miss Carte would call a costume parade and it was during one of these that I had my only encounter with her. Standing before her in my rather threadbare *Yeomen* costume, which had been handed down for some thirty years, she looked long and hard at my battered hat before saying to Albert, "This child's hat needs attention." With that, she swept on and so ended my only meeting with the head of the company. Norman Wilfred Wright remembers a costume call for *The Gondoliers* when she stopped and stared at the trousers of Howard Williamson, who was standing next to him. Looking round for Albert, she was too embarrassed to say out loud that Howard needed to wear an athletic support, but mumbled and waved her hands in the direction of the problem until Albert caught her drift. This, of course, reduced Norman and Howard to stifled giggles. Heaven forbid that she should use the term 'jock strap', but that was her reserved and old-fashioned nature. Rather more comfortable with John Reed, whom she got to know well, she once invited him to have dinner with her just to discuss a new hat for him as 'Bunthorne' in *Patience*, asking his opinion as to what he thought would be suitable. His response was that something similar to the floppy black beret she was wearing would be ideal and it very soon appeared.

When *The Sorcerer* was reintroduced into the repertoire in 1971, Bridget's relationship with the designer, Osbert Lancaster, was uncomfortable at best, the two seeming to rub each other the wrong way. Maybe the colourful, larger than life style of his costumes was not to her taste, but they didn't seem to like each other very much. Peter Riley, who got on well with Miss Carte, thought that keeping the two apart for the dress rehearsal of the new production was a good idea, so he asked his wife, Abby Hadfield, to take her out for the day. Abby, who had by then left the company but was staying with Peter in Manchester, said she wanted to strangle him, but she did as she was asked and invited Bridget on a day out to Buxton. Albert Truelove was, as usual, in tow. Having shown her around the pretty Peak District spa town, with its beautiful Frank Matcham Opera House, Abby took her into a shop which sold items crafted from the local Blue John stone. Ignoring the smaller pieces, Bridget's eye alighted on a pair of small vases which took her fancy. Informing the shop assistant that she wished to buy them, the young lady told her that they were extremely expensive and really only for display purposes. Not to be put off her purchase, she asked to speak to the manager, who confirmed that the vases were very costly, but she eventually got a price out of him. Abby relates that Bridget then produced her Coutts Bank cheque book, affirming her wealth by grandly announcing that the account number ahead of hers belonged to Queen Elizabeth, the Queen Mother. Suitably flabbergasted, the manager had the vases wrapped and Miss Carte departed, leaving the shop staff open-mouthed.

On the drive back to Manchester, Miss Carte said she was getting hungry, putting an anxious Abby into a quandary about somewhere suitable to eat. Doubtfully asking her if she liked curry, the great lady said she did, so Abby, who was from the area, took her to the Taj Mahal restaurant in Stockport, which she knew well. The meal, washed down with lager, was very much enjoyed, so much so, that Bridget asked the owner of the restaurant if it would be possible to buy some of the curry spices the cook had used to take back for her chef at The Savoy Hotel! It was certainly a very relieved Abby who dropped her charges back in Manchester after a successful mission. A footnote to this day trip happened some time later when Peter and Abby were invited by Miss Carte to have supper at her apartment at The Savoy, where a curry using the spices from Buxton was served and Abby spotted the two Blue John vases adorning the mantelpiece in the sitting room. Bridget, despite her shyness, had a fondness for one or two of her company members and it was not unknown for her to have dinner at John Reed's London home, where she seemed able to kick off her shoes and relax away from the demands of her business life.

Bridget D'Oyly Carte had a generous and supportive side which showed itself when people in her opera company became ill, there being several instances of her helping them both practically and financially. In Guy Matthews' first season with the company in 1974, he developed an abscess on his tonsils which made him very poorly. With Bridget's ready agreement, Frederic Lloyd made arrangements for him to see a Harley Street doctor, the company picking up the bill, and Guy remembers her making regular enquiries as to his progress, asking, "How is the young man?" It would be typical that she did not know his name, but cared sufficiently about his welfare to pay for his medical treatment. Alan Barrett also had good reason to be grateful to her after his wife, Mary Sansom, had a miscarriage, when they were sent away for two weeks holiday to help Mary recover, Miss Carte paying all their expenses. It was not the only time she took a personal interest in Mary's health, which was not always good. Alan tells that Mary was taken seriously ill when the company was playing in Blackpool and he feared for her life. Miss Carte insisted that Alan ring her every evening with a progress report, promising the services of a Harley Street doctor if necessary and then sending them on holiday to Devon when Mary was sufficiently recovered to travel. Guy Matthews recalls

John Ayldon telling him that John Webley and Doreen Carminay, both of whom suffered from cancer, received great kindness from Miss Carte during their final days, when she showed a caring nature which belied her aloof manner. Alan Styler was another to benefit from her thoughtfulness during his bouts of illness, as his widow, Vera Ryan confirms.

"In the summer of 1962, I think it was, Alan was quite poorly with lung trouble and then cancer and had to have radiotherapy, which was nasty and left him feeling sick. Bridget was very good and insisted on paying him full wages during this time. We moved to Manchester from Redditch before our daughter, Bridget, of course, was born in April 1964. Miss Carte came to lunch at our house there and asked Madeleine, our eldest at five, whether she had any pets, to which she replied, "We had a kitten, but it pooped all over the kitchen, so we gave it away." Miss Carte's response was, "How fascinating!"

Despite these illustrations of the caring side to her nature, Bridget was not a person to cross, as Barbara Lilley knows only too well. Barbara joined the company as principal soprano in 1975 and was delighted when her husband, Peter Lyon, replaced Michael Rayner as principal baritone in 1979 prior to the tour of Australia and New Zealand. At home discussing their respective salaries, she was shocked to discover that Pete had been offered more money at the beginning of his company career than she was earning after four years. She tackled Frederic Lloyd about this and finally got him to agree to give her a rise, but the management did not forget. As soon as she became pregnant in 1981, she received a phone call from Mr. Lloyd to say that her contract was to be terminated with immediate effect. Stunned by this news, she asked why and was told that Dame Bridget, as she was by then, thought her condition 'inappropriate' and that there were health and safety issues to consider. Barbara was not prepared to accept this decision, particularly as she would not be the first principal soprano to continue working for some time into a pregnancy, so she took advice on her legal rights before writing a formal letter of complaint to Mr. Lloyd, after which she was put on 'maternity leave' and paid in full to the end of her contract.

The D'Oyly Carte's approach to management may have been infuriating at times, but that was the way it worked and nobody got the better of them, however important they were. After the American tour of 1978, John Reed, like many others, was not happy about the prospect of another five months away from home with the company due to go to Australia and New Zealand the following year. When he suggested that he might not go, he was left in little doubt by the management that he was considered critical to the success of the tour; the Australian promoter wanted John Reed at any cost. John told them the conditions under which he would sign his contract, to which Frederic Lloyd, after consultation with Dame Bridget and the other Trustees, reluctantly agreed. The cancellation of the prestigious tour would have been disastrous for the company, not least, because there would be no alternative UK tour dates in place. John felt that an unfair amount of pressure had been put on him and resolved that if he was to continue with the company after Australia, it would, again, be on his own terms.

Just a few weeks into the 1979 Australian tour, the management was anxious to settle matters for the following UK tour so, at a meeting with Frederic Lloyd and Peter Riley in Brisbane, John set out his demands for staying with the company, adamant that he would leave if they were not met. Unfortunately, his conditions were deemed completely unreasonable, particularly as the management felt it had already bent over backwards to accommodate his terms for going on the tour of Australian and New Zealand. Peter says that despite a counter offer being made, there was no resolution to the impasse so, with neither side prepared to back down, a contract was neither offered nor expected and John Reed left the D'Oyly Carte Opera Company after twenty-eight years. Dame Bridget was fond of him, but not to the point of allowing him to dictate the terms of his employment within her company. Happily, John was to return for guest appearances during the company's farewell 1981-2 season at the Adelphi Theatre, his fans delighted he had come home.

Peter Riley laughed when recalling that Bridget could be a problem when she attended auditions, her eccentric attitude to some of the candidates leaving them with little chance of being accepted into the company. Sometimes, when asked what she thought about a young lady's potential, the reply was, "She's a blonde." Unmoved by the reminder that she would have to wear a wig if she joined the company, would come the response, "That's not the point. She will still be a blonde and we don't want blondes." She also had a problem with women who had fat legs and would pass comment on this after they had left the stage. "But, Miss Carte, she will be wearing a crinoline, or long dress." Completely unfazed by this argument, she would say, "Under which she will still have fat legs." Peter remembers one talented young soprano who auditioned for the company at least four times without success, but who went on to have a spectacular career and was made a Dame for her services to opera. Bridget, for some reason, never liked her, but Peter did not mention whether or not she was a blonde with fat legs! She was known to ask men who were auditioning if they were married and had children. If the answer was in the affirmative, she would tell them that being on tour all year would, very likely, mean the end of their marriage. If they were not married, she would later ask the others on the panel, "Do you think he's a queer?" Long before homosexuality was legalised, the company was happy to employ people they assumed to be gay, because they were seen as far more likely to stay with the company, thus avoiding frequent and inconvenient changes of cast.

Being the head of an opera company reasonably entitled the owner to have input into the selection of new recruits, but the basis on which Bridget D'Oyly Carte made some of her decisions was odd to say the least. If the Director of Productions and Music Director recommended taking on a singer then, surely, she should have bowed to their superior ability to recognise the talent needed to perform the works of Gilbert and Sullivan at a high professional level. But, in the D'Oyly Carte, it didn't work like that. If Miss Carte was at an audition, Albert Truelove would also be there, pen and notebook in hand to offer his opinion on the suitability of candidates, sometimes alongside technical and managerial staff who were sitting in on the proceedings. It was little wonder there was a company joke that new recruits were selected solely on their suitability to fit into the costumes vacated by the people leaving.

Bridget was a contradiction: always shy and reserved, but often kind and compassionate, at other times high-handed, standoffish and as far removed from her company members as could be imagined. Her lifelong passion for child welfare and good causes never diminished so, in 1972, she founded the D'Oyly Carte Charitable Trust to support the charities closest to her heart. In 1975, the opera company's centenary year, she was created a Dame of the British Empire for her services to charity and the theatre. D'Oyly Carters, who had to get used to her being referred to as 'Dame Bridget' instead of 'Miss Carte', noticed no other difference and still saw very little of her. For company members who had to endure the trauma of the final performance in 1982, a few words of farewell, condolence, thanks, or good luck wishes from Dame Bridget would have meant a great deal, but none came. She stayed at the front of the Adelphi Theatre with her fellow D'Oyly Carte Trustees, friends and invited dignitaries, whilst the distraught cast got changed for the last time. It was, undoubtedly, a night of great personal sadness for her, but not to come backstage or, at least, send a representative to bid us goodbye, did her no credit and such lack of thought on her part taints the memory of an intriguing woman.

Although not officially a part of the management, Albert Truelove certainly had the ear of Bridget D'Oyly Carte, the two of them sometimes appearing to be joined at the hip. He was much more than her personal secretary, he had influence with her and, sometimes, his own agenda. Peter Riley clearly remembers the time when Sir James Hanson, one of the Trustees, wanted to modernise the company's decrepit publicity department and asked Peter to become involved with this. A great deal of money, provided by Barclay's Bank, was spent on new colour photographs and a campaign was launched on London transport, featuring adverts at tube stations and on the sides of buses, even on parking meters, advertising the works of Gilbert and Sullivan as 'The World's Greatest Musicals'. Peter was anxious that Dame Bridget should see these ground-breaking adverts for the company's London season and took her to the offices of Allen Berrisford, the company dealing with the new publicity. She was thrilled with what she saw and said to Peter, "Riley, this is wonderful, just what my father and grandfather would have loved." A few days later, he was taken aside by Albert, to be told, "The Dame hates this new publicity" which Peter immediately recognised as the sign that Albert didn't like it. Frederic Lloyd dubbed him a 'complicator', because he always saw a problem with anything new.

There is a story of Albert arranging a meeting at The Savoy with two people he thought might be helpful with an idea he had for the opera company, which he was anxious to keep from Bridget until it proved viable. Walking with his visitors along the corridors of the hotel, Albert was horrified to hear voices, one of which was Bridget's; she was coming in their direction. Without hesitation, or explanation, he opened the door to a large cupboard and bundled his two guests inside! After a brief chat with Bridget and her companion, a relieved Albert let his captives out and continued to their meeting in his office. This amusing near miss sounds unlikely, but it was related to me by a friend of one of the victims of this subterfuge. If true, it demonstrates a devious side to Albert's dealings with his employer. He was certainly a character; a small, plump man with his trademark 'comb-over' hairstyle and large, thick-rimmed spectacles, he was not to be underestimated. Be it Savoy Hotel business, or opera company affairs, wherever Bridget went Albert was never far behind, exerting his hold over her.

Peter Riley says that Albert had a reputation for being completely chaotic when it came to paperwork. He was in the London office one day when Albert was on holiday, when Bridget came in and announced that she had, at last, had the chance to tidy his desk, a rare opportunity for her to find out what was really going on. To her dismay, she discovered her tax returns going back four years, which Albert had not bothered to submit to the Inland Revenue. She told Peter she was afraid she might end up in prison. This indifference to pushing a pen is confirmed by stalwart of the D'Oyly Carte office, Margaret Bowden, who tells that, when his office was cleared after his death, a number of uncashed cheques, donations to the 'Save the D'Oyly Carte' campaign, were discovered on his desk.

Bridging the managerial gap between Bridget D'Oyly Carte and her employees in the opera company was the General Manager, Frederic Lloyd. A tall, distinguished-looking man, with stooped shoulders, he walked with a heavy limp and used a walking stick, but it was his trademark monocle which completed the image of a character who stood out from the crowd. Despite his eccentricities, he was a shrewd operator who kept a tight reign on the company's business operation for thirty-one years and who did what he could, despite the diehard traditionalists amongst the Trustees, to take the company forward when it was beginning to fail. He had a wry sense of humour and a smooth tongue which bamboozled many a principal determined not to leave his Savoy Hill office without a pay increase at their annual contract review. He had the air of a man of authority who commanded respect and most of the company would, probably, admit to being a little bit scared of him.

There are many anecdotes about Frederic Lloyd and one of the funniest is a favourite memory of Peter Riley. After concerns were expressed that a principal soprano was struggling with her roles, the decision was made to end her contract and Lloyd had the unenviable job of breaking the news to her. She did not react well and demanded to know the reason, to which he is reputed to have given the following explanation: "Well, my dear, it seems that your voice is too low for the high notes and too high for the low notes." Another classic Freddie Lloyd story comes from Robin Wilson, son of the former Prime Minister, The Rt. Hon. Sir Harold Wilson, who was a D'Oyly Carte Trustee. One evening, Sir Harold was having dinner with Lloyd at the Garrick Club, when he witnessed Freddie's monocle fall into his quail's egg soup!

But, as General Manager, he could be ruthless when he felt it was necessary and Alan Barrett was on the receiving end of one of Lloyd's hard-nosed moves when the part of 'Samuel', in *The Pirates of Penzance*, was taken from him and given to a newcomer in the chorus, who would only join the company if given a part. Angry and disappointed, Alan tackled Herbert Newby, who was Director of Productions at the time, to be told that Bert knew nothing about it and that it was a decision taken by the London office without reference to the touring management. The irony of the situation was that the newcomer did not make a good job of the part, which was then given to Alan Styler, so Alan Barrett lost out again. In later years, anyone joining the D'Oyly Carte was not able to dictate such terms. A new chorister might be given understudies and small parts, but that was, usually, because they were replacing someone already in possession of those responsibilities.

Christene Palmer was anther to fall foul of the London management's occasional tough tactics. She relates the story of the time, just prior to the filming of *The Mikado* in 1966, when Philip Potter, who was to play 'Nanki-Poo', asked her what she thought of the contract for the film work. She told him that she had not received one and, on finding out that all the other principals had got theirs, immediately tackled Bert Newby. He reluctantly told her that the management wanted Gillian Knight to play 'Katisha' in the film. Christene was, understandably, hopping mad and told Bert that if she was not good enough to play the role for the film, they had better find someone to play it for the rest of the tour. Whether or not the management took heed of her warning she does not know, but she did, eventually, get a contract for the filming. Some years later, she was in conversation with Gillian and mentioned what had happened regarding the *Mikado* film. Gillian was astounded and told Christene she knew nothing about it and that she had definitely not been approached by the Carte management about playing 'Katisha' for the film. How ridiculous that the London office should send contracts to the confirmed principals before the casting was finalised. Frederic Lloyd must, surely, have realised that Christene would find out and be filled with righteous indignation, but she still has no idea what was behind the Savoy Hill scheming.

Frederic Lloyd was, undoubtedly, a clever manager who could be tough, but he also had a sympathetic side to his nature as I found out in one of my rare encounters with him. I had been in the company for about three years, when I received a letter from Mr. Lloyd stating that it had been brought to his attention that I had been off ill, particularly at weekends, far too often and that if my attendance record did not improve, my contract might not be renewed. I was staggered by this, because it was completely untrue. Fortunately, in those days, I kept a daily diary and so, after carefully checking back over the previous couple of years, I sent a letter to Mr. Lloyd asking him to consult the company records, from which he would see that I had been unfairly accused. This he must have done because, within a few days, he wrote again, apologising for what had happened, admitting that he had acted on information given to him which he had assumed to be correct. His regret seemed genuine and I don't think he was very pleased about being put in such an embarrassing position, but I very much appreciated his frankness. A short time later, when he was at Sadler's Wells Theatre, he took me aside to say how sorry he was about what had happened. I had a strong inkling as to who was responsible for trying to get me into trouble, but I had absolutely no idea why. I could not think of any disagreement or confrontation that might have prompted such a spiteful act. It was certainly not a clever move to pick on something to throw at me that could be so easily disproved.

Peter Riley, who knew Frederic Lloyd as well as anyone, is always happy to talk about a man whom he describes as "a thoroughly decent human being", a man who shed tears when he had to tell the popular, long-serving tenor chorister, William Palmerly, that his contract was not being renewed. But, he also recalls him being an expert at passing the buck. Lloyd was secretary of the D'Oyly Carte Opera Trust and, towards the end of the company's life, he and Peter had lunch prior to a Trustees' meeting, during which they discussed ideas to help the company move forward. Freddie particularly liked one of Peter's suggestions, but was concerned that, if the Trustees didn't approve of it, they might not be happy about the younger man having input, so he volunteered to claim the proposal as his own and take any criticism that might arise. On Dame Bridget saying, "Lloyd, that's a terrible idea; whatever were you thinking?" came the smooth retort, "Well, actually, it was Mr. Riley's idea."

Lloyd's distinctive mannerisms were great fodder for company mimics and impersonations of him were always good for a laugh. Both Gareth Jones and James Conroy-Ward were brilliant at taking him off, but James was not unknown to do it when in conversation with Mr. Lloyd himself, who always took it in the intended spirit of fun. James got the voice exactly right, copied the limp and by using his own 'Major-General' monocle, completed the effect to perfection. Gareth's version often included one of the comments for which Freddie was famous. When asked his opinion of gay people, he is reputed to have said: "That sort of thing's all right as long as it doesn't frighten the horses." Lloyd was devoted to the D'Oyly Carte Opera Company. A smooth-talking businessman, he was pleasantly eccentric, often charming and witty but, above all, he was an expert negotiator. When it came to getting the deals he wanted from company employees, he knew exactly which buttons to press. Unlike most of the D'Oyly Carte hierarchy, Frederic Lloyd was a progressive, anxious not only to secure the company's financial future, but also to see it flourish in the modern theatre world. Regrettably, he was frustrated by the incurable traditionalists amongst the Trustees, who wanted the company to continue as it had always done, unchanging and independent of outside influence. It seems out of character, but his day-to-day responsibilities in running the opera company seem to have obscured what was obvious to one of the company's London office staff. In 1979, Margaret Bowden, who had joined the company's accounts department in 1974, was working as assistant to the company accountant, John Harper, in the Savoy Court offices, when she realised, much to her consternation, that the financial position of the company was extremely precarious.

"Sir James Hanson had become a Trustee and asked for a weekly cash flow statement, which I prepared for him. When I was on holiday, it was not done and Sir James' secretary couldn't believe there was nobody else in the office to carry out this task. I was able to reassure them that, in my absence, there had been no major transactions taking place. We were a small office and ran a very tight ship. It was through preparing the cash flow statement every week that I began to realise the company was losing too much money and I could not see how this could continue. Gradually, the investments were disappearing just to keep going, but John Harper did not accept what I was saying. At that time, Peter Riley had joined the office staff after many years of touring and I confided in him my concerns about our future. He became as alarmed as I was and referred the matter to Frederic Lloyd. From then on, it was a matter for the Trustees."

When Bridget D'Oyly Carte set up the D'Oyly Carte Opera Trust after the expiry of copyright in 1961, the appearance on the scene of the Trustees made a big difference to the way the opera company was run. What, for so many years, had been her personal property to operate as she saw fit, became an organisation run by a committee of people with differing points of view. Although a Trustee herself, she did not become chairman of the Trust until The Bishop of London, The Rt. Rev. Robert Stopford, resigned the chair late in 1975. Looking through the list of the people who were Trustees over the years begs the questions, how, and why, were these people appointed? The obvious answer would seem to be that they were, very likely, chosen because they were prominent in their fields of expertise; had been knighted or boasted impressive numbers of letters after their names; were well-known in the field of politics or business; were friends and associates of Bridget D'Oyly Carte, or were in the wealthy London society set. It is unlikely that anyone would have accepted appointment to the Trust if they were not lovers of

Gilbert and Sullivan, but did this make such a diverse group of people suitable to oversee the running of a long-established and iconic opera company? They were not theatre people with knowledge of singing and acting techniques, or the artistic vision to develop policies to keep the company's productions apace of the modern theatrical world. Yet they had the power to appoint music and production staff, regardless of the fact that most of them did not have the expertise to differentiate between someone whom they thought would be able to do the job and someone who could do the job. Their lack of understanding sometimes left employees frustrated. Paul Seeley's work in the music department involved scoring and re-orchestration, which he loved doing, but not with his hands tied behind his back.

"I feel there was so much that could have been done, but we were hampered by the short-sightedness and ignorance of the Trustees. The company hierarchy was so paranoid about copyright, that we on the music staff did not use full scores. When *Princess Ida* was in preparation, I had to go to the Bodleian Library to make notes from the Sullivan manuscript. Yet the Trustees could have engaged a top academic to edit new full and vocal scores, with new band parts, for the company to publish, thereby having some copyright control and royalty income."

The first chairman of the D'Oyly Carte Opera Trust was Mr. A.W. Tuke and it would be fascinating to know the connection between he and Bridget D'Oyly Carte that led to his involvement. After his decision to resign the chair in 1972, the following tribute to his service appeared in the company's in-house magazine, *The Savoyard*.

"After being chairman of the Trustees since the D'Oyly Carte Opera Trust was set up more than ten years ago, Mr. A.W. Tuke has decided that it is time for him to vacate the chair, though he has agreed to remain a Trustee. No one who has been in close contact with the Trustees and the management during these ten years can fully appreciate the value of the services which Mr. Tuke has rendered to the D'Oyly Carte organisation and to the cause of Gilbert and Sullivan. He has not missed a single Trustees' meeting and has always been readily available to Miss D'Oyly Carte and to the management whenever they have wished to obtain his advice or his approval of some course of action. As a former Chairman of Barclays Bank, he brought wisdom and diplomacy to the conduct of the Trustees' meetings; as a fervent devotee of the operas, he attended performances whenever they were within reasonable reach, giving constant encouragement to those responsible for their presentation; and with his wide sympathy and understanding of people he was of invaluable assistance to those members of the staff with whom he came in contact. Mr. Tuke is being succeeded as Chairman by the Bishop of London, and the latter's place as Vice-Chairman is taken by Sir Cecil Parrott, K.C.M.G., O.B.E. The Trust is fortunate in having such men available to guide its affairs and willing to devote their leisure to assisting in the promotion of its aims."

So, we know Mr. Tuke loved G&S; saw the company whenever he could; encouraged the production staff; was always on hand to give advice and never missed a meeting, but it is significant that no mention is made of him being in contact with the performers, or soliciting opinions about company matters from their point of view. The very fact it is stated that the Trust was lucky to have such distinguished men willing to give up their free time in the cause of the company suggests the amateur nature of their association. Also serving as a Trustee in the early years was Dr. Charles Budd, a lover of G&S who attended many performances when the company was playing in Bristol. He was a great friend of Donald Adams and gave parties for the company at his home. By coincidence, he was the doctor who attended the scene of the car crash in 1931 which involved principal contralto, Bertha Lewis, who later died from her injuries in hospital, and patter man, Henry Lytton, who was seriously injured in the accident. Dr. Budd's reward was to be appointed a Trustee of the D'Oyly Carte Opera Company. The resignations of two of the original Trustees, of whom little is remembered, Mrs. Ruth Grandcourt and Professor Daniel Jones, saw new Trustees announced in *The Savoyard* of December 1964.

"We are delighted to welcome as new Trustees Sir Ashley Clarke, G.C.M.G., G.C.V.O., a former British Ambassador in Rome, Mr. Alfred Francis, O.B.E., Vice-Chairman of T.W.W. Ltd. (Television for Wales and the West) and Mr. Colin Prestige, whom many Associate Members have already known as Chairman of the Gilbert and Sullivan Society." Through the following years, there were comings and goings within the Trust which saw the departure of Bishop Stopford and the appointments of Sir Anthony Tuke, son of the first chairman of

Trustees who, like his father, was chairman of Barclays Bank, James E. Hanson and the Prime Minister, The Rt. Hon. Harold Wilson, O.B.E., F.R.S., M.P., as was gleefully reported in *The Savoyard* of January 1976.

"We are delighted to announce that the Prime Minister has accepted the Trustees' invitation to join them. It would be too much to hope that, with the heavy preoccupations in his official life, Mr. Wilson will be able to attend all meetings of the Trust, but he has already shown that his advice and encouragement will always be available, and indeed his practical help and support. Another new Trustee is Mr. James Hanson, an industrialist, founder of the Hanson Trust and Chairman of Trident Television. He is already a Governor of the Sadler's Wells Foundation, and has taken more than a passing interest in the annual appearances of the D'Oyly Carte Company at that theatre."

Two later appointments to the Trust were Sir Edmund Liggins, T.D., a Warwickshire solicitor who went on to become President of the Law Society and, finally, Sir Charles Mackerras, C.B.E., the latter being the first Trustee with the highest credentials in the performing arts. Not only was he a great conductor of worldwide reputation in both the orchestral and operatic repertoires, but his extensive knowledge of Gilbert and Sullivan was legendary, as witnessed by his brilliant ballet suite, *Pineapple Poll*, an ingenious compilation of Sullivan's Savoy Opera scores. At last the Trust had a member who could offer advice and guidance from a theatre professional's point of view. If only he had been appointed sooner, it could have made a big difference to the selection of the company's artistic and performance staff but, as it was, his input could be described as too little, too late. But there was another Trustee, one who was there from the formation of the Trust to the closure of the company in 1982, Sir Hugh Walter Kingwell Wontner, G.B.E., C.V.O., D.Litt., and with him lay the real power base within the Trust.

Sir Hugh Wontner was The Savoy group, being the first person to be both its Chairman and Managing Director since Richard D'Oyly Carte, taking full responsibility for the Savoy Theatre, The Savoy Hotel and its sister hotels, Claridge's, The Berkeley and The Connaught (Bridget D'Oyly Carte's favourite of all her hotels), when Rupert D'Oyly Carte died in 1948. The son of an actor-manager and actress, he loved the theatre and was a member of England's oldest amateur dramatic society,

249

'The Old Stagers'. He was a prominent figure in the City of London and served a term as its Lord Mayor. Widely-admired as a brilliant businessman, he had a reputation for unorthodox, even outrageous, methods. No one, apart from Albert Truelove, knew Bridget D'Oyly Carte better and his influence over her was well-known in D'Oyly Carte circles. Peter Riley, who was able to observe their relationship when he became a member of the management, describes him as her 'Svengali', such was his hold on what she thought and did. It is probably true to say that he made sure she relied on him for advice.

It is clear to see that the Trustees were, in the main, people of power, influence and social status; famous names in the upper echelons of British industry, business and politics who were deemed to have the clout to make a success of the D'Oyly Carte Opera Company's affairs. It seems odd that no former D'Oyly Carte performer was ever invited to serve on the Trust. Such operatic luminaries as Valerie Masterson, O.B.E. and Gillian Knight owed much to their D'Oyly Carte careers and both ladies retained great affection for the company. They knew the company from the sharp end and their advice as renowned international singers could have been invaluable. It might be argued that one of the mistakes made by the Trustees was their failure to consider bringing the company's artistes into the consultation process when the future was looking bleak. They, more than anybody, were the people who recognised that many of the productions were creaking with age and who longed for a fresh creative approach under a Stage Director of proven quality.

With the exception of Anthony Besch, who actually gave direction to the principals for his ground-breaking production of *The Gondoliers*, there was never a director with whom they were able to share the creative process, or respect. Everything regarding the acting of Gilbert's inspired dialogue was left to them and they were stuck with staging that was often uninspired. Brilliant artistes such as John Reed, Kenneth Sandford, Patricia Leonard and John Ayldon, might have given invaluable help to the Trustees, but it is unlikely that such an idea would have entered the heads of people used to being in charge of their own affairs. Ken Sandford longed for the chance to tell the Trustees what he thought about the way they did things, but would they have taken any notice? They always thought they knew best and this led to unsuitable appointments being made to the artistic staff.

Surely, the experience and advice of such acclaimed G&S performers could have been utilised by the Trust to help in making vital decisions towards the end of the company's life? They certainly knew the world of professional theatre and what was needed to enhance the company's artistic standards but, most likely, as mere employees, it would not have been deemed appropriate for them to sit in on Trust meetings. If no stone was to be left unturned in the effort to save the company, this could be seen as a missed opportunity.

It cannot be denied that it was useful to have Sir Anthony Tuke to help secure the small-scale, but vitally important, sponsorship from Barclays Bank in the latter years of the company. Likewise, Sir James Hanson had the contacts in industry to help in getting Benson and Hedges, the international tobacco giant, to sponsor the programme for the tour of Australia and New Zealand. However, they and their fellow Trustees struggled to raise sufficient money to secure a future for the D'Oyly Carte, so Peter Riley was charged with the responsibility of seeking sponsorship to keep the ailing company afloat. That he duly did, with a sum of £80,000 promised from Datsun, the Japanese car manufacturer, to sponsor *The Mikado* and £100,000 pledged by Imperial Tobacco. Both offers were rejected by the Trustees as 'inappropriate'; the first, according to Peter, because they would have preferred a British company to be associated with the D'Oyly Carte name; the second, because they did not wish to appear to be encouraging smoking. Some two years earlier, the Trust had been glad to accept financial help from Benson and Hedges, so how did that make sense? The expression 'beggars can't be choosers' was never more appropriate. Such money would have kept the company going for a time and given the Trustees breathing space to look for support elsewhere.

In 1981, James Conroy-Ward recollects being asked to appear on a television programme in Manchester, in which the former Prime Minister, Sir Harold Wilson, was to be interviewed about his life. Sir Harold had requested James to sing one of his favourite pieces, 'When I Was a Lad' from *HMS Pinafore*, to represent his love of Gilbert and Sullivan. At a reception in the Green Room after the transmission, Sir Harold approached James and told him that the company was safe, a six-figure sum having been promised to keep it afloat, but he did not disclose the name of the donor. James assumed the money to be coming from Sir Charles Forte, whose ambition to take over The Savoy chain of hotels was common knowledge. However, Peter Riley, who knew all about Forte's designs on The Savoy, asserts that Sir Harold could not have known about the secret talks Peter had held with Forte and was not known to have had any association with him, so this assertion remains a mystery. But more of this later.

Failure to secure large-scale investment in the company led to the Trustees' decision to make an application to The Arts Council of Great Britain for a grant. Frederic Lloyd, who had, for some time, seen the writing on the wall, had already quietly met with Jack Phipps, the director of touring opera, ballet and drama in that organisation. They discussed possible funding and, according to Peter Riley, Lloyd was told that, with a few compromises, financial support could be available. True to his progressive instincts, Lloyd had also made discreet enquiries with some of the country's leading opera companies with a view to securing the services of top-class Musical and Stage Directors. Once the application to The Arts Council had been submitted, a report on the D'Oyly Carte's operation was prepared and it was little short of damning. Although the company's tight business operation was praised, its production values and musical standards came in for severe criticism, as did its artistes, who were dubbed 'tired and wooden'. This was hardly fair to them given that they were performing as directed, but the mud stuck. However, a conditional offer of financial support was made. Providing the D'Oyly Carte management would agree to reduce the number of shows it toured, introduce operettas other than those by Gilbert and Sullivan into its repertoire (Messager's *Veronique* being one suggestion), and accept an Arts Council representative on the board of Trustees, money would be made available to allow the company to continue. Peter Riley was later told by Frederic Lloyd that although the progressives amongst the Trustees, Sir Charles Mackerras, Alfred Francis and Sir James Hanson, could see the advantages of the offer, the votes of the majority of the Trustees meant the refusal of the conditions, the prospect of having an outsider in their midst proving one of the main sticking points. They preferred to take their chances and go it alone. The Arts Council was later seen by the British public as the villain of the piece for its 'refusal' to fund one of Britain's oldest and best-loved theatre companies.

A 'Save the D'Oyly Carte' campaign was launched by the Trustees to raise public awareness of the imminent loss of a great British theatrical institution, with the aim of attracting donations to aid its cause. Publicity events were arranged, including an open-top bus ride through the streets of London. With company members in costume and a BBC reporter on board, a petition containing many thousands of signatures from company supporters was handed in at the offices of The Arts Council, whilst television cameras covered an interview with Sir Harold Wilson and the former Lord Chancellor, Lord Elwyn-Jones, outside the Houses of Parliament. The cast of *HMS Pinafore* was invited to appear on the BBC's 'Omnibus' programme, where they were given the chance to talk about the D'Oyly Carte's plight. Wherever the company was appearing, local media covered the probability of its imminent closure, one of the most memorable occasions seeing the cast of *Pinafore* photographed aboard *HMS Victory* in Portsmouth. Another event was arranged in Blackpool, with the chorus in *Pirates* costumes cavorting on the beach for the benefit of the cameras.

Behind the scenes at this time of frantic money-chasing, the historic relationship between the D'Oyly Carte Opera Company and The Savoy Hotel stirred up decidedly murky water. Sir Charles Forte's desire to own the world-famous hotel was fanatical, but he was up against a fierce opponent in Sir Hugh Wontner. Some years before, Wontner had foiled a takeover bid for the hotel by splitting The Savoy shares into two types, 'A' and 'B', the latter becoming the important voting shares, which were not easy to acquire. It was widely considered to be an outrageous move, but it did the job and the hotel was kept in D'Oyly Carte hands. It served its purpose again by making it very difficult for Forte to buy the voting shares he needed to complete a takeover. The animosity between the two men spawned a bout of mutual insults, but a newspaper article about the possibility of Forte supporting the ailing D'Oyly Carte gave Peter Riley an idea.

"I told Freddie that I was going to send an anonymous letter to Forte suggesting that if he pledged to support or save the opera company in tandem to his bid to gain control of the Savoy, that his bid might be looked on more favourably by some of the shareholders, but that there should be 'no strings' attached. The only other person who knew about this was James Hanson; he was my trustworthy contact on the board of Trustees and we were in contact quite a lot. He warned me to be wary of Forte, describing him as "a slippery character", and also told me to watch my back from The Savoy camp as well. In fact, I remember his very words, and I quote: "It's shit or bust Peter, and I admire your courage. Good luck." He also told me he would support me to the hilt, but he, personally, would not want to be involved in any negotiations with Sir Charles.

"I delivered the said letter to the Forte office by hand, under cover of darkness (real James Bond stuff this). In the letter, I suggested that perhaps an approach should be made to the Trustees. The upshot of this was a letter in *The Stage* from Edward Martell, an associate of Forte, suggesting that if a member of the management of the D'Oyly Carte Opera Company contacted Sir Charles, he might well be prepared to support the opera company on a completely 'no strings' basis. Absolute horror from the Directors' corridor at 1, Savoy Hill; emergency meetings everywhere; it was like World War Three had been declared. Meanwhile, I waited for the dust to settle, then contacted Martell, who suggested an initial meeting between Forte, Martell and myself. I then declared that I had been approached by Martell and it was agreed that I go ahead with the meeting and report back to Sir Hugh Wontner and Dame Bridget. It was also agreed that I should be the only liaison between the opera company and Forte, and that no one from The Savoy Hotel should be involved.

"I subsequently met with Forte and Martell in Forte's office at The Grosvenor House Hotel, when Sir Charles told me that he had always been a great fan and admirer of both the operas and the company, and that he was prepared to do anything possible to ensure the survival of the company. He said that his offer would not in any way be linked with his attempt to take over the Savoy group. Needless to say, many meetings followed and it was suggested that I should arrange a meeting with Forte and Martell with a representative of the Trustees. Consequently, a lunch meeting was arranged, and I was accompanied by Colin Prestige, who was a solicitor, from the Trust. A further meeting followed with myself, Sir Anthony Tuke (as chairman of the Trustees), Forte and Martell. As a result of all this, it was agreed that a separate trust should be formed, to be called 'The Gilbert & Sullivan Trust', and Edward Martell would be the formulator. The Trustees would be Sir

Charles Forte, Edward Martell, George Proctor (on Forte's staff as chief legal adviser), Sir Anthony Tuke, Lord Delfont, Sir Norman St.John Stevas (another Forte acolyte), Louis Benjamin (Stoll-Moss Theatres) and yours truly, with Dame Vera Lynn as chair person. The Queen Mother was approached and agreed to act as patron. A strange mix you might think, so did I!

"Another upshot: I was contacted by Fred Hitch, who acted on behalf of Lady Ellerman, widow of Sir John (Ellerman Shipping Lines), a major shareholder in The Savoy, and a great supporter of the opera company. Mr. Hitch indicated to me that Lady Ellerman might be prepared to sell her shares (substantial) in the Savoy if it would lead to the continuance of the opera company. Private talks took place between Dame Bridget, Lady Ellerman and the Ellerman Trust. Nothing was forthcoming, and I can only assume that it was as a result of the close friendship of the two women that Lady Ellerman was persuaded to hang on to her voting shares. If she had sold them, no doubt they would have been snapped up by Forte and control of The Savoy would have passed to 'The Milky Bar Kid' (Sir Hugh Wontner's nickname for Forte because he had opened London's first Milk Bar)."

Early in all these negotiations, Sir Hugh had warned Peter that he was treading on dangerous ground, his dislike of Forte expressed in the most snobbish way. "You see, Peter, he will never be an hotelier, he is a caterer. We might save the opera company, but we would lose the hotel." It was a traumatic time, as Peter concludes.

"I feel sure that, with respect, members of the company never knew how hard some of us tried to save it all, so if you ever wondered when I saw you all in late 1981, early 1982, that I looked tired and washed-out, I was working very hard. In the end, we did not get the support from the Trustees, apart from Hanson and Mackerras. The others sat on the fence; they were, quite likely, 'manipulated' by Wontner. Everyone failed to realise that The Savoy Hotel came from Gilbert, Sullivan and D'Oyly Carte and they were too afraid to save the opera company."

And so, all efforts to keep the D'Oyly Carte going came to nothing and Peter remembers being at the Trustees' meeting at which the decision was made to close the company after its final performance at the Adelphi Theatre in London on February 27th 1982. At this dreadful news, he immediately walked out of the room, never to see any of the

255

Trustees again. For a young man of thrity-five, who had joined the company as Props and Baggage Master when he was just seventeen, and who had worked his way up to managerial level, it was a bitter blow. He had given his all in trying to help save the company and he knew that money to aid its survival had been offered, but rejected by the Trustees, sounding the death knell for the famous old company. It might be argued that the Trustees, under the leadership of Dame Bridget, were well-intentioned but, in reality, the all-important majority of them did not seem to know how to go about developing the opera company's future in a theatrical world so different from the one known by Gilbert, Sullivan and Richard D'Oyly Carte. The Trustees had the opportunity to embrace change; develop a sustainable touring policy; make compromises to enable them to accept offers of sponsorship, and engage artistic staff capable of bringing the highest production values to the staging and music of the Savoy Operas. Keeping the D'Oyly Carte alive should have been of paramount importance, but however successful the Trustees were in their own careers, they were, with one or two exceptions, amateur Gilbert and Sullivan enthusiasts running a professional opera company. It is true to say that even had a financial lifeline been thrown to the company, its continuance may not have been assured for more than a few years, but it would, at least, have had a chance of surviving.

During the course of my research for this book, I have spoken with many D'Oyly Carte members and the consensus is that the company was responsible for its own demise. The perennial autocratic style of management and decision-making of Trustees so far removed from the work face was, in their opinion, why the world-famous company went down. That such a renowned theatrical institution, some 107 years old, was allowed to slip away is nothing short of a tragedy and a cause of great regret to the generations of talented performers who built its fine reputation. The three great men who gave life to the wonderful Savoy Operas, along with their many devotees around the world, would have wished it otherwise.

CHAPTER ELEVEN

MAGIC MOMENTS

The terrible sadness of Gilbert and Sullivan aficionados worldwide at the loss of the historic D'Oyly Carte Opera Company was matched only by that felt by the many performers who were proud to have served under its name. For those employed by the company at the time of its closure, who had gone through the awful experience of seeing hopes for survival raised and dashed, was the prospect of unemployment and a very different life. Statutory redundancy payments were not enough to pay their bills for very long, so most immediately embarked on the necessary round of auditions or job interviews and, happily, many of them went on to enjoy successful careers in the theatre. But the memories of their life in the Carte have never diminished, although the distance of time has certainly lent enchantment to the days of year-round touring, eight shows a week and endless travelling, hardships tempered by the companionship and mutual support of wonderful people. It was not an easy way to earn a living, but every D'Oyly Carter has their own favourite stories of company life, so it is fitting to end with a selection of magical moments which sum up the spirit and camaraderie of a theatrical institution like no other.

Early in the 1960s, Pauline Wales was on her second American tour and struggling to come to terms with the fact that her marriage to chorister, John Maguire, was breaking down. Alone in her hotel room after a show, she was in tears, lonely and distraught, when a knock at the door brought a friendly face concerned that she might be in need of company. It was Valerie Masterson. Seeing Pauline's obvious unhappiness, Valerie insisted she go with her to her room for a drink, after which she decided more action was needed to raise a smile on Pauline's face. Completely out of the blue, she broke into a charleston, which Pauline describes as "absolutely brilliant", showing that Valerie was more than a wonderful singer, she was a great dancer, too. The ploy worked, cheering up Pauline who, despite having being so miserable, laughed in delight at Valerie's antics and she has never forgotten the thoughtfulness shown to her that night. Was there ever a better example of how D'Oyly Carters looked after each other?

Pauline has another lovely story about the delightfully quirky side to Valerie's nature, which always makes her chuckle. Convinced that having to smile so much during the 'Three Little Maids' scene in the first act of *The Mikado* would give her wrinkles on her face, Valerie would exit with her 'sisters', Pauline and Peggy Ann Jones and immediately begin to pull her face into a frown in order to reverse the effects of ten minutes with a fixed smile on her face. It must have worked, she still looks amazing.

Whilst talking about *Mikado*, I remember that Kenneth Sandford loved to relate the story about once having an 'out of body' experience during Act One of the show. Anyone who knew Ken would consider him the least likely person imaginable to make such a claim, so to hear him describe himself as "floating high up in the flies", looking down on himself as 'Pooh-Bah' in conversation with 'Ko-Ko' and 'Pish-Tush' seems very much out of character. He told me this during my research for his biography. I did express some doubt as to his sobriety at the time, but he assured me he hadn't touched a drop of the hard stuff and that he experienced this strange phenomenon on several subsequent occasions. Far from being frightening, Ken found the sensation quite pleasurable, particularly as he was extremely impressed by his own acting!

Another of Ken's favourite recollections involved John Reed. As the Kings, 'Hildebrand' and 'Gama' respectively, in *Princess Ida*, both had almost an hour off the stage after Act One so, when they were sharing a dressing room, and he had finished *The Daily Telegraph* crossword, John would have some fun by sculpting his wart. It needs to be explained that John always made a large, bent nose from special theatrical putty, the final touch to his disfigured appearance as 'Gama', to which he added a large wart. It was not the most comfortable thing to wear, so he would remove the nose after the first act and stick it to his dressing room mirror until he had to put it back on for the third act. Ken would watch in fascination as John carved the wart into the shape of a lighthouse, or castle, or some other edifice, marvelling at the intricacy of his work. Once on the stage, the wart looked just that to the audience but, close to, the detail of the building was clear to the cast and Ken, who had earlier had a good laugh, was able to maintain the necessary stern facade of 'King Hildebrand' as his colleagues tried to suppress their mirth. If only the audience had known!

Lorraine Daniels, one of the great D'Oyly Carte characters, would admit that, way back in the 1970s, she was not the best cook in the world, but she was a trier. In conversation one day with Beti Lloyd-Jones in the dressing room of Cardiff's New Theatre, the subject of hummus came up and Beti gave her a recipe so that she could try making it. At the time, many of the company were staying in holiday chalets at Lavernock Point, so having a kitchen meant that Lorraine could try out Beti's recipe. Unfortunately, her efforts left her less than satisfied, the mixture being too lumpy and extremely pungent, so she decided to take it to work the following day to ask Beti where she had gone wrong. As it took over half an hour to get to the theatre, the car owners took turns to drive and the day the hummus went to town, it was Barry Clark who drew the short straw. With a full car and Lorraine in the front seat clutching her disastrous hummus, the overpowering smell of garlic proved too much for the driver and his passengers, so Barry insisted that she wind down the window and hold out the aluminium foil parcel at arm's length for the whole of the journey. It may have been freezing in the car, but it was better than being overpowered by garlic fumes!

One of Vera Ryan's favourite memories, as ever, involved her husband Alan Styler. Whilst the company was playing a season in

Harrogate, the male principals and ladies' chorus went to the local rugby club to give a short concert and enjoy the hospitality of the members in return. Vera can't remember why there were no male choristers or principal ladies present, but the odd arrangement of voices led to a very funny moment. Alan was to sing 'The Captain's Song' from *Pinafore* and asked the ladies to fill in as sailors for the chorus responses. At the start of the second verse, he sang, 'I do my best to satisfy you all' to the ladies, who replied with, 'And with you we're quite content', reducing everyone to fits of laughter. Ever the cheeky chappie, it is not unlikely that Alan had realised the potential for some fun and set up the girls accordingly.

The mystique of being a glamorous leading lady in a famous opera company was well and truly shattered for Barbara Lilley, after a backstage fall left her with a painful coccyx. The following day, she was still in considerable pain, so she went to see a doctor. Flat out, with her rear end being prodded, she was bright red with embarrassment when the doctor told her how much he was looking forward to seeing her on the stage the following night! Another painful moment for her came when she once made a hurried visit to the loo before the dramatic dialogue scene and duet with 'Ralph Rackstraw' in the first act of *HMS Pinafore*. Finding the toilet devoid of paper, she used the tissue tucked into the sleeve of her dress. Unfortunately, she had forgotten that, as was her habit, she had dabbed menthol and eucalyptus oil all over it. The discomfort which followed sorely tested both her singing and acting skills to the limit, her watering eyes caused more by pain than emotion!

During the 107-year history of the D'Oyly Carte, there were many married couples within the company, some relationships standing the test of time whilst others failed. Company weddings were always a cause for celebration, none more so than that of Vivian Tierney and Gareth Jones during the 1978 tour of North America, which saw them tie the knot at a New York community church (by coincidence, now the meeting place for the New York Gilbert and Sullivan Society) in the shadow of the Empire State Building. With the whole company in attendance, the bride was given away by Gordon MacKenzie and her bridesmaid was Suzanne O'Keeffe, whilst Barry Clark was Gareth's best man. With the happy couple whisked away by limousine to their honeymoon hotel, those invited to the reception waited in great anticipation for a truly showbiz occasion, because it was to be held at the famous restaurant, Sardi's, in the heart of Broadway's theatre district. Traditionally the place where theatre folk awaited reviews in the small hours after the opening of a new show, the walls covered in photographs of so many great stars formed the backdrop to a memorable D'Oyly Carte event. It was a magical day.

Some twenty-three years earlier, the D'Oyly Carte was playing a season in New York and Cynthia Morey remembers the thrill of the company being invited to present excerpts from the Savoy Operas live on the iconic Ed Sullivan show. She, along with Joyce Wright and Beryl Dixon, was asked to perform 'Three Little Maids from School'. It was the most exciting event of the company's New York calendar and was particularly special because television was so new to them in those days. On a later tour, Jennifer Toye tells that the company again appeared on the famous Sunday night TV show, which was broadcast nationwide from New York, in which Nat King Cole was topping the bill. Charming and friendly with the company members, he chatted with them during the rehearsal, revealing that he had always loved Gilbert and Sullivan and that he was very thrilled to be appearing on the same show as the D'Oyly Carte Opera Company.

The great American cities provided many wonderful experiences, but the simplest of pleasures could provide magical memories of times across the pond. During the California leg of the 1978 tour, a group of Carters went to San Diego's Sea World theme park. Three of the men, Geoffrey Shovelton, Kenneth Sandford and James Conroy-Ward, made a bet to see which of them would make the worst-dressed British tourist. Needless to say, James Conroy-Ward came in a distant last, his contribution to sartorial inelegance amounting to nothing more than sporting a sailor cap and having an open-neck shirt. The other two, however, went to town, with Ken Sandford shading it in white and green check shorts, with a shirt of navy and white horizontal stripes, topped off by a large floppy sun hat. He looked truly awful! The rest of the group, which included Beti Lloyd-Jones and Gordon 'Mike' MacKenzie walked a long way behind them.

Touring year-round, everyone understood the need for having fun to keep spirits high and Maggie Bourgein has fond memories of two of her greatest Carte friends, John Ayldon and Michael Rayner, who were past masters at keeping everyone entertained, as she relates.

"John was very keen on opera and for some reason had a thing about *La Traviata*. He spent a week or so, when we were doing *Pinafore*, pretending to be 'Violetta', clinging to the rigging and staggering violently in the wings as if in the throes of consumption. It reduced me to a quivering jelly. Mike played the 'Sergeant of Police' in *Pirates* and so had Act One off. On a Saturday matinee, he would listen to the football scores in his dressing room, then come on marching round the stage shouting out any relevant scores, with particular attention to West Bromwich Albion, Roberta's team."

A matinee in Wimbledon in the mid-1970s produced a moment that was hardly magical, but it was certainly memorable. During the break between shows, the principals had been asked to remain in costume and be available for new *Mikado* photographs to be taken on the set at the end of the afternoon performance. Astonishingly, as the house curtain was taken out for the photographer to start, an elderly man, who had attended the matinee, was discovered asleep in his seat. Closer inspection proved that, sadly, he was not asleep, but had quietly passed away. The shock and distress felt by those present was understandable, but the practical implications of the situation had to be addressed if the evening performance was to go ahead on time. Before the poor chap could be taken from the theatre, the police and coroner had to be summoned for the formalities to be completed, but he made his final exit just in time for the show to go on. Gareth Jones loved to relate this story, which always concluded with the comment on the day's tragic events he attributed to Julia Goss: "I didn't think we were that bad."

A favourite moment for Peter Riley happened just after he took over as Stage Manager from Jack Habbick in 1966. Jack had suggested he should go to check out the technical facilities for his first company visit to Leicester's De Montfort Hall and he was grateful for the advice. The main space hardly resembled a theatre, with no orchestra pit or proper proscenium arch. It had a low stage and curtains which stretched right across the width of the hall. Having surveyed the scene with a dubious eye, Peter was in conversation with the caretaker of the venue, who was showing him round. He asked, "What are the acoustics like?" to which came the reply, "We haven't got any." A footnote to this story involves James Conroy-Ward. Not long after he had taken over as understudy to John Reed, the company was playing the same venue. Standing in the wings watching John on the stage, he leant against the non-existent wall he expected to be behind the end of the open curtain and fell through into the orchestra. Bar a few bruises and battered ego, James survived unscathed, but he gave quite a shock to the double bass player and the audience!

I have two magic D'Oyly Carte moments of my own and would almost sell my soul to re-live them just once more. Both happened in the 'old' production of *Iolanthe*, which served the company for so many years before the Bruno Santini-designed production of 1977. The first happened early in the second act, when the chorus of fairies had to skip round the stage in two lines, arm in arm, prior to singing 'Strephon's a Member of Parliament'. I had to lead on the contralto line, alongside soprano, Anne Egglestone. Anne was a pretty, buxom woman, who was very strong and every now and then, she would get the devil in her to give me the ride from hell. Setting off from the wings at great speed, she gathered so much momentum that, by the time we passed 'Private Willis' standing in front of his sentry box I, being on the downstage side of Anne with further to travel, got perilously close to the edge of the stage at an angle of forty-five degrees. So fast were we going, that we had to mark time to allow the other girls room to make their entrance. By the time the fairies had formed two straight lines across the back of the stage, I had completely corpsed and was incapable of singing a note. I found it absolutely hysterical which, of course, Anne knew full well, but her trick was not to do it too often, so I never knew when it would happen. Oh, how I would love to do that again!

The second of my favourite *Iolanthe* incidents would often happen during the second act finale. With the fairies and peers happily paired, singing 'Up in the Air Sky High, Sky High', the men had to lift their ladies off the ground several times so that the girls could adopt a pose as if flying off to fairyland. If there was a chorus lady missing, two men had to share one fairy and this meant that I sometimes got Jeffrey Cresswell and Bill Palmerly as my partners, so I knew exactly what to expect. Both being tall, strongly-built chaps, they would each get a firm grip on me by putting a hand up the back of the bodice of my fairy costume and, instead of gently lifting me, they would throw me up in the air as high as they could. This instantly reduced me to a giggling wreck as I soared head and shoulders above the other fairies. The three of us found it absolutely hilarious and I would give anything to experience that silly moment once more.

A bizarre event to live long in the memory of company members playing in Cleveland, Ohio on the 1964 North American tour, was finding themselves playing next door to a circus, which shared backstage areas with the theatre space. Many of its performers were staying in the same hotel as the Carters and Kenneth Sandford relates, in his biography, that he soon got used to riding in the elevator with the circus clowns, many of whom made up and dressed in their hotel rooms. However, he never got accustomed to having to sing, or deliver dialogue, to the accompaniment of lions roaring, nor to being startled by the sight of clowns' faces peering down from the fly gallery above the stage. Pauline Wales, too, vividly remembers what an extraordinary season it proved to be and, in particular, John Reed having to sing the touching 'Tit Willow', in *The Mikado*, with elephants trumpeting in the background! The joy she felt at being able to cuddle a baby chimp has always stayed with her, but it was an altogether more dramatic moment which really stands out in her memory. She had been very taken with a handsome young lion tamer, but on arriving for a rehearsal one morning, she was horrified to see him being taken away on a stretcher, having been attacked by one of the lions. She later learned that the young man's father, who had a wooden leg, had gone into the cage to try and rescue his son, but he suffered a heart attack in the process and it was left to his daughter to go in and calm down the lions!

During the company's one-week season in Wellington, New Zealand in 1979, a large store devoted to selling sheepskin products was a favourite haunt of Carters, who bought everything from boots, gloves and coats, to rugs to have shipped home. When Patricia Leonard went in with her husband, Michael Buchan, she saw the rugs made from two sheepskins joined together and was taken with the idea of buying a bed cover if she could find anything large enough. Without further ado, she approached a male shop assistant and asked, "Do you have a four skin?" Completely unperturbed, the young man smoothly replied, "Certainly, madam, the quad skins are over there." Mike was so embarrassed by his wife's faux pas, to which she was oblivious until later on, that he walked out of the store and waited outside whilst she sealed the deal. Needless to say, when word got round the dressing rooms of Tricia's blooper, she was never allowed to forget it and Mike still chuckles about his late wife's unerring ability to put her foot in her mouth. Later on, when the wife of the tour organiser, Derek Glynne, saw everyone sporting sheepskin, she was heard to tartly remark: "We're paying them too much." That went down well.

In the early 1970s, John Reed and his faithful dog, Sheba, were staying with friends in Market Bosworth for the company's week-long season at the De Montfort Hall in Leicester. His host was very proud of his pristine lawn and had a hatred of dandelions appearing in the immaculate swathe. John could not resist the temptation to have some fun and went to the local park to collect a large bagful of the yellow flowers. Keeping them out of sight until his friends had gone out, John then set about arranging the flower heads to form the word 'LOVE' across the lawn, knowing that it would be seen from his host's bedroom when he opened the curtains the following morning. The cursing he heard from the next room suggested he had done a good job with his floral tribute. The joke was taken in good spirit, but John was warned, in no uncertain terms, that if any of the flowers took root, he would be looking for somewhere else to stay!

One of Anne Egglestone's favourite recollections happened in the second act finale of *Patience*. During a moment of boredom in the ladies' chorus room, it was suggested that the girls black out their teeth for the final entrance, in which they had to dance on in elegant red and white dresses. They kept tight-lipped fixed smiles on their faces until the 'Duke of Dunstable', played by Ralph Mason, entered at the back of the stage to say, 'Approach such of you as are truly lovely.' As the girls rushed upstage, with their backs to the audience, they flashed their gummy smiles at him and reduced the surprised Dragoon Guards' officer to fits of laughter and almost unable to continue his dialogue. Standing, very unamused, in the wings was Director of Productions, Michael Heyland, known to company members by his nickname, 'P Three' (due, in part, to him giving everyone numbers when staging a new production), who duly admonished the ladies after the final curtain, but it was too late by then, the fun had been had. Anne is adamant that the idea was not hers and lays the blame for the scheme on her great friend, that D'Oyly Carte stalwart, Beti Lloyd-Jones. Not that Anne was unknown to do something daft: she once went on for the opening ladies' scene of *The Mikado* in her fluffy slippers, having forgotten to change into her show sandals after the break between the matinee and evening performance. Another moment that always makes her laugh whenever she thinks about it happened at the time when many of the ladies of the chorus took up knitting to while away the time in the dressing room. She can remember Susan Maisey's wool and needles making an unscheduled appearance in 'The Mikado's Entrance', when they got caught up on the back of her kimono. As she made her exit at the end of the scene, the ball of wool rolled down the stage, unravelling as it went and Susan was the only one not to notice!

Lorraine Daniels remembers another occasion when teeth were blacked out and it was by my good self. Whilst singing 'When a merry maiden marries' in *The Gondoliers*, she had to perch on the edge of an ornamental well and my position was slightly downstage left of her. With my back to the audience, I was looking directly at her, so she always used to say that she sang the number to me because I smiled at her and never took my eyes from her face. After my years of devotion to lending her support, I chose her final performance as 'Tessa' to break from professional behaviour by using black tooth enamel to blank out one of my front teeth. The alluring gap almost caused Lorraine to fall down the well, but she managed to overcome her giggles and finish the number with her usual panache. She was always a good sport.

A moment of sheer magic for the audience came at London's Saville Theatre in 1965, during a matinee of *Princess Ida*. As Donald Adams finished the first verse of his Act Three aria, 'This Helmet, I Suppose', the choristers tasked with removing the helmets and armour from the three brothers stepped up, but the one taking off the helmet from 'Scynthius', accidentally removed his wig as well. Each piece of armour removed was immediately carried into the wings, so poor George Cook was left cringing with embarrassment, his short-cropped grey hair on display, part of his forehead without make-up and the elastic holding on his beard clearly visible to one and all! Most of the cast were laughing uncontrollably and barely able to sing, but Donald,

266

with remarkable self-control, carried on as if nothing had happened. That, or he had not noticed what was going on to his left. George's misery continued for another three verses, when he was, at last, able to slip off into the wings to retrieve his wig. It is hardly surprising that, thereafter, he dreaded the approach of that point in the show but, fortunately, it never happened again.

Those principal sopranos in the D'Oyly Carte who played the title role in *Princess Ida* always dreaded the moment at the end of the second act when they had to fall from the battlements at the back of the stage, to be 'rescued' from a raging torrent by 'Prince Hilarion', who had to leap off after her. Making the fall look realistic whilst delivering dialogue was never easy for 'Ida'; having to move backwards without obviously looking round to judge the place where she had to fall took some doing. Had the audience been able to look behind the scenes at this dramatic moment, they would have seen the less than glamorous sight of a pile of battered old mattresses placed to break her fall and a couple of backstagers to pick her up. Creating the illusion of reality is part of every performer's bag of tricks and one of Kenneth Sandford's occasional forays into schoolboy humour resulted in a splendid example of theatrical ingenuity. In the second act of *Yeomen*, Ken, as 'Wilfred Shadbolt', had to run onto the stage carrying an arquebus after the loud bang created in the wings to represent a gunshot. In the days when smoking backstage was not considered unthinkable, he would light a cigarette just before making his entrance and blow the smoke down the barrel of the gun, which would still be smoking when he arrived at the front of the stage. What delightful fun!

Another very happy, but unusual, moment for Ken happened after he had struggled through a performance with a painful big toe. The next morning, he decided that it needed attention, so he took himself off to Edinburgh Royal Infirmary, where he was informed that the toe was septic and needed cauterising. He was given a general anaesthetic for the procedure and told, after he came round, that he must not drive for twenty-four hours, but nothing was said about working. Leaving his car in the hospital car park, he took a bus to the theatre in something of a haze and performed very much under the influence. Having floated happily through his dialogue and songs on a cloud of anaesthesia, the next morning he could remember nothing at all about the show, except that he had enjoyed it very much and wished he could bottle the feeling for the times when he had to perform when tired, or under the weather.

Edwin Rolles dines out on the story of a company reception at which Dame Bridget D'Oyly Carte was present. She offered to buy everyone a drink so, taking advantage of this unusual hospitality, everyone ordered the most expensive drinks. Ever the gentleman, Eddie volunteered to accompany her to the bar to help with the large order, where she announced that she had not got her wallet in her bag, leaving the unfortunate Eddie feeling obliged to offer to pick up the hefty tab, which she accepted with grateful thanks. Why was Albert Truelove not a step behind her on that occasion, one might wonder?

The Sorcerer was always a welcome change from the usual weekly performance fare. Being presented much less frequently than the other operas, it was a show which offered plenty of opportunity for fun, because it was less-regimented than most of the productions. For the chorus, the freedom to move around naturally and create individual characters was always appreciated. There was an occasion when one of the three 'old ladies' took watches and jewellery from the dressing tables of her colleagues and pinned them on the inside of her large woollen shawl. During the first act finale, she moved quietly around the stage as 'Aline' and 'Alexis' sang their romantic duet 'Oh, Love', showing off the goodies inside her shawl and offering the items for sale, enjoying the look of surprise on the faces of those recognising their belongings! From a performance point of view, everyone on the stage enjoyed watching John Broad's fantastic interpretation of 'The Notary'. John was a genius with make-up and created a skull-like face which complemented his ability to turn his tall, slim frame into a stooped and doddering old man. But it was his hands which fascinated everyone. Swathed in grey gloves, they seemed to have a life of their own. Whatever he was doing, the fingers slowly moved independently of each other to create a truly horrible impression of subtle lechery. It was theatrical magic.

One of Alan Barrett's magic moments also involved a skull. Expert at character make-up, to while away a couple of dreary hours between a matinee and evening performance, he decided to create a skeletal face. So pleased was he with the result, that he popped down to John

Reed's dressing room to show off his handiwork. Unfortunately, John was entertaining visitors, who were taken aback by Alan's shocking appearance, but John joined in the fun by telling them, "This is Alan Barrett, he's not feeling very well today."

Audience members occasionally caused distraction for those on the stage, but it was unusual for them to create mayhem in the orchestra pit. One of Musical Director, Royston Nash's, favourite tales was of the time at Sadler's Wells Theatre when a 'cellist went into the pit early to tune his instrument, before propping it carefully against his chair and going back to the orchestra room. When he returned with his colleagues a few minutes later for the start of the performance, he found his 'cello smashed to matchsticks. In the short time he had been away, a front-row member of the audience had fallen through the curtain dividing the pit from the auditorium and landed on top of his prized 'cello. The show had to go on without him, but the inconvenience of having to find a good replacement and make an insurance claim was considerable. It was a memorable moment for all the wrong reasons.

D'Oyly Carte auditions, as we have seen earlier, could be slightly eccentric to say the least, but few people outside of the company would have a clue as to just how quaint were its selection methods. A tradition going back to the earliest times of the company was the filing system used for auditionees, which featured pink cards for the ladies and grey for the men, these being kept on file for possible future use. Comments, sometimes in code, were written on them and it was widely believed by company members that one such code was 'NFU', the polite translation being 'not for us'. It was also thought that when Bridget D'Oyly Carte's secretary, Albert Truelove, attended auditions, one of his codes was 'NBGS', which stood for 'nice boy, grey suit'. I have it on good authority from Peter Riley that these amusing insights have a basis in fact.

The annual Last Night of a London season was a tradition which provided many magical memories. Eagerly-anticipated by performers and audiences alike, they developed over the years from sedate, amusing affairs to riotous and exuberant celebrations of the talents of company members. Originally intended to be something of a party for loyal London audiences, they were, in truth, for the benefit of the cast, who were able to let down their hair for one night of the year and showcase their versatility as performers. Such was the demand for tickets, they were allocated by ballot, unless, of course, they came via an inside source. Robin Wilson, for example, was always pleased to get a ticket from his father, company Trustee, Sir Harold Wilson. Performers, too, could usually get hold of a couple of tickets for friends or family but, otherwise, it was the luck of the draw for those desperate to be in on the fun.

During the 1950s, these occasions were modest affairs and might consist of doing one act from two different operas, or *Trial by Jury* with the jury box and public gallery filled by characters from the operas. There was one Last Night when 'Mad Margaret', in the guise of Joyce Wright, was in the public box interrupting proceedings with shouts of 'Basingstoke!' By the late 1960s, the practice of deviating slightly from a usual performance gradually changed to something more adventurous and there was a memorable year when John Reed reflected the 'Swinging Sixties' and the cult 'Flower Power' movement by appearing as 'Reginald Bunthorne' in *Patience* dressed as a hippie. Aided and abetted by the colourfully-attired lovesick maidens, he delighted the audience with his trendy interpretation of Gilbert's 'fleshly poet'. In later years, John appeared twice more as 'Bunthorne'. Firstly, leather-clad as a punk rocker complete with chains, and secondly, alongside Kenneth Sandford as 'Archibald Grosvenor', when the two veteran D'Oyly Carters poked fun at themselves by appearing as doddery old men, cleverly meandering between the dialogue scenes they shared in the various operas as if they were in their dotage, much to the delight of an appreciative audience.

In the last few years of the company, Last Nights became increasingly sophisticated, filled with big production numbers and well-rehearsed routines which really showcased the talents of company performers. Alan Spencer's choreography to Paul Seeley's brilliant arrangements of Sullivan's scores proved hugely popular with cast and audiences alike. One of the more unlikely ideas saw Barbara Lilley, dressed as a charlady with a cigarette dangling from the corner of her mouth, singing 'I Cannot Tell What This Love May Be' from *Patience*. Behind her were some of the ladies' chorus, also wearing nylon overalls, with head-scarves tied into turbans in classic cleaning lady style. Armed with mops and buckets, they tap-danced through the number to huge applause. The joy of these madcap performances for the audience was not knowing what to expect and the 1980 Last Night at Sadler's Wells Theatre was no exception.

The Australian tour of the previous year gave Kenneth Sandford the idea to make a second, and final, appearance as 'Dame Edna Everage', the famous Australian housewife character created by female impersonator, Barry Humphries, whom Ken had so successfully imitated at the fancy dress party in Sydney. The Act Two scene of *The Gondoliers*, in which 'Don Alhambra del Bolero' berates 'Marco' and 'Giuseppe' for their crazy ideas about kingship, was in the programme, so Ken, who had kept the trademark spectacle frames he had made for the Sydney party, once again borrowed a dress and wig to enter looking uncannily like Dame Edna. It took the astonished audience some time to work out who was in the evening gown, but their delight when they heard his familiar voice as the 'Don' was greeted with wild enthusiasm. Another year saw the gentleman of the chorus dressed as American sailors singing the 'Peers' Chorus' in big band 'swing' style. With the tap-dancers from the ladies' chorus also in sailor outfits, the number was a huge success. Yet another of Alan and Paul's collaborations provided a great routine for 'The Magnet and the Churn' from *Patience*. Performed in the style of the musical *Grease*, Ken Sandford was a cool John Travolta, ably assisted by Patricia Leonard as Olivia Newton-John.

These are but a few examples of what made D'Oyly Carte Last Night performances so wonderful on either side of the footlights. More than that, such shows gave a platform for the artistes to demonstrate their diverse theatrical talents. The great majority of them were classically trained singers and many could act and dance to a high standard, but they were employed by the company to perform in the house style, so opportunities to use their wider skills were infrequent. Having said that, it must be made clear that performing Gilbert and Sullivan is not as easy as some may think. How often D'Oyly Carters have heard it said, "Oh, it's only G&S", the implication being that performing the Savoy Operas is not difficult. The musicals of their Victorian time, they require singers with excellent technique to cope with the demands of Sullivan's music. They also require actors with the skills to bring out the best in Gilbert's brilliantly-satirical dialogue and performers to do justice to the numerous joyous dances which pepper Sullivan's scores. Many grand operas do not require all of these attributes, yet they are perceived to be far more demanding of the performer and of greater artistic value.

Working for the D'Oyly Carte provided the chance to hone stagecraft like no other company and many of its performers went on to successful careers in opera and musical theatre, grateful for their grounding in the hard world of professional theatre. Both Valerie Masterson and Gillian Knight have told me how important their time in the Carte had been in helping them towards their distinguished careers in grand opera. For new principals, learning the art of delivering dialogue, timing and performance values from their established colleagues was key to their success. The generosity of experienced principals in giving a helping hand to newcomers was legendary and Jennifer Toye perfectly captures this tradition of new principals being taken under the artistic wing of their more experienced colleagues.

"I took over my parts in 1958 and was coached by Bill Cox-Ife. Ann Drummond-Grant gave me coaching in dialogue and general performance. She was wonderful and helped me so much, giving tips I doubt many other sopranos would have had. She had, after all, been in the company for many years and knew the pitfalls and secrets as to how to get the best out of my performance. I shall always be in her debt and never forget her wonderful sense of humour and kindness." There was no obligation on principals to provide this care, or money paid for their time and trouble; it was the D'Oyly Carte and, in the absence of production staff with the ability to do this important job, they just got on with it. Likewise, within the chorus, anyone joining was always given the help and advice they needed. Matriarch of the ladies' chorus, Beti Lloyd-Jones, may have been a little scary to any newcomer, but she was always there watching, helping and advising, whilst the men's chorus had such stalwarts as Jimmie Marsland, Jack Habbick and Jon Ellison to get the new boys up and running.

Looking after each other was what you did in the D'Oyly Carte. During long tours away from home, you were everything to each other. Friends, surrogate parents, lovers and playmates pulled together on and off the stage to survive what was a very hard way of life. It was a company like no other and all its surviving members still refer to 'the family' with enormous fondness. The D'Oyly Carte Opera Company's many wonderful characters and its way of theatrical life must not be forgotten, because there will never again be a touring repertory company like it.

One might argue that, with the D'Oyly Carte Opera Trust still in existence, there is always the outside possibility that the company might be resurrected but, more than thirty years after the closure of the original company, what would it be like? More importantly, would it be welcome at both London and provincial theatres at a time when G&S is being performed less and less? With the present day cost of touring shows, it would seem unlikely that anything other than the most popular operettas could be included in the repertoire, so the lesser-known gems would, probably, be excluded and that would be a pity. The short-lived New D'Oyly Carte Opera Company made little impact on G&S audiences, so how would it be possible to bring it back again in a format that would mirror the long-lasting success of the company given his name by Richard D'Oyly Carte in 1879? Although interest in the company and its performers is still strong amongst older people, the new generation of G&S devotees is too small to ensure a demand for professional productions of Gilbert and Sullivan in this country. This can only be addressed if young people are encouraged to realise that performing in, and watching, the Savoy Operas can be as much fun as any modern musical. There is an urgent need for talented directors with sufficient understanding and love of the genre to stage productions which would appeal to younger people whilst bringing out the best in Gilbert's satire and Sullivan's music. The Savoy Operas are historic pieces which deserve to be performed at the highest level; they are a window into the past, but should still be a part of our theatrical future.

So, how might this rebirth be possible? If many millions of pounds are spent each year by individuals who buy prestigious football clubs, there must be a wealthy philanthropist somewhere out there who cares sufficiently about Gilbert and Sullivan to see the D'Oyly Carte name returned to our theatres. There are still enough surviving company members with the expertise in Gilbert and Sullivan to offer advice to a new generation of performers and, I believe, most would be delighted to help nurture such a project. If funding was made available to the present D'Oyly Carte Trustees, the benefactor might stipulate that they take advice from established theatre professionals in the setting up of a new performing company, one which could succeed both artistically and financially.

Pie in the sky? Yes, of course, but why not have the dream? All it needs is one entrepreneur with a passion for Gilbert and Sullivan and a very large bank balance. This is the challenge I lay down before it really is too late. If such a philanthropist is out there, please give the money that could rejuvenate the appreciation of Gilbert and Sullivan and put it back in the hands of a new, vibrant and sustainable D'Oyly Carte Opera Company. It is not possible to go back in time, but we can look to the future and then, maybe, in fifty years time, another D'Oyly Carte performer might echo the words of Lorraine Daniels:

"It was such a wonderful company. We were, we still are, unique!"